Recommended Industry Standards of
the People's Republic of China

中华人民共和国行业推荐性标准

Design Guidelines for Highway Safety Facilities

公路交通安全设施设计细则

（英文版）

JTG/T D81—2017（EN）

Editing organization for English version: Highway Branch of China Association for Engineering Construction Standardization

Approval authority: Ministry of Transport of the People's Republic of China

Effective date: January 1, 2018

China Communications Press

人民交通出版社

Beijing

图书在版编目(CIP)数据

公路交通安全设施设计细则：JTG/T D81—2017：EN/中国工程建设标准化协会公路分会编译. — 北京：人民交通出版社股份有限公司, 2024.4

ISBN 978-7-114-19169-5

Ⅰ.①公… Ⅱ.①中… Ⅲ.①公路运输—交通运输安全—安全设备—安全设计—英文 Ⅳ.①U491.5

中国国家版本馆 CIP 数据核字(2024)第 060974 号

Classification of standards: Recommended Industry Standards of the People's Republic of China
Name of standards: Design Guidelines for Highway Safety Facilities
Code of standards: JTG/T D81—2017(EN)
Editing organization in charge: Highway Branch of China Association for Engineering Construction Standardization
Production editor: Pan Yanxia
Publisher: China Communications Press
Address: No.3, Waiguanxiejie, Andingmenwai, Chaoyang District, Beijing 100011, China
Website: http://www.ccpcl.com.cn
Sales telephone: 8610-59757973, 8610-85285930
Chief distributor: Distribution Department of China Communications Press
Printed by: Beijing Communications Printing Co., Ltd.
Page size: 880×1230 1/16
Sheets: 20
Word counts: 585 thousand
Edition: First edition in April 2024
Impression: First impression in April 2024
ISBN 978-7-114-19169-5
Price: 300.00 yuan($40.00)

(The Press is to replace books with printing or binding defects.)

中华人民共和国交通运输部

公 告

第 48 号

交通运输部关于发布《公路交通安全设施设计细则》英文版的公告

为促进公路工程行业标准的国际合作与共享,现发布《公路交通安全设施设计细则》英文版[JTG/T D81—2017(EN)]。

本细则英文版的管理权和解释权归中华人民共和国交通运输部,日常管理和解释工作由英文版编译单位中国工程建设标准化协会公路分会负责。

本细则英文版与中文版在技术内容上出现异议时,以中文版为准。

如在使用过程中发现问题或有修改建议,请函告中国工程建设标准化协会公路分会(地址:北京西土城路 8 号,邮政编码:100088,电子邮箱:h.chai@rioh.cn)。

特此公告。

中华人民共和国交通运输部
2023 年 9 月 20 日

交通运输部办公厅　　　　　　　　　　　　2023 年 9 月 21 日印发

英文版编译出版说明

标准是人类文明进步的成果,是世界通用的技术语言,促进世界的互联互通。近年来,中国政府大力开展标准化工作,通过标准驱动创新、合作、绿色、开放、共享的共同发展。在"丝绸之路经济带"与"21世纪海上丝绸之路",即"一带一路"倡议的指引下,为适应日益增长的全球交通运输发展的需求,增进世界连接,促进知识传播与经验分享,中华人民共和国交通运输部组织编译并发布了一系列中国公路行业标准外文版。

中华人民共和国交通运输部发布的公路工程行业标准代号为JTG,体系范围包括公路工程从规划建设到养护管理全过程所需要制定的技术、管理与服务标准,也包括相关的安全、环保和经济方面的评价等标准。

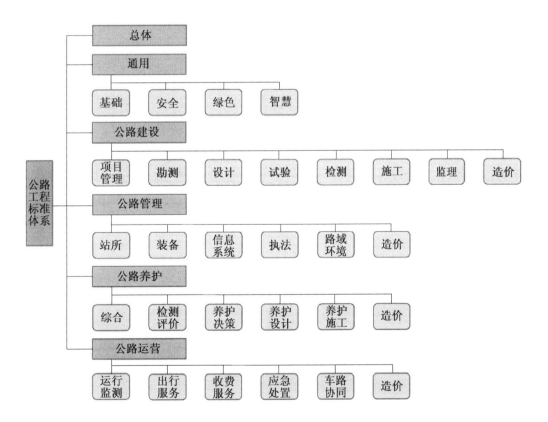

公路交通安全设施是公路的重要组成部分，在预防和减少交通事故、降低事故伤害、保护生命、提升公路交通安全方面发挥重要作用。作为指导公路交通安全设施设计的重要标准，中华人民共和国交通运输部于1994年发布了《高速公路安全设施设计和施工规范》(JTJ 074—94)，后于2006年修订发布了《公路交通安全设施设计规范》(JTG D81—2006)和《公路交通安全设施设计细则》(JTG/T D81—2006)，又于2017年再次修订发布了《公路交通安全设施设计规范》(JTG D81—2017)和《公路交通安全设施设计细则》(JTG/T D81—2017)。《规范》属于强制性标准，主要规定公路交通安全设施的功能要求和设置原则；《细则》属于推荐性标准，主要规定实现交通安全设施功能的手段和方法，以及推荐的形式和材料。《细则》充分吸收中国相关科研成果和大量工程实践经验，并借鉴了国际先进理念和技术，总体指标经济适用，部分指标高于国外相关标准。该英文版可与此前已发布的《公路交通安全设施设计规范》(JTG D81—2017)英文版一并配套使用。

《公路交通安全设施设计细则》(JTG/T D81—2017)英文版的编译工作由交通运输部委托中国工程建设标准化协会公路分会主持完成，并由交通运输部公路局组织审定。

感谢本细则中文主编刘会学在本英文版编译期与审定期给予的协助与支持。

如在执行过程中发现问题或有任何修改建议，请函告英文版主编单位，(地址：北京西土城路8号，邮政编码：100088，电子邮箱：h.chai@rioh.cn)，以便修订时研用。

英文版主编单位：中国工程建设标准化协会公路分会

英文版主编：柴华

英文版参编人员：毛煜菲，侯相琛，盛洁，王健，唐琤琤，于楠楠，胡晗，胡晓伟

英文版主审:王忠仁,Timothy B. Luttrell

英文版参与审查人员:张慧彧,邝子宪,聂志光,姚海冬,丁遥

The People's Republic of China
Ministry of Transport
Public Notice

No. 48

Public Notice on Issuing the English Version of *Design Guidelines for Highway Safety Facilities*

The English version of JTG/T D81—2017 (EN) *Design Guidelines for Highway Safety Facilities* is issued hereby for international cooperation and standardization of highway transportation industry.

The general administration and final interpretation of the English version of the *Guidelines* belong to Ministry of Transport, while particular interpretation for application and routine administration of the English version of the *Guidelines* shall be provided by the China Committee of Highway Engineering Standardization, the editing organization in charge of the English version.

In the event of any ambiguity or discrepancies on the technical contents between the English version and the Chinese version of the *Guidelines*, the Chinese version shall be referred to and accepted.

Comments, suggestions and inquiries are welcome and should be addressed to Highway Branch of China Association for Engineering Construction Standardization (Address: No. 8, Xitucheng Road, Beijing, Postal Code: 100088, E-mail: h. chai@ rioh. cn). The feedbacks will be considered in future revisions.

It is hereby announced.

Ministry of Transport of the People's Republic of China

September 20, 2023

General Office of Ministry of Transport   Printed on September 21, 2023

The People's Republic of China
Ministry of Transport
Public Notice

No. 47

Public Notice on Issuing the *Design Specifications for Highway Safety Facilities* and *Design Guidelines for Highway Safety Facilities*

Hereby the *Design Specifications for Highway Safety Facilities* (JTG D81—2017) is issued as one of the Highway Engineering Industry Standards to become effective on January 1, 2018, and the *Design Guidelines for Highway Safety Facilities* (JTG/T D81—2017) is issued as one of the Highway Engineering Recommended Industry Standards to become effective on January 1, 2018. The previous edition of the *Specification for Design of Highway Safety Facilities* (JTG D81—2006), and its English versions, and the *Guidelines for Design of Highway Safety Facilities* (JTG/T D81—2006) shall be superseded from the same date.

The general administration and final interpretation of the *Specifications* and the *Guidelines* belong to Ministry of Transport, while routine administration and particular interpretation for application of the *Specifications* and the *Guidelines* shall be provided by the Research Institute of Highway, Ministry of Transport, the editing organization for the Chinese version.

Comments, suggestions and inquiries are welcome and should be addressed to the Research Institute of Highway, Ministry of Transport (No. 15, Huayuandong Road, Haidian District, Beijing, Postal Code: 100191). The feedbacks will be considered in future revisions.

It is hereby announced.

Ministry of Transport of the People's Republic of China
November 17, 2017

General Office of Ministry of Transport　　　　Printed on November 20, 2017

Introduction to English Version

Standards reflect the achievement of civilization, provide common language for technical communications, and improve global connectivity. In recent years, the Chinese government has been proactively implementing a strategy on standardization to stimulate innovation, coordination, greening, opening up and sharing for reciprocal development in China and worldwide. In the light of mutual development along the Silk Road EconomicBelt and the 21st-Century Maritime Silk Road (so called 'the Belt and Road Initiative'), the Ministry of Transport of the People's Republic of China organized translation and published an international version of the Chinese transportation industry standards and specifications to cater for the increasing demands for international cooperation in world transportation, achieve interconnected development and promote knowledge dispersion and sharing experience.

JTG is the designation referring to the standards and specifications of the highway transportation industry, issued by the Ministry of Transport of the People's Republic of China. It covers the standards and specification in terms of technology, administration and service for the process from highway planning through to highway maintenance. The criteria for safety, environment and economic assessment are also included.

Highway safety facilities are important parts of the highway system, which play critical role in traffic accident prevention and decrease, reduction of traffic accident severity, life protection, and the improvement of highway safety. As the technical guidance for highway safety facilities design, the *Design and Construction Specifications for Motorway Safety Devices* (JTJ 074—94) was issued in 1994 by the MOT China, the updated version the *Guidelines for Design of Highway Safety Facilities* (JTG/T D81—2006) was issued in 2006, and the updated version the *Specifications for Design of Highway Safety Facilities* (JTG D81—2017) and the *Guidelines for Design of Highway Safety Facilities* (JTG/T D81—2017) in 2017. The *Specifications for Design of Highway Safety Facilities* (JTG D81—2017) is a

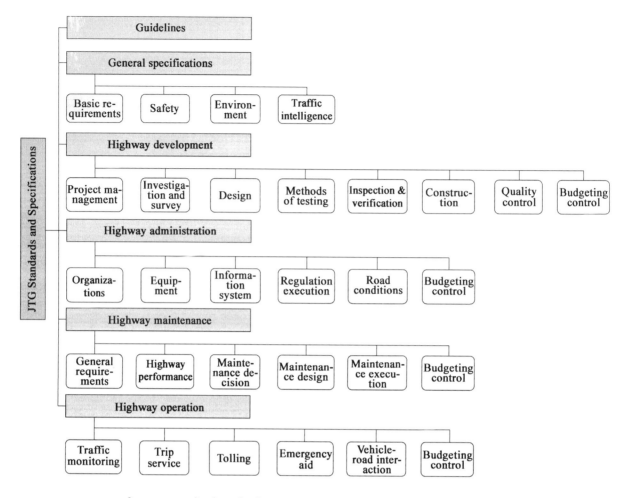

mandatory standard, which specifies the functional requirements and placement of highway safety facilities, the *Guidelines for Design of Highway Safety Facilities* (JTG/T D81—2017) is a recommended standard, which specifies ways and methods for deployment of highway safety facilities. The *Guidelines for Design of Highway Safety Facilities* (JTG/T D81—2017) is fully absorbing relevant Chinese scientific research results and engineering experience, and drawing on international advanced theory and technology, the overall indicators are economical and practical, some of indicators are higher than the indicators of the overseas standards.

The English version of the *Design Guidelines for Highway Safety Facilities* (JTG/T D81—2017) may be applied in conjunction with the previously published English version of the *Design Specifications for Highway Safety Facilities* (JTG D81—2017).

The revision and updating of the English version was conducted by the Highway Branch of China Association for Engineering Construction Standardization under authorization of the Ministry of Transport (MOT) and approved by the Highway Department of MOT.

The great gratitude is given here to Liu Huixue for the valuable assistance and suggestions during the editing and approving of the English version.

Comments, suggestions and inquiries are welcome and should be addressed to editing organization in charge of the English version (Address: No. 8, Xitucheng Road, Beijing, Postal Code: 100088, E-mail: h.chai@rioh.cn). The feedback shall be considered for future editions.

Editing organization for English version:
Highway Branch of China Association for Engineering Construction Standardization

Chief editor for English version: Chai Hua

Associate editors for English version:
Mao Yufei, Hou Xiangchen, Sheng Jie, Wang Jian, Tang Chengcheng, Yu Nannan, Hu Han, Hu Xiaowei

Chief reviewers for English version: Wang Zhongren, Timothy B. Luttrell

Associate reviewers for English version:
Zhang Huiyu, Julian TH Kwong, Nip Chi Kwong, Yao Haidong, Ding Yao

Foreword to Chinese Version

Following the requirements of *Notice of Planning for Compilation and Amendment Program of Highway Engineering Standards in* 2011 (TGLZ [2011] No. 115) *issued by the General Office of Ministry of Transport*, the updating of the *Guidelines for Design of Highway Safety Facilities* (JTG/T D81—2006) was carried out by the Editing Organization, Research Institute of Highway Ministry of Transport.

This edition the *Design Guidelines for Highway Safety Facilities* (JTG/T D81—2017) (hereinafter refer to as 'the *Guidelines*') is an overhaul of its former edition of the *Guidelines* (JTG/T D81—2006). The *Design Guidelines for Highway Safety Facilities* (JTG/T D81—2017) is issued and implemented after approval.

Taking the characteristics of highway operation environment and the trend of highway development in China into account, and according to the functions and technical parameters, traffic, and terrains of classified of highways, the updating of the *Guidelines* is conducted based on the research achievement and design practice during the implementation of last edition, and by referring to the experiences and technologies developed in other countries. Special research of key technical issures were conducted, and nationwide consultation were made during the updating. This edition of the *Guidelines* was then finalized after several rounds of discussion, revision and trial application.

This edition of the *Guidelines* comprises 12 chapters and 4 appendices, namely including: general provisions, design nations, overall design, traffic signs, road markings, barriers and railings, visual guiding devices, fencing, netting, anti-glare devices, escape ramps, other highway safety devices.

The major revisions in this edition of the *Guidelines* are as follows:

1 According to the *Technical Standards for Highway Engineering* (JTG B01—

2014), the layout of chapters and sections has been adjusted, highlighting the application functions of various safety devices.

2   A new chapter on 'overall design' is added to emphasize the coordination and interrelations among the highway civil engineering works, administration facilities and road service facilities, with detailed criteria for their application and structural design.

3   More details haven been given in chapter 4 and chapter 5, regarding the basic concepts and functional roles of traffic signs and road markings in terms of traffic safety facilities.

4   Tunnel portals have been taken as one of the particular design units for which the configulation of traffic signs, road markings, barriers and railings can be arranged in a systematic way.

5   To keep consistent with the *Standards for Safety Performance Evaluation of Highway Barriers* (JTG B05-01—2013), the 'containment level' of the barriers has been renamed as 'protection level' with an extension in classification. More details have been given for the configuration of curb barriers and the determination of protection levels of the barriers for effectiveness in practice. More detailed requirements have been specified for the barrier structures on various bridges, based on which a systematic method has been proposed for designing test pieces of bridge barriers. The performance requirements for highway movable barriers at median openings have been put forward. Details on the 'impact attenuators' have been added. The provisions on sample structures of various forms of barriers have been added and updated. Recommendations have been also given on the methods of altering barrier structures to fit site conditions.

6   In chapter 7 of the *Guidelines*, the chapter heading 'Delineator' has been changed to 'Visual Guiding Devices' with an extension in its coverage of application, to emphasize the importance of delineators on tunnels and in other special highway sections.

7   Adjustment has been made to the height and the grid size of isolation fencing according to the subjects to be isolated in a specific region, and the provisions have been added for the requirements of 'access gates'.

8   The type of netting has been expanded to two types, including the netting for falling objects and the rockfall netting.

9   A new chapter of 'Escape Ramps' has been added with provisions on location, structural composition, horizontal and vertical alignments, length, materials, and auxiliary facilities.

10   A new chapter entitled 'Other Highway Safety devices' has been added with the provisions on the application and placement of the safety facilities not stipulated in previous chapters, such as wind screens, snow fences, snow poles, height restriction gantries, speed humps, and convex mirrors.

Chapter 1 of the *Guidelines* was drafted by Liu Huixue, and Chapter 2 was drafted by Tang Chengcheng. Chapter 3 was drafted by Liu Huixue, Jia Ning, Ma Liang and Wang Wei. Chapter 4 was drafted by Zhao Nina. Chapter 5 was drafted by Song Yucai and Hou Dezao. Chapter 6 was drafted by Tang Chengcheng, Liu Huixue, Huang Chen, Li Yong, Ge Shufang, Zhang Shaoli and Gao Shuide. Chapter 7 was drafted by Song Yucai and Sun Bin. Chapter 8 was drafted by Sun Zhiyong. Chapter 9 was drafted by Song Yucai and Zhang Hua. Chapter 10 was drafted by Ge Shufang. Chapter 11 was drafted by Wu Jingmei, and Chapter 12 was drafted by Zhang Weihan. Appendix A was drafted by Song Yucai. Appendix B and Appendix D were drafted by Liu Huixue. Appendix C was drafted by Liu Huixue, Tang Chengcheng, Tai Yonggang, Deng Bao and Zheng Hao.

Comments, suggestions and inquiries are welcome and should be addressed to the current management team of the *Guidelines*.

Contact person: Liu Huixue (Address: No. 15, Huayuandong Road, Haidian District, Beijing, Research Institute of Highway, Ministry of Transport, Postal code: 100191, Tel: 62062052, Fax: 62370155, E-mail: hx. liu@ rioh. cn). The feedbacks will be considered in future revisions.

Editing organization in charge:
   Research Institute of Highway, Ministry of Transport

Associate editing organizations:
   Jiaoke Transport Consultants Ltd.

Guangdong Communications Group Co., Ltd.
Jiangxi Ganyue Expressway Co., Ltd.
Beijing Zhongluan Traffic Technological Co., Ltd.

Chief editor: Liu Huixue

Associate editors:

Tang Chengcheng	Song Yucai	Zhao Nina	Huang Chen
Ge Shufang	Hou Dezao	Jia Ning	Sun Bin
Li Yong	Ma Liang	Sun Zhiyong	Wu Jingmei
Zhang Weihan	Wang Wei	Tai Yonggang	Deng Bao
Zhang Shaoli	Zheng Hao	Zhang Hua	Gao Shuide

Chief reviewer: Chen Yongyao

Associate reviewers:

Li Aimin	He Yong	Li Chunfeng	Cheng Yinghua
Wu Huajin	Duan Liren	Pan Xiangyang	Xin Guoshu
Zheng Tiezhu	Gao Hailong	Zhang Yuhong	Bao Gang
Wang Jianqiang	Xia Fangqing	Wang Songgen	Shen Guohua
Guan Guiping	Xia Chuansun	Liu Guangdong	Sun Fuling
Hu Yanjie	Liu Xiping	Guo Min	Zhou Yubo
Ni Wei	Zhou Keqin	Ma Zhiguo	Peng Rui
Li Chunjie	Yin Dongsheng	Hu Jiangbi	Chen Weixia
Li Huichi			

Contents

		Page
1	**General Provisions**	1
2	**Design Notation**	7
	2.1 Notations for barrier design	7
	2.2 Notation for visual guiding devices design	10
	2.3 Notations for fencing design	11
	2.4 Notations for netting design	12
	2.5 Symbols for anti-glare devices design	14
3	**Overall Design**	15
	3.1 General	15
	3.2 Conceptual analysis on the project and road network	18
	3.3 Design objectives	19
	3.4 Scope of application	21
	3.5 Structural design standard	23
	3.6 Design coordination and interface demarcation	33
4	**Traffic Signs**	35
	4.1 General	35
	4.2 Provision principles	38
	4.3 Sign face design	41
	4.4 Materials	45
	4.5 Support forms and structures	50
5	**Road Markings**	53
	5.1 General	53
	5.2 Provision principles	54
	5.3 Material selection	66

			Page
6	**Barriers and Railings**		69
	6.1	General	69
	6.2	Subgrade barriers	71
	6.3	Bridge railings and railings	126
	6.4	Median opening barrier	146
	6.5	Impact attenuator facilities	148
7	**Visual Guiding Devices**		149
	7.1	General	149
	7.2	Installation principles	150
	7.3	Placement	153
	7.4	Delineator types	155
	7.5	Structural requirements	157
8	**Fencing**		158
	8.1	General	158
	8.2	Provision principles	159
	8.3	Form selection	160
	8.4	Structure requirements	162
9	**Netting**		166
	9.1	General	166
	9.2	Netting for falling objects	167
	9.3	Rockfall netting	168
10	**Anti-glare Devices**		174
	10.1	General	174
	10.2	Calculation of the shield angle	176
	10.3	Provision principles	177
	10.4	Form selection	181
	10.5	Structural requirement	183
11	**Escape Ramps**		187
	11.1	General	187
	11.2	Provisions of the escape ramps	187
	11.3	Geometric design of escape ramps	190

			Page
	11.4	Pavement materials and technical requirements of arrester beds and escape ramps	193
	11.5	Supporting facilities for safety and rescue	194
	11.6	Antifouling and drainage systems	196
12	**Other Highway Safety Devices**		**197**
	12.1	Wind fences	197
	12.2	Snow fences	203
	12.3	Snow poles	211
	12.4	Height restriction gantries	212
	12.5	Speed humps	214
	12.6	Convex mirrors	216
	12.7	Other devices	216

Appendix A	**A Sample of the Integrated Design of Safety Facilities at Tunnel Entrance and Exit**	217
Appendix B	**Calculation Methods for Clear Zone Width**	219
Appendix C	**General Structural Design Sample of Cable Barrier, Corrugated Beam Barrier and Concrete Barrier and Variation Method**	222
Appendix D	**Design Method of Testing Pieces of Bridge Railings**	267
Wording Explanation for the *Guidelines*		281
References		282
Technical Terms in Chinese and English		283

1 General Provisions

1.0.1 This edition of the *Guidelines* is developed according to the *Design Specifications For Highway Safety Facilities* (JTG D81—2017), for standardizing and unifying the design of highway safety devices so that the implemented devices are systematic, rational, advanced and practical to fully embody the functional and operational characteristics of the highways.

Background:

In July 2006, the Ministry of Transport issued the Guidelines for Design of Highway Safety Facilities (JTG/T D81—2006, hereinafter referred to as the Guidelines). As one of the recommended standards for highway engineering industry, it took effect on September 1, 2006.

Compared with the Specification for Design of Highway Safety Facilities (JTG D81—2006, hereinafter referred to as the Specification) that addresses 'What to do' in the design of road safety devices, the Guidelines focuses on 'how to do' and 'how to do better' in terms of road safety devices. The Guidelines outline the design principles and design procedures, describe the factors to be considered for the configuration of safety devices, explain how to select the types, forms and scales of safety devices, and illustrate the typical layout and profile sketches, which provides designers with useful methods for traffic safety analysis and helpful rules to tailor the design in line with local conditions. The Guideline will help avoid blind copying of the Specification by designers.

Since the issuance and implementation of the Guideline, China's highway construction has greatly improved. Highway safety devices are widely applied in all classes of highways. In these practices, it is found, however that there are still room for the current Guideline to be further improved to better meet the needs of large-scale highway construction in China. The main issues are identified as follows:

(1) Provisions

In terms of overall design, how to strengthen the provisions of proactive guiding devices and the principles for reasonably providing passive protection facilities are needed to be further refined.

How to determine the roadside clear zone distances based upon factors such as design speed or operating speed, traffic volume, and geometric alignments (horizontal, vertical, cross-sectional).

How to reflect the requirements of highway class, traffic volume, and landscape if provide median barriers.

How to refine the protection levels of barrier.

Considering the increasing trend of large vehicles in China, which measures can be taken in the Guideline to improve traffic safety for relevant highways.

(2) Barrier deformation after impacts

The requirements on the allowed deformation of various barriers after impacts are needed to be proposed.

(3) Form selection

How to select a barrier form to better reflect the safety and landscape, and how to adopt economically effective protection measures for lower class highways are needed to be further clarified.

(4) Structural calculations

The calculation models and methods for the structural design of bridge railings are needed to be further refined; treatments for various types of barriers are needed to be further refined, especially in the sections of retaining wall and bridges.

(5) General structure design models

The Guidelines emphasize the principles of customized design according to site conditions. However, many design agencies still hope the Guidelines can provide more general structure design models of barriers to be used in design.

In addition, the specifications of new problems of safety facilities brought by the development of *multi-lane motorways, lower class highways, reconstruction and upgrading projects, and the development of highway network are not completed or not detail enough. The operability is still needed to be largely improved.*

The main purposes of the revision of the Guidelines are to comprehensively summarize the pratices of highway safety facilities since 2006. By applying advanced experiences and failures of the highway construction and highway safety researches in China and abroad, it adjusts unsuitable terms in the Guidelines to make improvements of new problems of road safety facilities brought by the development of multi-lane motorways, lower class highways, reconstruction and upgrading projects as well as the changes of highway operations, further improvements of the pertinence and maneuverability so that the Guidelines can be more scientific, practical and easy-to-use.

1.0.2 The *Guidelines* is applicable to the design of highway safety facilities of all the classes of new constructed highways as well as upgrading and reconstruction projects.

Background:

After the implementation of the Guidelines on September 1, 2006, the scope of application extended to all the classes of new constructed as well as reconstruction and upgrading projects. This revision adjusts the scope, and the new scope includes the safety facility design of all the classes of new constructed highways as well as reconstruction and upgrading projects. As for the reconstruction and upgrading projects of existing highways, the design of road safety facilities should comply with the principles. For details, may refer to the Guidelines for Design of Traffic Engineering and Facilities of Expressway Reconstruction and Extension (JTG/T L80) and other industry standards.

1.0.3 The design of highway safety facilities covers traffic signs, road markings (including raised pavement markers), barriers and railings, visual guiding devices, fencing, netting, anti-glare devices, escape ramps and other highway safety devices such as wind fences, snow fences, snow poles, height restriction gantries, speed humps, and convex mirror.

1.0.4 The overall design of highway safety facilities shall be carried out on the basis of integration of road network with technical conditions, terrains, traffic conditions, and environment. There shall be coordination between different highway safety facilities, and between highway safety facilities and civil engineering works or other facilities. Their deployment shall also be complementary to each other.

1.0.5 The design of highway safety facilities shall comply with four principles: user-orientation, proactive intent, systematic design and key subjects in priority. On the basis of comprehensive analyses of road safety or the findings and suggestions by road safety audits, and in the perspective of highway users, the active guiding devices shall be provided as the priority, and passive protection facilities shall be provided according to the needs. Active guidance and passive protection will be integrated, which will make the full-funcational of the design plans, and the operations will be well suited.

1.0.6 The affects of roadway widening, road resurfacing, overlay, snowfall and other related factors during highway operations should be taken into accounting the design of safety facilities on a new constructed highway, and the relevant technical measures should be applied, as shown in Figure 1.0.6. The design of road safety facilities on a reconstruction and upgrading highway shall be carried out on the basis of investigation and evaluation of existing roads and in accordance with the road, traffic and environment after reconstruction and upgrading for reutilization of the existing devices and remediation of defects if there is any.

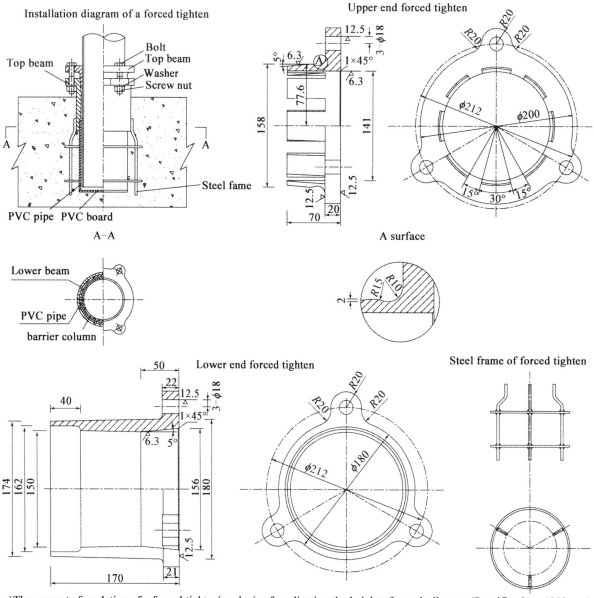

a) The concrete foundation of a forced tightening device for adjusting the height of guardrail posts (Specification: $\phi 140$ mm) (Dimension unit:mm)

Figure 1.0.6

b) an example of the structure design of the overhead traffic signboard gantry widened for future needs of roadway extension
Note: in the circle highlighted is the flange for existing gantry beam.

Figure 1.0.6　Example of operation-oriented configuration of safety facilities

Background:

The overlay or resurfacing of a road pavement may somehow affect the existing safety devices such as the height of a barrier or the height of a posted sign. The designers may take appropriate countermeasures to mitigate such effectiveness, for example, to appropriately increase the height of the traffic signs, to raise the level and select single-slope type of the concrete barriers; to pre-reserve additional bolt holes for further extending the columns of the corrugated beam barriers or cable barriers, or to adopt the forced tightener and re-changeable concrete foundation for barrier post installation, as shown in Figure 1.0.6 a) (in which the tighteners are made of cast steel material).

For the safety facilities installedon the sections which roadways may be extended in future, some appropriate structural forms may be selected to utilize the existing devices. Taking the situation shown in Figure 1.0.6 b) as an example, in the case when the roadway is to be widened to three or more lanes, the signboard gantry will need to be added with one additional cross beam, one pair of additional flanges, and one additional foundation only, and the major parts of the existing device will sustain for utilization.

For the reconstruction or upgrading projects, the designers need to fully consider the traffic safety and the operation characteristics of the existing highways, and carry out the design of highway safety devices on the basis of surveys and evaluations, and in accordance with the post-project conditions (such as highway classes, design speeds and so on), traffic conditions, and environmental conditions. For the purpose of resource conservation and environmental protection, the existing safety devices should be reasonably utilized and the existing defects should be fully remedied.

1.0.7　The design traffic volume for highway safety facilities shall be the design traffic volume of the highway projects. The outline dimensions of the design vehicles, the representative vehicle types, etc. shall comply to the prevailing *Technical Standards for Highway Engineering* (JTG B01) and the *Standard for Safety Performance Evaluation of Highway Barriers* (JTG B05-01).

1.0.8 The application of reliable new technologies, new materials, new techniques and new products shall be encouraged, subject to the safety and functional requirements.

1.0.9 In addition to meeting the provisions of the *Guidelines*, the design of highway safety facilities shall comply with the requirements of relevant prevailing national and industry standards.

2 Design Notation

2.1 Notations for barrier design

2.1.1 A notation used for the barriers to be installed on road shoulders is composed of three generic symbols, namely the symbol of structure form, the symbol of protection level and the symbol of embedment condition. Each of them is defined as follows:

1 Structural forms
　Gr—Corrugated beam barrier
　Grd—Composite corrugated beam barrier
　Gc—Cablebarrier
　RrF—Cast-in-place F-shaped concrete barrier
　RrS—Cast-in-place single slope concrete barrier
　RrI—Cast-in-place reinforced concrete barrier
　RpF—Precast F-shaped concrete barrier
　RpS—Precast single slope concrete barrier
　RpI—Precast reinforced concrete barrier

2 Protection levels
　C—Roadside Level 1
　B—Roadside Level 2
　A—Roadside Level 3
　SB—Roadside Level 4
　SA—Roadside Level 5
　SS—Roadside Level 6
　HB—Roadside Level 7
　HA—Roadside Level 8
　Bm—Median Level 2

Am—Median Level 3
SBm—Median Level 4
SAm—Median Level 5
SSm—Median Level 6
HBm—Median Level 7
HAm—Median Level 8

3 Embedment conditions

nE—Barrier footing embedded in soil with post spacing in n meters

E_1—Concrete barrier footing embedded in soil

E_2—Concrete barrier footing connected to the structures beneath

nB_1—Buried in structures such as foot bridges, passageways and open culverts with embedded sleeve as foundation and barrier post spacing is n meters

nB_2—Buried in structures such as foot bridges, passageways and open culverts with embedded anchor bolt as foundation and barrier post spacing is n meters

nC—Buried in a concrete foundation set independently and barrier post spacing is n meters

4 Format

1) General form

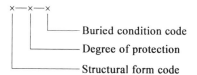

2) Sample

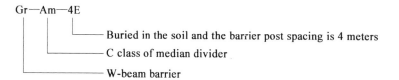

2.1.2 The notations used for the barriers on a bridge consists of three generic notations namely of structure notation, protection notation and intallation notation, which are defined are as follows:

1 Structural forms

Bp—Beam guardrail

Rcw—Reinforced concrete barrier

Cm—Composite barrier

2 Protection levels
B—Roadside Level 2
A—Roadside Level 3
SB—Roadside Level 4
SA—Roadside Level 5
SS—Roadside Level 6
HB—Roadside Level 7
HA—Roadside Level 8
Bm—Median Level 2
Am—Median Level 3
SBm—Median Level 4
SAm—Median Level 5
SSm—Median Level 6
HBm—Median Level 7
HAm—Median Level 8

3 Installation conditions
B—Footing buried in concrete
Fp—Bridge railings fixed on bridge deck by flange connection

4 Format

1) General form

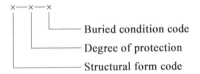

2) Example

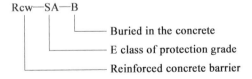

2.1.3 The notations of barrier ends and transition treatment consist of notations of structural form and protection levels of barrier ends and transition treatment. The provisions are as follows:

1 barrier end and transition treatment structural forms
AT1—Roadside upstream terminal: AT1-1 flared buried type; AT1-2 flared round type; AT1-3 energy-absorbing type

AT2—Roadside downstream terminal

BT—Corrugated beam barrier and concrete barrier transition structures: BT-1 wing-wall type; BT-2 lap-joint type

CU—Crash cushions

CT—Highway barriers of median opening ending structure (Median opening end treatment?)

DT—Barrier triangle ending structure (not clear to me)

FT—Tunnel portal end structure

2　Protection levels of anti-collision end treatment or crash cushions

TB—Level-1

TA—Level-2

TS—Level-3

3　Notation

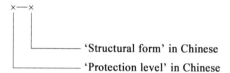

1) Sample

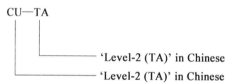

2.2　Notation for visual guiding devices design

2.2.1　Visual guiding device design are composed of type noation of visual guiding devices, structural forms selection and installment conditions evaluation which are defined as follows:

1　Visual guiding devices

V_G—Visual guiding devices

2　Structural forms

De—Delineator

De (Rbw)—Delineator (white reflector plate)

De (Rby)—Delineator (yellow reflector plate)

De (Rsw)—Delineator (white retroreflective sheeting)

De (Rsy)—Delineator (yellow retroreflective sheeting)

Cv—Merge warning signs
Gca—Alignment guide signs
Dt—Tunnel outline belts
Wp—Warning posts
Wb—Warning blocks
Ip—Intersection posts

3 Installation
E—Embedded in the soil
At—Attached
At1—Attached to the corrugated beam barriers
At2—Attached to the concrete barriers
At3—Attached to the walls of tunnels
At4—Attached to cable barriers
At5—Attached to the safety walk near the edge of traveled way

4 Notation

1) General form

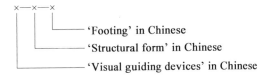

2) Sample

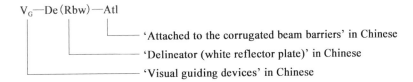

2.3 Notations for fencing design

2.3.1 Fencing design are composed of type notation of fencing, structural form selection and installation condition evaluation, which are defined as follows:

1 Fencing
F—Fencing

2 Structural forms
Em—Expanded metal
Ww—Welded web
Wn—Woven net
Bw—Barbed wire
Wb—Wall building

3 Footing
E—Embedded in soil
C—Buried in concrete

4 Notation

1) General form

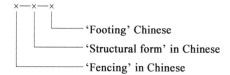

2) Sample

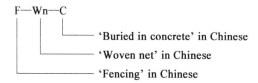

2.4 Notations for netting design

2.4.1 Netting for falling objects are composed of netting, structural forms and footing, which are defined as follows:

1 Netting for falling objects
Bf—Netting for falling objects

2 Structural forms
Em—Expanded metal
Ww—Welded web
Wn—Woven net
Mp—Metal plate

3 Footing

B—Buried in or attach to the multiple span structures

4 Notation

1) General form

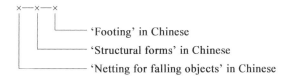

2) Sample

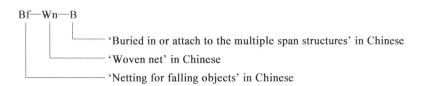

2.4.2 Symbols of rockfall netting are composed of notations of rockfall netting and structural forms, which are defined as follows:

1 Rockfall netting
Sf—Rockfall netting

2 structural forms
Rs—Wire mesh
Cs—Circular meshes

3 Notation

1) General form

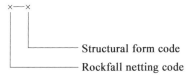

2) Example

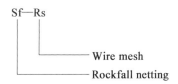

2.5 Symbols for anti-glare devices design

2.5.1 Anti-glare devices design covers anti-glare devices, structural forms selections and footing evaluation. The design elements are codified as follows:

    1 Anti-glare devices
    Gs—Anti-glare devices

    2 Structural forms
    P—Anti-glare board
    N—Anti-glare nets

    3 Footing
    E—Embedded in soil
    C—Embedded in concrete
 Gw—Installed on concrete barriers
  Gr—Installed on corrugated beam barriers

    4 Notation

    1) General form

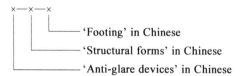

    2) Example

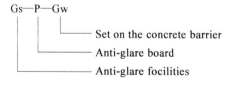

3 Overall Design

3.1 General

3.1.1 For any classified highway, the traffic safety devices shall be designed, implemented and put in operation in paces with the progress of the civil engineering works.

3.1.2 As one of the integrated parts of the overall design for a proposed highway engineering project, the design of highway safety devices shall comply with the following provisions:

1 Coordinating design interfaces: including clarifying the relationships and interfaces between the highway safety devices and the highway civil engineering works, service facilities, or administration facilities, and determining the design priorities among various specialties.

2 Unifying design principles: if the highway engineering is proceeded in stages, highway safety devices are needed to be synchronized designed and implemented in stages of highway civil engineering; if the highway engineering is designed by two or more departments, the one shall be specified to take charge of unifying design principles, technical standards, construction scope and major technical indicators of different design departments.

3 Requirements for documentation: the composition and specific contents of design documents at each stage are needed to be proposed according to the characteristics of highway engineering and the requirements of different design stages.

3.1.3 The overall design of highway safety facilities shall be carried out on the basis of sufficient collection of information such as the plans of the project and the road network where the project locates, the technical requirements, relevant maps and drawings, as well as the conclusions of road safety audits, and site investigations.

3.1.4 The overall design of highway safety facilities shall include the analyses on the project and its road network, the design objectives, as well as the scope of configuration and the criteria for structural design, the design coordination. and the demarcation of interfaces.

3.1.5 In addition to the provisions stated in Clause 3.1.4 in the *Guidelines*, the overall design of highway safety facilities for a highway upgrading or reconstruction project shall include a plan of reutilization of existing facilities, and a plan of temporary highway safety facilities to be used during construction, based on the conclusions of investigation and comprehensive analyses on the existing highway.

3.1.6 The data that shall be collected for the overall design of road safety facilities shall mainly include:

 1 The drawings and files on civil engineering works, service facilities and administration facilities

  1) Overall design

   ① Civil engineering design description, including the technical indicators of the main routes, interchange ramps and intersected roads at intersections, the natural and geographic features of the area, and the design traffic volumes and traffic compositions.

   ② The position and direction of the route in the road network.

  2) The road geometry, subgrade, pavement and drainage

   ① Vertical and horizontal alignment drawings

   ② Tables of tangents, curves and deflection angles

   ③ Design drawings of typical cross-sections

   ④ Stations of starts and ends of cut and fill sections

   ⑤ Stations of median openings

  3) Bridge and culvert

   ① The list of the super-large, large, medium and small bridges and their layout drawings.

② The list of of passageways, culverts and pedestrian overpasses and their overall layout drawings.

4) Tunnel

① Vertical and horizontal alignment design drawings of tunnels (including the design drawings of traffic island on both side of tunnel portals);

② The clearance profiles of tunnels construction and the detailed structure drawings of communication cable trenches;

③ The layout and related tables of tunnel ventilation, fire prevention and lighting facilities.

5) Intersections

① The lists of intersections (including the overpass bridges and the pedestrian overpasses aross over the main route) and the layouts of grade separations.

② The layout plans of interchanges, the cross-setional drawings of the main roadways and ramps at interchanges. Detailed drawings of all connections of all connections of at-grade intersections and interchanges are additionally collected later at the stage of detailed design.

③ The traffic volumes and traffic compositions at the entrances and exits of interchanges.

④ The at-grade intersections and interchanges at main service areas.

6) Service and administration facilities

① The layouts and location stations of service facilities and administration facilities such as service areas, parking areas, administration agents, maintenance agents and toll stations.

② The lists and the layouts of field devices for traffic surveillance.

7) Cost estimating and budgeting

The tables about the material price and rate in the estimates and budgets documents of civil engineering design.

    2   Data to be collected by site investigation inquiry

        1) Current situations, problems and suggestions in relation to the safety devices on surrounding roads of the highway networks shall be surveyed by inquiring the highway operators, maintenance departments, traffic administration departments and various highway users.

        2) The historic design drawings of safety devices in the surrounding road networks shall be collected, focusing the functional allocation and traffic management methods among the highways in the region, the information coordination and continuity of traffic signs, and the layout of highway service facilities, in accordance with the new project.

3.1.7　In addition to the provisions of Clause 3.1.6, and for the overall design of safety facilities of a reconstruction and upgrading project, the following data shall be collected:

    1   Statistics of traffic crash history on existing roads, Road Safety Audit reports, and project as-built documents for safety facilities, etc.

    2   Information about current situations, problems and suggestions in relation to the safety facility installed on the existing highway shall be collected by inquiring highway operators, highway maintenance undertakers, traffic administration agents and various highway users.

    3   The reports on condition survey of existing highway safety facilities.

3.2　Conceptual analysis on the project and road network

3.2.1　The analyses on project-related information shall include the following:

    1   Functions and location of the highway project within the road network.

    2   Scope of direct service and indirect service of the highway project.

    3   Locations of important roadside facilities, such as transportation hubs, scenic areas, and protected zones of drinking water source.

    4   Technical standards, terrains, traffic features and environment.

3.2.2 The analyses on relationship of the project and the road network where the project belongs to shall include the following:

1 Information on chainage in relation to the starting point and ending point of the project;

2 Information of the start points and end points of the highway sections overlapping with other highways;

3 Information of the start points and end points of the highway sections passing through urban areas;

4 Information in relation to multi travel route options;

5 Information on the naming and numbering of related routes;

6 Information on highway intersections, railway crossings and acrossings over navigation channels.

3.2.3 The comprehensive analysis of traffic safety on the proposed highway in the point of road users' view shall include the following:

1 Potential safety risks and hazardous sections during highway operation;

2 Critical aspects in the safety designs for highway safety facilities.

3.3 Design objectives

3.3.1 The design objectives of highway safety facilities shall be proposed from the perspectives of service, safety, administration, environment, and costs in conjunction with the analysis outcomes of the project and road network.

Background:
Combined with functional requirements and construction costs of highway safety facilities, this Clause proposes the design objectives of highway safety facilities from the perspectives of service, safety, management, environment protection and costs. It does not mean that all the five objectives shall be fully accomplished in every project. The design objectives shall be determined rationally based on project features and site characteristics. For example, the design objectives for touring

highways are proposed mainly from the perspectives of service, safety, and environment protection, whereas costs may not be taken as a critical objective.

3.3.2 From the perspective of 'user priority', the design of highway safety facilities shall provide technical supports to satisfy highway user's needs of driving information guidance, driving comfortability, and safe travel.

Background:
Highway safety device designers are needed to pay sufficient attention on the coordination with the project developers and the civil work designers, and accurately appreciate the ideas and concepts embodied in civil engineering design, so as to idenrity to whom and in what extent the traffic safety devices can be provided.

3.3.3 The objectives of designing safety facilities shall be guided by the safety assurance concept, and focus on the major safety issues, safety risks and hazardous sections (or places) as stated in Clause 3.2.3 above.

Background:
Detailed design objectives include specific requirements for the reflection of traffic signs and road markings, the impact energy of barriers, the protection level of barriers at median openings, and so on.

3.3.4 The objectives of designing highway safety devices shall be conducive to highway maintenance, highway operation and traffic safety management.

Background:
The designers of highway safety devices can be kept tight coordination with the highway operators, maintenance undertaker and traffic management agents to accurately learn the needs of highway operation and management, such as speed control, permitted vehicles, and clearance profile.

3.3.5 The design of highway safety facilities shall put forward the objectives of nature harmonization, and insist on conservative policy in environment vulnerable areas.

Background:
For highways that pass through environment sensitive areas, such as touring highways, the design of highway safety facilities are need to minimize the impact on the natural environment. Relevant countermeasures such as the use of graphical traffic signs, and the provisions of hollow structured barriers are encouraged.

3.3.6 Based on 'life-cycle cost' concept, the design of safety facilities shall pursue the objective of maximizing the benefit to cost ratio and minimizing the operation and maintenance costs.

Background:
The design of highway safety facilities shall pay attention not only to the construction costs, but also the subsequent costs of maintenance and restoration, such as the costs of routine maintenance, incident remedy, material stocking and relevant overhead costs. The design of safety facilities must also be forward-looking, that is, after being put into use, it should not lose or greatly reduce its functional abilities due to the small amount of pavement overlay, covering and other maintenance work that occurred later in the process.

3.3.7 The objectives of the recycling of existing facilities and the installation of temporary safety facilities shall be put forward in highway upgrading and reconstruction projects.

Background:
The reutilization of the highway safety facilities generally includes direct utilization, reuse by transformation, use as temporary facilities and use as materials. From the perspectives of resource conservation, highway upgrading or reconstruction projects shall take the reutilization ratio of existing devices as one of the design objectives. In addition, in order to meet the needs of construction during traffic operation, some design objectives for configuration of temporary safety devices, such as the layout of traffic signs and protection levels of barriers, shall be proposed.

3.4 Scope of application

3.4.1 The scope of implementation for highway safety facilities shall be determined based on the adopted design objectives with considerations on the road network planning, highway function, technical classification, traffic volume and traffic composition, and highway environment.

1 A highway system consists of road users, vehicles and environment. The provisions of highway safety facilities shall improve road safety, driving behavior and road adaptability of vehicles.

2 Customized solutions for highway safety facilities shall be provided according to the various features of highway sections.

3.4.2　Primary arterials, which consist of all motorways, shall be provided with systematized and complete traffic signs, road markings, visual guiding devices, fences, necessary nettings and glare screens as specified in the *Guidelines*. Roadside barriers must be installed on bridges and in high embankment sections. For the sections where the clear zone distances are inadequate, designers shall make decisions whether barriers shall be provided in accordance with the concepts for barrier configuration. Median barriers must be continuously installed where the median width of an integral formation is less than or equal to 12 m. Transition designs shall be carried out for the connections of barriers with different rigidity. Movable medians must be equipped at median openings. Crash cushions shall be installed at the exit ramp/connector gores.

3.4.3　Secondary arterials, which consist of motorways, Class-1 and Class-2 highways, shall be provided with complete traffic signs, road markings, visual guiding devices, fencing and netting devices as specified in the *Guidelines*. Roadside barriers must be provided on bridges and high embankment sections. For the sections where the clear zone distances are inadequate, designers shall make decisions whether barriers shall be provided in accordance with the concepts for barrier configuration. For sections of Class-1 highway where the median width of its integral roadways is less than or equal to 12 m, median barriers must be continuously installed. Transition design shall be carried out for the connection of barriers with different rigidity. Movable barriers must be equipped at median openings on a motorway section. Anti-glare devices shall be provided for Class-1 highway as needed.

3.4.4　Main collector-distributors, which are Class-1 and Class-2 highways, shall be provided with fairly complete traffic signs, road markings, any necessary visual guiding devices and fencing as specified in the *Guideline*; for bridges or sections with high embankment, roadside barriers must be applied, for the sections below the suggested clear zone distances, barriers shall be provided complying with the provisions of barriers; traffic separating devices to enhance traffic safety shall be placed at the medians of Class-1 highways with integral formation.

3.4.5　Minor collector-distributor highways, which are Class-2 and Class-3 highways, shall be provided with fairly complete traffic signs, road markings, and any necessary visual guiding devices as specified in the *Guidelines*. Roadside barriers shall be installed on bridges and in the high embankment sections. For the sections with inadequate suggested clear zone distances, designers shall make decisions at discretion whether barriers shall be provided.

3.4.6　Local highways, which are usually Class-3 and Class-4 highways, shall be installed with the traffic signs as specified in the *Guidelines*, and provided with road markings and any necessary visual guiding devices in the sections of inadequate sight distances, sharp curves or steep grades. Roadside barriers shall be installed in the sections of inadequate clear zone distances, at steep cliffs, deep valeys or water banks.

3.4.7 For any continuous long downhill grade, designers shall make decision on whether an escape ramp shall be provided according to the relevant provisions of the *Guidelines* and the comprehensive road safety evaluation. Traffic signs, road markings, and traffic separation devices, protection and impact attenuation devices shall be installed where an escape ramp is provided.

3.4.8 For road sections vulnerable to wind or snow damages, wind screens, snow fences, snow poles, and other related safety devices shall be provided according to the *Guidelines*. Height restriction gantries, speed humps and convex mirrors and other devices may be provided based on the needs of operation and traffic management, according to the *Guidelines*.

3.5 Structural design standard

3.5.1 The classification of actions, representative values and combination of actions shall comply with the provisions as follows:

1 The actions for structural design of highway safety facilities shall comply with provisions listed in Table 3.5.1-1. The standard value of the vehicle transverse impact load for bridge railings shall comply with the provisions in the *Guidelines*, but the standard values, representative values and combination of action design values shall be all calculated according to provisions of the prevailing *General Specifications for Design of Highway Bridges and Culverts* (JTG D60). When there are other non-negligible actions on the structure, the calculation of standard values, representative values and combination of actions design values shall be in accordance with relevant specifications.

Table 3.5.1-1 Loading conditions for structural design of highway safety devices

Type of devices	Name of actions	Classification of actions
Barriers	Structural gravity (including additional gravity of structure)	Permanent actions
	Gravity of soil (at-grade barrier)	
	Lateral earth pressure (at-grade barrier)	
	Prestressing force (cable barrier)	
	Wind load	Variable actions
	Load on sidewalk or bikeway railing	
	Vehicle impact load	Accidental actions

continued

Type of devices	Name of actions	Classification of actions
Traffic signs, netting for falling objects, fencing, anti-glare devices, wind fences, snow fences, height restriction warning gantries	Structural gravity (including additional gravity of structure)	Permanent actions
	Gravity of soil (place at the subgrade)	
	Lateral earth pressure (place at the subgrade)	
	Wind load	Variable actions
	Temperature effect	
Anti-collision height restriction gantries	Structural gravity (including additional gravity of structure)	Permanent actions
	Gravity of soil (place at the subgrade)	
	Lateral earth pressure (place at the subgrade)	
	Wind load	Variable actions
	Temperature effect	
	Vehicle impact load	Accidental actions
Raised pavement markers	Wheel load	Variable actions

2 According to the actions that may occur simultaneously in the structure during operations, the actions for structural design of highway safety facilities should be respectively combined based on the limit states under ultimate loadings and normal loadings, and the worst unfavorable combination shall be used for design.

3 Where the structural design of highway safety facilities is designed according to the limit state under ultimate loadings, the following two types of combination of actions shall be adopted:

1) Fundamental combination. Combination of design values of permanent action and variable action, the formula of the effects of fundamental combination actions are as follows:

$$S_{ud} = \gamma_0 \left(\sum_{i=1}^{m} \gamma_{Gi} S_{Gik} + \gamma_{Q1} S_{Q1k} + \psi_c \sum_{j=2}^{n} \gamma_{Qj} S_{Qjk} \right) \quad (3.5.1\text{-}1)$$

$$\text{or } S_{ud} = \gamma_0 \left(\sum_{i=1}^{m} S_{Gid} + S_{Q1d} + \sum_{j=2}^{n} S_{Qjd} \right) \quad (3.5.1\text{-}2)$$

Where:

S_{ud}—Design value of the effects of fundamental combination of actions at ultimate limit state;

γ_0—Important factor of a structure, shall be selected according to the structural design safety level as specified in the current *Unified Standard for Reliability Design of Highway Engineering Structures* (GB/T 50283), as shown in Table 3.5.1-2; the safety levels of structural design may be adjusted in accordance with the specific situation of the location of the safety facilities, but shall not be lower than the level as specified in Table 3.5.1-2.

γ_{Gi}—Partial safety factor for the ith permanent action, shall be adopted as specified in the provisions of Table 3.5.1-3;

S_{Gik}, S_{Gid}—The ith standard and design value of actions with permanent actions;

γ_{Qj}—Partial safety factor for the jth variable actions, in which the γ_{Q1} is the partial safety factor of dominant variable actions and $\gamma_{Qj} = 1.4$;

S_{Qjk}, S_{Qjd}—The jth standard and design value of actions with variable actions, in which the S_{Q1k} and S_{Q1d} are the controlling values of the variable actions;

ψ_c—Factor for combination value of other variable actions in addition to dominant variable actions: where permanent action and dominant variable action combine another variable action, the coefficient for combination value of another variable $\psi_c = 0.8$; where there are two or more other variable actions besides the dominant variable action, $\psi_c = 0.7$;

m—The amount of permanent actions in the combination;

n—The amount of variable actions in the combination.

Table 3.5.1-2 Safety class of structural design of highway safety facilities

Safety class of structural design	Type of facility	Importance factor of a structure γ_0
Level 2	Bridge railings, netting for falling objects, wind fences and snow fences installed on super-large bridges Cantilevered traffic signs and gantry traffic signs on motorways or Class-1 highways	1.0
Level 3	Structures of other highway safety facilities	0.9

Table 3.5.1-3 Coefficients for permanent actions

Type of actions	Partial safety factor of permanent actions	
	Detrimental to the structural loading capacity	Favorable to the structural loading capacity
Gravity of structure	1.2	1.0
Gravity of soil	1.2	1.0
Lateral earth pressure	1.4	1.0
Prestressing force	1.2	1.0

2) Accidental combination. Combination of characteristic value of permanent action, one representative value of variable action and the standard value of accidental action. The formula of combination of accidental actions are as follows:

$$S_{ud} = \gamma_0 \left(\sum_{i=1}^{m} s_{Gik} + \psi_{f1} S_{Q1k} + \sum_{j=2}^{n} \psi_{qj} S_{Qjk} + S_{Ad} \right) \qquad (3.5.1-3)$$

Where:

S_{ud}—The combination action design value of accidental actions in the limit states under ultimate loading capacity;

ψ_{f1}—Coefficient for frequent value of dominant variable actions: where the action is wind load, $\psi_f = 0.75$; where the action is the load on railings for pedestrians or bicyclists, $\psi_f = 1.0$; where the action is temperature, $\psi_f = 0.8$; where the action is others, $\psi_f = 1.0$;

ψ_{qj}—Factor for quasi-permanent value of the jth variable actions: For wind load, $\psi_q = 0.75$. For the load on railings for pedestrians or bicyclists, $\psi_q = 0.4$. For temperature gradient action, $\psi_q = 0.8$. For other actions, $\psi_q = 1.0$;

S_{Ad}—The standard value of accidental actions (impact load).

4 Where the strucutres of highway safety facilities are designed according to the limit state under normal operations, the frequency combination of the actions shall be adopted, that is, the permanent action standard value is combined with the frequent variable value of dominant variable actions and quasi-permanent value of other variable actions. The formula of combination action are as follows:

$$S_{fd} = \sum_{i=1}^{m} S_{Gik} + \psi_{f1} S_{Q1k} + \sum_{j=2}^{n} \psi_{qj} S_{Qjk} \qquad (3.5.1\text{-}4)$$

Where:

S_{fd}—Design value of the effects of frequent combination actions at the limit state under normal operations;

ψ_{f1}—Factor for frequent value of dominant variable action; For the load on railings for pedestrians or bicyclists, $\psi_f = 1.0$. For wind load, $\psi_f = 0.75$. For temperature gradient action, $\psi_f = 0.8$. For other actions, $\psi_f = 1.0$;

ψ_{qj}—Fatctor for quasi-permanent value of the jth variable actions: For the load on railings for pedestrians or bicyclists, $\psi_q = 0.4$. For wind load, $\psi_q = 0.75$. For temperature gradient action, $\psi_q = 0.8$. For other actions, $\psi_q = 1.0$.

Background:

1 *Loading safety of structures are the basis for the functions of safety facilities. The structural design of safety facilities is based on the process of carrying out the calculation of the loadings, and is also one of the contents of the design of safety facilities.*

The structural types of highway safety facilities are various and there are numerous types of functions involved. The main considerations for carrying out the calculation of structures of safety facilities are listed in the Table 3.5.1-1. For other effects, such as the shrinkage and creep actions of concrete barriers, there are currently no conditions for calculation, therefore, they are not listed in Table 3.5.1-1. However, in the design, it is still necessary to consider the possible effects of this type of action on the use of the structure and to adopt appropriate treatments.

The actions are classified as permanent action, variable action, and accidental action according to the variation of time change. Permanent action refers to the action that the value of the magnitude does not change with time or its change is negligible compared with the average value during the design reference period. Variable action means that the value of the magnitude changes with time in the design reference period and its change is not negligible compared with the average value. Accidental actions are those that do not necessarily occur during the design reference period, but once occur, they have a large value and a very short duration.

2 *Limit state of ultimate loading capacity is generally based on the fact that structure internal force exceeds its bearing capacity or is not suitable for continued bearing, such as the longitudinal bent or break of barriers after the vehicle impacts, the slip and overturning of roadway barrier foundation or the damage of deck slab of bridge railings, the column bending or overturning of structural supports for signs under wind load, and the raised pavement markers crashed by wheels.*

The limit state of normal use is generally based on structural deformation, cracks and vibration parameters which exceed the allowable limit of normal service or durability. The design of limit state of normal use of structural supports for highway signs mainly considers the deformation of the structure not exceeding the allowable limit, especially the deformation of traffic signs, fences, anti-glare devices, wind fences, snow fences and height restriction gantries under wind load and temperature change.

For the limit state under consideration, where determining the actions, all possible actions can be combined. The total value of actions of the combinations in the structure is obtained, and the worst unfavorable group in all possible combinations can be selected to be the design basis for the ultimate state.

3&4 *The design of the ultimate state of the loading capacity of the safety facility structure can be divided into two combination actions according to the possible functions, namely the basic combination and the accidental combination. The basic combination refers to the combination of the design value of permanent action and the design value of variable action, which is applied in the conventional design of the structure and shall be considered in all safety facility structures. Accidental combination refers to the standard value of permanent actions and the action of a certain representative value of variable actions and the standard values of accidental actions, which is to be used in some special cases of design rather than the structures of all safety facilities, mainly for the stress check calculation of impact load on barriers and height restriction gantries.*

The design of normal use limit state of safety facility structures mainly considers the deformation of traffic signs, fences, anti-glare devices, wind fences, snow fences and other structures under the combination actions. In the process of using, the deformation limit is allowed to be exceeded in a short or not long time overall. Therefore, short-term action can be only considered and designed according to frequent composition. (Long-term action is applicable to the normal use limit state associated with the number of overload, such as the design of human comfort where the structure vibrates, according to the quasi-permanent combination design).

The Equation (3.5.1-1) and Equation (3.5.1-2) are the load effect expression of ultimate limit state commonly used in various structural design specifications. The basic parameters of the former adopt standard values, and then multiplied by the partial safety factor; the latter expresses the basic design parameters by the design value after multiplying the standard value by the partial factor. The two equations are essentially the same.

Structural design safety class is divided based on the severity of the consequences of structural damage, which reflects the difference of reliability of different structures. The Unified Standard for Reliability Design of Highway Engineering Structures (GB/T 50283—1999) stipulates that the design safety level of highway engineering structure includes Level-1, Level-2 and Level-3. According to the severity of the possible consequences of damages to the structures of safety facilities, the design safety level is stipulated as Level-2 and Level-3. The types of safety facilities corresponding to different safety levels are listed in Table 3.5.1-2. Designers may also agree with the owner to adjust the structural design safety levels in accordance with specific conditions of the safety facility structure, but shall not be lower than the level specified in Table 3.5.1-2.

The load has variability. It is not possible to directly quote various statistical parameters that reflect the variability structural design. Through complex probabilistic operations, it is necessary to give a specified value to the action, which is called representative value. Actions have four representative values, which are standard value, frequent value, quasi-permanent value and combination value. The standard value is the basic representative value of action, the magnitude of which must take the possible maximum value which may appear in the structure design in prescribed time limit, which is generally determined by the value of a certain quantile of the maximum probability distribution that is applied to the design reference period. Frequent, quasi-permanent and combination values are the representative values of variable actions. Since various variable actions are unlikely to act simultaneously on the structure at the same time, if all the standard values are accumulated, the calculation results tend to be conservative. Therefore, the frequent, quasi-permanent and combination values are reduced by multiplying the standard value by the corresponding factor. Frequent value refers to the value of variable action that occurs relatively frequent in structure and is large in value, which is obtained by multiplying the standard value by frequency coefficients less than 1. The quasi-permanent value refers to the value of variable actions frequently occurred in structures, but it is smaller than the frequency value of the variable actions, which is obtained by multiplying the standard value by a quasi-permanent value coefficient smaller than frequency coefficient. The combination value is the variable action value that makes the combination action of the variable action more consistent with the corresponding probability where the load appears alone during the design reference period, or the variable action value that makes the structure have a uniform and reliable index after combination.

The values of combination action expressions [Equation (3.5.1-1)-Equation (3.5.1-4)], as well as the function sub-item coefficient, frequent coefficient, quasi-permanent coefficient and combination coefficient are determined according to the relevant provisions of the prevailing General Specifications for Design of Highway Bridges and Culverts (JTG D60).

3.5.2 Permanent action shall conform to provisions as follows:

1. The standard value of structural weight may be calculated according to the design dimensions of the structural elements and the unit weight of materials.

2. Prestressing force, gravity of soil and lateral earth pressure shall be calculated in accordance with the provisions of the prevailing *General Specifications for Design of Highway Bridges and Culverts* (JTG D60).

3. The design of concrete barrier and steel-concrete barrier should take into consideration the shrinkage and creep of concrete.

Background:

1 *Unit Weight of common materials as shown in Table 3-1.*

Table 3-1 Unit weight of common materials

Material	Unit weight (kN/m^3)	Material types	Unit weight (kN/m^3)
Steel	78.5	Cement mortar	20.0
Cast iron	72.5	Glass fiber reinforced plastic (GFRP)	14.0-22.0
Reinforced concrete	25.0	Aluminum alloy	28.0
Plain concrete	24.0	Aluminum	27.0
Earth fill	17.0-18.0	Mortar rubble	23.0

3 *Due to the shrinkage and creep actions of concrete, cracks, especially vertical penetrating cracks are found in concrete walls of the concrete barriers and composite barriers. Concrete*

material is discontinuous in the cracks, however, the safety protection role of barriers as a longitudinal continuous structure would not be adversely affected thanks to the rebars embedded in the barriers, although the development of cracks will lead to the rusting of the rebars and thus affect the durability of the barriers. Therefore, the design of concrete barriers and composite barriers should take concrete shrinkage and creep into account to avoid abrupt change of cross-sections to reduce the uneven shrinkage of concrete and the constraints on the displacement of deformation. Loadings due to concrete shrinkage and creep also shall be considered and the resulting cracks shall be controlled.

3.5.3 Variable loadings shall conform to provisions as follows:

1 The standard value of wind load shall be calculated in accordance with provisions of the prevailing *Wind-resistant Design Specification for Highway Bridges* (JTG/T D60-01). The return period of basic wind pressure shall be 50 years.

2 The standard value of wheel load for raised pavement markers shall be 70 kN. The tire contact length and width shall be 0.6 m × 0.2 m.

3 The standard value of temperature shall be calculated according to provisions of the prevailing *General Specifications for Design of Highway Bridges and Culverts* (JTG D60).

4 The standard value of the horizontal thrust on the top of railing columns on sidewalks or bikeways shall be 0.75 kN/m; the standard value of vertical force on handrails shall be 1.0 kN/m.

Background:
2 *The standard value of vehicle wheel load for raised pavement markers and the landing size of wheels are determined according to the current General Specifications for Design of Highway Bridges and Culverts (JTG D60), and the ground pressure of tires calculated from this is about 0.6 MPa.*

4 *The standard values of the load on railings for pedestrians or bicyclists are determined according to the prevailing General Specifications for Design of Highway Bridges and Culverts (JTG D60).*

3.5.4 Accidental impact loading shall conform to provisions as follows:

1 Impact vehicle type, impact speed, and impact angle adopted in the structural design and

safety performance evaluation of barriers shall meet the requirements of the prevailing *Standard for Safety Performance Evaluation of Highway Barriers* (JTG B05-01). When a particular vehicle type in the traffic composition of the actual highway section is not included in the specified impact vehicle types, the vehicle type does not need to be considered in the structural design and safety performance evaluation.

2 When designing a test piece for bridge railings, the standard value of the vehicle transverse impact load on the test piece shall comply with provisions as shown in Table 3.5.4. On the basis of comprehensive analysis of factors such as roadway alignment, degree of roadside hazards, operating speed, traffic volume and traffic composition etc., the vehicle transverse impact load shall be calculated according to Level 1-C when the adopted protection level is lower than Level 1-C. The vehicle transverse impact load shall be determined according to the actual impact conditions when the adopted protection level is higher than Level 8-HA.

Table 3.5.4 Standard values of vehicle transverse impact load for bridge railings

Protection level	Code	Standard value (kN)		Distribution length (m)
		$Z = 0$ m	$Z = 0.3\text{-}0.6$ m	
1	C	70	55-45	1.2
2	B	95	75-60	1.2
3	A	170	140-120	1.2
4	SB	350	285-240	2.4
5	SA	410	345-295	2.4
6	SS	520	435-375	2.4
7	HB	650	550-500	2.4
8	HA	720	620-550	2.4

Note: Z is the maximum lateral dynamic deflection value of the bridge railings.

3 The vehicle impact load on a height restriction gantry may be calculated with Equation (3.5.4). The direction of impact is in accordance with the direction of travel. The point of action is located at the geometric center of the beam.

$$F' = \frac{m|v_t - v_0|}{T} \quad (3.5.4)$$

Where:

F'—The vehicle impact load on the height restriction gantries (kN);

m—The total mass of the design vehicle (tonne), which shall be determined in conjunction with the on-site survey data of traffic flow for the sections;

v_0—The operating speed of the vehicle before impact (m/s), which shall be determined based upon the actual observation result of traffic flow;

v_t—The operating speed of vehicle after impact (m/s), which shall allow the impact vehicle to stop with emergency braking power in front of the bridge or tunnel with vertical clearance limitation;

T—The duration (s) of a vehicle impact on the height restriction gantries. It varies from 0.1 s to 1 s, 1 s for flexible height restriction gantries and 0.1 s for rigid height restriction gantries.

Background:

1 *The design and safety performance evaluation of every barrier structure are carried out according to the impact vehicle types, impact speeds and impact angles under the corresponding protection levels in the current Standard for Safety Performance Evaluation of Highway Barriers (JTG B05-01). Therefore, the safety protection of barriers is premised on the impact test conditions that the corresponding protection level is not exceeded under real impact conditions. The impact vehicle types stipulated in the current Standard for Safety Performance Evaluation of Highway Barriers (JTG B05-01) reflects the traffic composition under normal conditions. For the special highway such as touring highways and freight specialized highways, the traffic compositions do not include the specified impact vehicle type (for example the touring highways may not have trucks and freight specialized highways may not have large and medium-sized coaches), barrier structural design and safety performance evaluation may not consider the vehicle types.*

3 *Height restriction gantries are classified as overheight warning gantries and crash-worthy height restriction gantries in accordance with the different functional requirements. The functions of height warning gantries are to alert and warn the drivers that there are height restriction bridges or tunnels so that overheight vehicles cannot pass; the anti-collision gantries have certain crash-worthy capability and can absorb part of the kinetic energy of impact vehicles. After impact into crash-worthy gantries and brake with emergency braking power, overheight vehicles shall be able to stop in advance of the bridges or tunnels.*

The vehicle impact load Equation (3.5.4) of the crash-worthy gantries is based on the momentum theorem. The method involves fewer parameters, which is simple in calculation and easy to use. In the equation, the vehicle operating speed v_t after impact can be determined by the horizontal distance between the crash-worthy height restriction gantries and the height restriction bridges or tunnels. Where the distance is far, the driver will have more reaction and braking time after the impact with height restriction gantry, so the vehicle operating speed v_t after a impact can be set to a higher value, thereby reducing the force requirements on the height restriction gantries and vice versa.

It is not possible to accurately calculate the time where the anti-collision gantry structure is designed, and the Equation (3.5.4) stipulates the approximate value of the rigid height restriction gantry that does not substantially deform after the impact as 0.1 s, and that of the flexible height restriction gantry which deform greatly after the impact is approximately 1 s, which lead to a certain amount of errors in application of the equation. Therefore, the equation applies to the design of crash-worthy height restriction gantries, and the tests of specific design functions is supposed to rely on computer simulation and other techniques.

3.5.5 The structural design of highway safety facilities shall be based on the most probable and worst loading combinations that may occur concurrently during operations. The loading combinations shall be selected from the bearing capacity limit states and service limit states respectively. The structural design of highway safety devices shall concurrently meet structural and technological requirements.

3.6 Design coordination and interface demarcation

3.6.1 The coordination of highway safety facilities with highway civil engineering and construction, service facilities and administration facilities shall be improved; the provisions of civil engineering and constructions, service facilities and administration facilities shall be optimized from the perspective of operational safety to avoid the missing or omission of items and the potential safety risks. The overall design of highway safety facilities shall conform with provisions of the overall design of the highway.

3.6.2 For highway safety devices that affect the design of highway civil engineering and construction, service facilities and administration facilities, the relevant design standards, schemes or requirements shall be proposed by the responsible party for the design of highway safety facilities according to requirements of the design procedures.

1. For the sections of the Class-3 or Class-4 highways that require barriers, the widened value of shoulder width for sections installing barriers is needed to be provided by the design agency for highway safety facilities.

2. For the motorways and Class-1 highways, the designing agencies of road safety facilities shall take protection form and capability of the median barriers into consideration and put forward the width value.

3. For the safety facilities on bridges, tunnels and other structures, the design agency of safety facilities shall put forward the placement locations, stress conditions and requirements.

3.6.3 In the layout plans of highway safety facilities, the locations of field devices for traffic surveillance, light supports and other administration facilities or service facilities along the highway shall be labeled, the rationality of placement of highway safety facilities shall be checked to avoid visual blockage, omission or duplication. The successive traffic signs and VMS or lighting poles should be placed in suitable spacing with the number of poles consolidated; when different devices block each other, they shall be adjusted in position or installed on the same pole. Traffic signs and road markings shall be provided for service facilities and administration facilities.

3.6.4 The design interface of highway safety facilities with highway civil engineering and constructions, as well as service facilities and administration facilities shall be clearly specified in accordance with the prevailing *General Specification of Freeway Traffic Engineering and Roadside Facilities* (JTG D80).

4 Traffic Signs

4.1 General

4.1.1 The types, colors, shapes, lines, characters, graphics, dimensions and settings of traffic signs shall comply with the requirements of the prevailing *Road Traffic Signs and Markings* (GB 5768).

4.1.2 The information provided by traffic signs shall be entirely related to the needs for safety, services, and management of traffic. The layout and support structure of traffic signs shall not be accompanied by commercial advertisements and other irrelevant information.

4.1.3 The design of traffic signs shall allow the devices to be clearly recognized, correctly understood and properly located to allow for sufficient perception-reaction time by drivers. Highway functions, technical classes, road network, as well as traffic conditions and environment, demand of road users and traffic management shall be comprehensively analysed in design stage, and the following rules shall be follow:

1 Serving function. In order to serve the functions of highways, some factors such as construction purpose, conditions, service objects shall be fully concerned.

2 Systematic design. From the perspectives of system, the design of traffic signs and road markings, signals, yellow flashing signals or other safety devices shall be planned as a whole without contradiction or ambiguity.

3 Consistency. On the same highway section, the design principles, scope of implementation, shapes and styles of the same typed traffic signs shall be consistent.

4 Coordinated design. The installed place of traffic signs shall be coordinated with other

devices such as lighting, monitoring facilities, cables and pipelines, and plantings. Traffic signs shall not be blocked by other devices.

Background:

1 *Serving function. Serving function is the most basic foundation for the design of traffic signs. The purpose of traffic signs is to serve the functions of highways. For example, Class-2 and above highways adopt high or relatively high technical standards, and serve for high traffic volume, they often operate as the arterials, therefore, highway users need more guide signs; national and provincial highways of other classes serve for a large demand of mid-distance and long-distance trips, the demand for guide signs is also high. In above cases, the guide signs have the priority for placement. For example, after the guide signs are installed at intersections, intersection warning signs with similar meanings are not necessary to be provided. But in terms of some lower classes local highway, after engineering feasiblity study, relevant warning signs shall be installed in sections of roads where there is something different from the expectations of drivers due to geometric alignment, pavement, weather and other factors, in order to warn drivers to decelerate or take other actions.*

2 *Systematic design. Based on the safety of highway traffic, from the system perspective, the design of traffic signs and other safety devices such as road markings, traffic signals, and yellow flashing signals shall be coordinated. There shall be no information contradiction and ambiguity between devices and advantages of the system shall be fully played. The placement and change of a certain traffic sign call for the synchronized change of related traffic signs, road markings, signals, etc.*

3 *Consistency. In order to maintain the good visibility of the layout and structure of traffic signs, to meet the driver psychological expectations and make road users quickly obtain the information, reduce information processing time, and enhance understanding and impressions, the design principles, scope of implementation, shapes and styles of traffic signs on the same road are supposed to stay the same. Besides, the same types of signs are best to adopt the same templates and supporting modes, in particular, the templates of the highway numbering signs shall be consistent nationwide.*

4 *Coordinated design. Traffic signs, lighting, cables and pipelines, and plantings shall be designed in a comprehensive and coordinated manners, and their locations shall be reasonably determined so as to avoid visual obstructions, affecting the functions of traffic signs.*

4.1.4 The design of traffic signs shall be based on the approach of overall planning, step-wise progression and focused provisions taking into consideration information demands at different levels for the road networks, route itineraries and road sections. The following steps shall be complied with during the design:

1 The analysis of road network layout, traffic flow and traffic operation;

2 The selection of guide instructions and control information of regional road networks;

3 The design standards, scope of implementations and shape styles of road sections;

4 The analysis of safety features and information demands of key road sections;

5 The tests for overall coordination and adjustments for partial optimization.

Background:

The design of traffic signs is a complicated process. In order to make the design process more scientific and rational, in addition to requiring the designer to have professional knowledge and experience, it also needs rational design methods, so that the entire process of the design complies with scientific and rational design procedures. In general, the provisions of highway traffic signs and road markings should take into consideration of the information requirements at different levels of road networks, routes and road sections, and adopt methods of overall layout, advancing layer by layer, and key provisions. The focus of advancing layer by layer through 'plane-line-point' is as follows:

(1) The 'area' level

Based on the highway network, features of the highway traffic flow in each level of the road network are needed to be analyzed according to traffic engineering theories. Demand characteristics for sign information under different conditions of highway network level, different traffic flow, and different land layout are needed to be analyzed. Considering the entire road network structures, traffic volume, the directions of traffic flow and information guidance requirements, overall plans and general layout for traffic signs are needed to be made to determine the guidance direction, control information, provision levels, and divisions of right-of-way.

(2) The 'line' level

In the road network environment, the scope and standard of traffic signs along the whole highway are determined according to the function, technical class, technical conditions, traffic conditions, and environment of the single highway in the design project. Traffic sign system of a road network contains many kinds and a huge amount of traffic signs. For a route or a road network, it is not easy to fully achieve the functions of traffic signs without a unified provision principle. Therefore, in the design of traffic signs, the overall layout of the entire system is needed to be determined systematically, logically and humanely. According to road network planning, highway functions, technical classes, technical conditions, traffic conditions, and environment, the provision scales, standards and the design key points are needed to be determined to achieve unified construction standards.

(3) The 'point' level

Traffic signs are needed to be designed specifically for important nodes such as interchanges, rest areas, intersections, high-risk sections and other special sections in the road network. After providing initial plans, inspections and comprehensive considerations are needed considering the prevailing circumstances from aspects of the vision, security, overall layout, etc. Integrating, adding or reducing types, adjusting the information and locations, or optimizing the forms and structures of traffic signs are needed to be considered till the traffic signs of entire road network are continuous and uniform.

4.2 Provision principles

4.2.1 Traffic signs shall provide clear, definite and concise information for highway users who are unfamiliar with the road conditions but have planned for their itineraries.

4.2.2 The traffic signs shall target at specific road conditions and carry out the systematic layout and comprehensive installation on the basis of comprehensive analysis of safety so as to be compatible with actual traffic operations of the road sections. For road sections with potential safety risks, active guidance and warning instructions shall be strengthened; for multi-lane highways, the visual recognition of traffic signs to road users in different lanes shall be considered equally; for road sections with adverse weather conditions, the coordinated installation of static signs and variable message signs shall be enhanced.

4.2.3 Where there are dangerous locations that affect safety and are not easily found on the highway itself and the environment along the highway, the warning signs shall be installed based on sufficient demonstration. Warning signs shall not be overused.

4.2.4 Regulatory signs shall be provided at conspicuous locations near the start of a road section where certain traffic or pedestrian behaviors are prohibited or restricted. The provision of speed limit and associated signing shall be based on the comprehensively consideration of factors such as highway function, technical class, urbanization of roadside areas, geometric features, operating speeds, traffic operation, traffic crashes, and environment and so forth. Their needs, the speed limits and the forms of provisions shall be determined on the basis of a holistic analysis of road safety. Installation of speed limit signs is then subject to agreement by the responsible authority. The installation of speed limit signs shall meet the following requirements:

1. The speed limit should be implemented in the unit of road section, and the speed limit of the road section should not be changed frequently.

2. The speed limits may be different from the design speeds.

3. According to the operation characteristics of different vehicle types and the requirements of safety management, the speed limit for vehicle types may be adopted.

4. The speed limit signs shall be used in conjunction with other safety facilities.

Background:
The design of highway speed limit signs is a multi-factor decision and balance process, which must be analyzed and demonstrated in traffic engineering:

1. *The highways with the same design speed also differ in the linear index. The main reason is that the design speed stipulates the limit index of the restricted road section, but there is no regulation on the upper bound. The design standards and specifications also encourage designers to adopt higher technical indicators if the objective conditions permit. Therefore, a road adopting the unified design speed is likely to appear. The technical conditions and operating conditions of roads in different road sections are significantly different. In addition, operating conditions of some individual local road sections such as sharp bends, restricted viewing distances, tunnels, and sections affected by special weather and frequent-crash road sections are relatively special. Therefore, it is advisable to implement the speed limits of the road sections according to the specific road conditions so that the driver can have sufficient time to maintain a stable speed and make the vehicles run smoothly. Frequent changes in the speed limit must be avoided.*

2. *The design speed is a theoretical technical indicator, which is usually the representative value of the corresponding minimum technical indicator to be followed in terrain constrained road sections (such as small radius curves, steep grade, limited sight distance, etc.) on the premise of ensuring safety. The design speed has a direct relationship with the terrains along the highways, the cohesion of the design speed of adjacent road networks, and the construction cost. However, the design speed cannot represent the actual operating status of the highway, so the design speed is one of the important factors where considering the decision of the speed limit value, but not the only one.*

3 *The performance differences between trolleys and carts represented by minibuses in China are more prominent. The speed limit for different types of vehicles can be adopted based on traffic composition, the operating speeds and crashes with consideration of highway functions, operation efficiency, traffic safety and traffic management.*

4 *It is infeasible to improve road safety by simply lowering speed limit. Drivers should be be the priority during the selection of speed limits, and try to make the driver's driving expectation consistent with the highway and related environments. In order to achieve the goal, it is necessary to comprehensively use various types of safety facilities such as guide signs and warning signs and deceleration markings.*

4.2.5 According to the needs of traffic flow organization and traffic management, indicative signs shall be provided at sites where drivers and pedestrians are prone to be uncertainties or must comply with driving regulations.

4.2.6 Guide signs shall be laid out in a comprehensive manner according to the principle of integrated road network. It will be necessary to ensure that the information is well coordinated, and the phenomenon of insufficient, improper or excessive information must be avoided. On the basis of highway function, direction of traffic flow and the spatial distribution of urban areas along a route, information with larger traffic demands shall be given priority with respect to travel distance, population and the level of social-economic development.

4.2.7 The extent of guide signs towards tourist areas shall be rationally determined on the basis of the hierarchy of the tourist attractions and road network conditions. Other traffic signs have higher priority if there are conflicts with tourist area signs. Messages of tourist attractions may be incorporated into the sign face of guide signs provided that there is no overloading of information.

4.2.8 The provision of informatory signs shall not affect the provision and visual recognition of warning, regulatory, indicative and guide signs.

4.2.9 The comprehensive provision scheme of traffic signs at highway at-grade intersections shall be rationally determined based on factors such as traffic management method, physical form, technical class of intersecting highways, direction of traffic flow as well as following the principles of well-defined right-of-way, rational channelization, clear guidance, safety and orderliness. Traffic signs shall be coordinated with road markings to guide vehicles through the intersection.

4.2.10 The specific location of traffic signs shall comply with the requirements in the prevailing *Road Traffic Signs and Markings* (GB 5768) and meet the following requirements:

1 Traffic signs shall not affect the sight distance of highway and traffic safety.

2 Traffic signs shall not be too close apart, or obscuring each other; otherwise structural supports not blocking each other shall be adopted.

3 Traffic signs shall not be blocked by other devices such as overpasses, lighting devices, surveillance facilities and plantings.

4 Traffic signs on motorways and Class-1 arterialss shall not be installed within the roadside clear zone. Where they are necessary, the sign posts shall be of breakaway or energy dissipating systems, or else roadside barriers shall be placed according to their installation principles.

4.3 Sign face design

4.3.1 The layout of guide signs shall be concise and clear enough to reflect the name, location, direction and distance of routes, and the layout of information shall meet the following provisions:

1 In destination-distance signs, the destination shall be laid at the far left side and be arranged from near to far, and top to bottom.

2 Where there is a sign with information of two destinations in the same direction, it should be in one row or two rows with the sequence of near to far, left to right or top to bottom.

3 In the first line of motorway exit notice signs, this shall be the number (name) information of the exit links; and in the second line, this should be the information of one or two destinations that can be reached by the connecting highways.

Background:
The arrangement of the name, destination and distance in guide signs must be unified and arranged in a certain order, which conforms to the actual conditions of the road and the expectations of drivers, so as to help drivers to interpret and understand the information.

4.3.2 Indicating arrows in the guide signs should reflect the correct driving direction of the vehicle at a certain angle and meet the following requirements:

1 Where the arrow of a gantry sign or an attached sign on an overpass is used to indicate the

function of the traveled way or the destination, the arrow shall be pointed downwards and point to the center line of the traveled way.

2 Where indicating the advancing direction of vehicles rather than a specific road, the arrow shall be pointing upwards.

3 Where indicating the direction of the exit, the arrow shall be inclined upwards, and the angle of inclination shall reflect the alignment of the exit lane.

4 As for the arrow in the guide signs for at-grade intersections, it shall be pointing upwards where indicating straight travel direction, and shall be consistent with the alignment of the turning lane where indicating turns. Where the three directing arrows pointing up, left and right are arranged up and down, they shall be arranged from top to bottom in the order of up, left, and right, and the arrows pointing upwards and leftwards shall be put on the left, and the arrows pointing rightwards shall be put on the right. Where three directing arrows pointing to the up, right and left directions are arranged from left to right, they shall be arranged from left to right in the order of left, up and right.

5 Indication signs for interchanges and multileg at-grade intersections may use curved arrows that indicate the real shapes of interchanges and at-grade intersections. The graph patterns of arrows shall be clear and legible without ambiguity and complication.

6 In guide signs, where the indicating arrows are in the same layout with the geographical information and numbering information and arranged from top to bottom, the direction arrows shall be below the geographical and numbering information. Where arranged from left to right, the arrows directing leftwards and straight and shall be on the left and the arrow directing right shall be on the right.

***Background*:**
The arrow sign on the traffic sign is one of the important means to convey traffic management information. Human eyes tend to be more sensitive to arrows and other graphics than to texts. Therefore, a reasonable use of arrow graphics can play a fast and clear role in the information transmission, which can improve the efficiency of communication. The direction and angle of arrows establish the links among the destination indication, direction and traveled way, and it shall be selected according to functions and management requirements.

1 *Where the arrow of a gantry sign or an attached sign on a overpass is used to indicate the function of traveled way or the destination of travel, the arrow shall be downward and point to the centerline of the traveled way, as shown in Figure 4-1 a).*

2 *Where indicating the advancing direction of the vehicle rather than a specific traveled way, the arrow shall be upward, as shown in Figure 4-1b).*

3 *Where used to indicate the direction of the exit, the arrow shall be inclined upwards, and the angle of inclination shall reflect the alignment of the driveway exit, as shown in Figure 4-1c).*

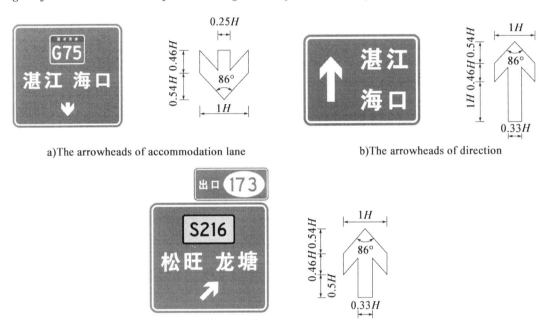

Figure 4-1 The arrows of exit

Note: *H* is the height of letters.

5 *The arrow graphic itself in the guide sign is also a kind of information, which requires the driver to take time to read and understand. Therefore, where using graphical information, the graphic shall be concise and clear, and the guidance shall be clear and direct, as shown in Figure 4-2. For complex at-grade intersections or interchanges, it is not appropriate to use complete geometric layouts as graphic information, so as to avoid more difficulty for drivers to read and bringing potential safety hazards.*

Figure 4-2 A design sample of graphical traffic signs

4.3.3 Ports, railway stations and airports in guide signs shall adopt the graphic symbols at the same time, as shown in Figure 4.3.3-1, and shall comply with the provisions of the current *Road*

Traffic Signs and Markings (GB 5768). The direction of aircraft head in the symbol of 'airport' heading left, up or right shall be consistent with the driving direction, as shown in Figure 4.3.3-2.

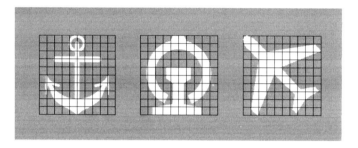

Figure 4.3.3-1 The symbol of large transportation hubs

Figure 4.3.3-2 The orientation of aircraft head

4.3.4 Traffic signs nested in use shall meet the following requirements:

1 The regulatory signs and indicative signs applied to the white plate without border are the signs that must be complied with, and their sizes of layout and graphics shall not be arbitrarily changed.

2 The stop and yield signs of prohibition signs shall not be used on the white plate without border.

3 Where prohibition signs and indicative signs are provided with auxiliary signs, they can be used together on white plate without border.

4 In the road sections with prohibition signs for vehicles, if the corresponding notice and warning signs are not installed at the appropriate positions before entering the road section, the regulatory signs patterns shall be nested in the guide signs.

5 Motorways and national highways should be nested on the traffic signs in the form of numbers. The urban street names should be nested on the motorway guide signs in blue background.

Background:

2 *Because of the legibility of the layout of the stop and yield signs of prohibition signs, they shall*

not be applied to the white plate without border in accordance with the provisions.

4.3.5 The dimensions of traffic signs and the height of characters shall comply with the provisions of the prevailing *Road Traffic Signs and Markings* (GB 5768), which shall be determined according to the design speed except for special provisions. Where the differences between operating speeds and design speeds of a road section is higher than 20 km/h, the layout specification and legibility of the traffic signs should be evaluated according to operating speeds. In special circumstances, the dimensions of traffic signs and the sizes of characters shall be appropriately increased or reduced based on sufficient demonstrations. The following provisions shall be met:

1 The determination of guide signs dimensions shall rely on the height of characters, the number of words in the layout, the demands for using other letters simultaneously, pattern layout and layout optimization and so on.

2 The warning, prohibition and indicative signs installed in areas with high traffic volumes, with multiple traffic lanes, or complex traffic conditions, the dimensions or height of characters may be larger than those determined by the design speed after demonstration.

3 Where the installation space is limited for signs of warning, regulatory and indication in median barriers to use post-type structural supports, the dimensions of signs may adopt the minimum value. The side length of triangle warning signs shall not be less than 0.6 m. The diameter of circular prohibition signs shall not be less than 0.5 m. The side length of triangle prohibition signs shall not be less than 0.6 m. The diagonal length of octagon prohibition signs shall not be less than 0.5 m. The diameter (or short side length) of indicative signs shall not be less than 0.5 m.

4 Where guide signs in tunnels or on bridges are restricted by construction gauge and structural bearing capacity, the height of the characters may be properly reduced, but it shall not be less than 0.8 times of the normal value, or a narrow font with an aspect ratio of 1 : 0.75 shall be adopted. However, the interrelationships between the various elements of the layout shall not be changed.

4.4 Materials

4.4.1 Materials for traffic signs shall be of sufficient strength, durability and corrosion resistance. The material and structure shall be appropriate, economical, light-weight and environment-friendly in accordance with local conditions, with considerations of aesthetics.

4.4.2 For highway upgrading and reconstruction projects or traffic sign replacements, the material for traffic signs shall be re-utilized according to the real conditions under the commitment of expected applied functions and the quality of the projects.

***Background*:**
The re-utilize of materials for traffic signs may be in many ways, such as replacing the retro-reflective sheeting, changing the layouts, displacing the signs, adding and deleting the contents of layouts. Under the commitment of expected applied functions and the quality of the projects, integrating the engineering needs and the performance status of the signs, the re-utilize of traffic signs usually adopts the following schemes:

(1) The original signs can be re-utilized as materials. In terms of materials for sign layouts, back supporting materials, etc., the materials shall be in the same or similar specifications as those on the original roads, so that although the original signs cannot be totally re-utilized, it can be fully utilized as accessories such as a steel pipe and an aluminum alloy chute for back support.

(2) The original signs can be re-utilized in other places after the layout transformation. For the upgrading of highways, most of signs on original mainline need to be replaced with the increased height of characters. In this case, the layout of these signs can be used in other places where the size is appropriate to take full advantage of them.

(3) The original signs can be directly re-utilized on new roads depending on the situation. If the performance of retro-reflective sheeting is decreased, it can be replaced.

(4) The original signs can be re-utilized as temporary signs. The traffic signs that have been rusted and no longer be used on new roads, can be used as temporary traffic signs.

4.4.3 The various materials used for the surface, panels and structural supports for the same traffic signs shall be compatible, which will help to avoid corrosion or damage to the sign board caused by electrochemical effects, and different thermal expansion coefficients or other chemical reactions.

4.4.4 The retroreflective performance of retroreflective sheetings used on traffic signs shall comply with provisions in the prevailing *Retroreflective Sheeting for Traffic Control* (GB/T 18833). The selection of retroreflective sheeting classes shall comply with the following principles:

1 For highways with strong influence from the environment, high speeds and high traffic volume, high class retroreflective sheetings should be used.

2   For highways with low traffic volume, retroreflective sheetings may be of a lower class than other highways depending on prevailing circumstances.

3   For special highway sections with complex traffic movements multilanes, varying cross-sections, sight distance restriction or large viewing angles, retroreflective sheetings for warning signs and regulatory signs should be of a higher class than those of other traffic signs of the highway.

4   For overhead traffic signs such as gantry signs, and cantilevered signs, etc., retroreflective sheetings should be of a higher class than those of roadside traffic signs.

5   For traffic signs on road sections susceptible to adverse weather conditions, such as rain and fog, higher class retroreflective sheetings should be adopted.

4.4.5   Class V retroreflective sheetings should be used for regulatory signs, indicative signs, and warning signs in the following circumstances:

1   Sections with small radius curves on the mainline of motorways and Class-1 highways, and small radius ramps of interchanges.

2   At-grade intersections or road sections with complex traffic movements, poor visibility, or excessively large viewing angles.

3   Sections with three or more lanes in one direction.

4   Sections with varying cross-sections.

5   Very high proportion of large vehicles.

4.4.6   Active luminous or illuminated signs should be adopted for the signs that indicate the emergency telephone, fire equipment, cross passageway for pedestrians or vehicles, evacuation in tunnel, etc. The materials and requirements of active luminous or illuminated signs shall comply with the provisions of current *Road Traffic Signs and Markings* (GB 5768).

***Background*:**
The driving environment of tunnels is different from that of general roads, which mainly reflect in the changes of illumination, field of view and ventilation, besides, many tunnels also have cross-sectional changes. All of these may have a greater impact on safety than the general road sections,

especially the signs indicating the emergency telephone, fire equipment, cross passageway for pedestrians or vehicles, evacuation in tunnel must be more easily identified and marked in any case.

4.4.7 Traffic signs plate may be made of aluminum alloy plate, extruded aluminum alloy profile, thin steel plate, synthetic resin plate, etc. The relevant indicators and production of the plate shall comply with the provisions as specified in the current *Road Traffic Sign Board and Supporting Part* (GB/T 23827). The thickness of the plate shall meet the strength requirements.

4.4.8 Large traffic signs may be made in blocks and assembled on-site, but the number of assembling blocks shall be reduced as much as possible. The joint part shall not overlap with the figures, characters and important symbols in the signs. The overall strength of the sign plate after assembling shall be not less than that of the whole plate.

Background:
Where selecting the traffic sign plate, it shall be determined according to the highway grades, meteorological conditions, economic conditions and comprehensive consideration of mechanics of materials, durability, construction convenience and other factors. Large-size sign plate (more than 5 m^2) are recommended to use aluminum alloy plate, which have the advantages of light weight, high strength, corrosion resistance and wear resistance. In terms of the plate with an area of more than 15 m^2, for the convenience of transportation, installation and maintenance, it is usually formed by extruding aluminum alloy plates. The section is shown in Figure 4-3. It is necessary that the number of assembling blocks shall be reduced as much as possible. The stitching seam must not overlap with the figures, words and important symbols in the signs, ensuring that the overall strength of the sign plate after splicing is not less than that of the whole plate.

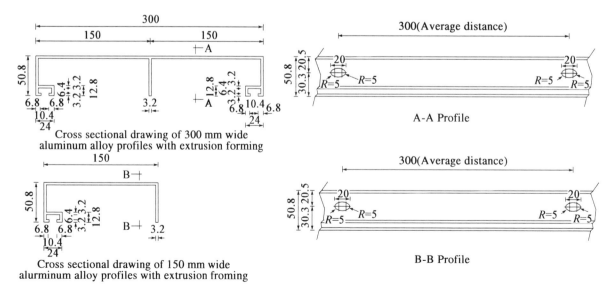

Figure 4-3

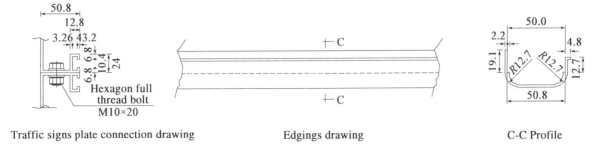

Figure 4-3 A sample of the cross section of traffic signs plate with extrusion forming (Unit: mm)

4.4.9 The materials used for the supporting structure of traffic signs shall meet the following requirements:

1 Traffic signposts and beams may be made of steel tube, H-beam tube, channel steel, wood, synthetic materials, and reinforced concrete materials, etc. posts and beams shall not be assembled in the length direction, and their terminal parts shall be provided with caps.

2 The steel components of traffic signs must be rust-proofed and anti-corrosion.

3 The base of traffic signs should adopt an enlarged base. Where the foundation is too large or the quality of soil at the base is poor, the pile foundation may be adopted.

Background:
This clause stipulates the materials commonly used in the structural supports for highway signs:

1 *Steel pipes, H-beams, channel steels, etc., as posts and beams of traffic signs, have the advantages of high strength and good processing performance, but it is corrosive and antiseptic treatment is required. Concrete-filled steel tube has the advantages of both steel pipe and concrete. With high strength and small deformation, it has greater advantages where the height of the signpost is more than 10 m. Wood can be used on the highways with lower classes and lower traffic volume or temporary traffic signs.*

2 *The steel components can be used only after anti-corrosion treatment, and hot dip galvanizing can be adopted.*

3 *Traffic signs generally apply reinforced concrete to expand the foundation. Floor-standing traffic signs located on the soft-base road sections can use station foundations. The buried depth of the post depends on the external force of the board and the bearing capacity of the foundation. The single-post traffic sign located at the bridge section can be based on a steel structural supports and attached to the bridge.*

4.5 Support forms and structures

4.5.1　The single-post supporting structure should be applicable to warning, regulatory, indicative signs and small guide signs. The double-post or multi-post supporting structures may be applied to the middle-sized or large guide signs. Where the terrain conditions are constrained, the post may be installed asymmetrically under this circumstance that driving safety and the function of signs are ensured.

4.5.2　In the following circumstances, traffic signs shall be mounted overhead using structures such as cantilevers or gantries:

1　Recognition of roadside traffic signs is blocked or interfered.

2　Sight distance or traffic safety is affected by roadside traffic signs.

3　Roadside space is constrained and post mounted traffic signs are not feasible.

4　There are three or more lanes in one direction.

5　Traffic volume is at or close to design capacity, or the proportion of large vehicles is very high.

6　Exit guide signs of interchanges between motorways, complex interchanges or interchanges with close spacing of exits.

7　Multilane exit ramps of interchanges or left exit ramps.

8　Advance guide signs and guide signs for at-grade intersections.

9　Sections with frequent lane changes.

10　Sections with high density of traffic signs.

11　Motorway sections in urban areas.

4.5.3　Where the exit ramp of interchange is located behind the overpass bridge and the distance is relatively close, an advance exit sign shall be attached to the overpass bridge.

Background:

The exit sign is installed in the triangle termination of the intercommunication exit and plays the role of identifying the exit location, so that the driver can confirm the exit. Where the exit ramp of interchange is located behind the overpass bridge and the distance is relatively close, it tend to block the signs at exit ramps and exit triangles. Therefore, the signs in the triangle terminal exit are usually attached to the overpass bridge, or an attached exit sign is added on the overpass bridge (Figure 4-4).

Figure 4-4 Example of exit guide sign mounted onto overpass in advance of an exit

4.5.4 The connection between the exit number signs and the main signboard to which it is attached shall be subject to stress calculation so as to select the appropriate connection method.

4.5.5 Removable anti-loose and anti-theft nuts may be used on the structure of traffic signs. Their average anti-unloading and anti-loosening torque should not be less than 200 N · m.

4.5.6 Where the traffic posts adopt the breakaway and energy-dissipating structure, the design shall comply with the following provisions:

1 The possible dangers to other vehicles and pedestrians after the dissipation of the post shall be taken full consideration so it should not be used in bus stops and pedestrian concentrated area.

2 It should not be installed in the side ditch of gutters, steep slopes and other places where vehicles are prone to jump after crash.

3 It should be ensured that safety and durability of disassembled facilities are not affected under wind load.

4 After the vehicle crashes into energy-dissipating structures, the height of the indissoluble parts remained in road or above the ground should not exceed 10 cm.

5 Where power equipment is installed up in the energy-dissipating structure, effective measures shall be taken to prevent fire and electric shock after crash.

6 The safety performance of energy-dissipating structures shall be verified by vehicle crash tests, and the test method and safety performance evaluation criteria may refer to the prevailing Evaluation Specification for Highway Safety Barriers (JTG B05-01).

Background:

The traffic signs (especially the posts) installed on the roadside are obstacles for vehicles driving out of the road. From the perspective of roadside safety, the farther the roadside traffic sign is from the highway, the better. Therefore, the visibility of the sign and the safety requirements of the roadside are a contradiction. In designing, both requirements must be taken into consideration. Due to land shortages and other reasons, most of the road traffic signs in China will be located within the roadside effective clear zone width. The traffic signs within the roadside effective clear zone width of the motorways and first-class highways shall be protected by energy-dissipating structures or barriers according to the specifications of the sign structures; as for the traffic signs within the roadside effective clear zone width of other roads, corresponding warning tips are necessary to ensure driving safety.

The energy-dissipating structure refers to the signposts, lampposts and traffic light poles which can absorb the crash energy through its own disintegration where hit by a vehicle, in order to reduce the severity of traffic crashes. First established in the United States in the 1960s, energy-dissipating structures have now become the basis of a tolerant design. So far, it has been widely used in the United States and Europe, and the United States has established a crash test standard. Manual for Assessing Safety Hardware (AASHTO 2009) and structural design standards Standard Specifications for Structural Supports for Highway Signs, Luminaires, and Traffic Signals (AASHTO 2013). There is no specific test standard for energy-dissipating structures in China, so in practice, it can refer to provisions as specified in the current Evaluation Specification for Highway Safety Barriers (JTG B05-01).

5 Road Markings

5.1 General

5.1.1 Road markings include all kinds of road markings, direction arrows, literal symbols, object markers and raised pavement markers, etc. The classifications, definitions, and colors of the road markings shall be in accordance with those specified in the current *Road Traffic Signs and Markings* (GB 5768).

5.1.2 The design of road marking shall meet the following general provisions:

1 Road marking design shall take full account of human, vehicles, roads, environment and other factors, and conduct a comprehensive investigation and analysis to ensure that the design is targeted and systematic.

2 Road marking design shall guide the traffic properly and ensure the orderly driving of vehicles.

3 Road markings and traffic signs shall be used cooperatively and the meanings of them shall not be contradictory.

4 The material of road markings shall perform well in durability, skid resistance, convenience and economy of construction. In the normal service life period, it also shall have good visibility.

5.1.3 Design of road markings may be implemented in the following order:

1 Collect the following basic information: cross-sections, interchanges, at-grade intersections, service facilities, bridges, tunnels and climate conditions, etc.

2　Well design and deploy road markings by taking road and traffic conditions, environment, traffic management, materials and other factors in to account.

Background:
Road markings placed on highways play an important role in providing road users with travel guidance and information services. In some cases, road markings can be used as a supplement to traffic signs and signals. Road markings can also be used alone to provide regulatory, warning and guiding information that other devices cannot perform.

Of course, road markings also have limitations. The visibility will be constrained by snow, debris, and pavement hydrops. The durability of road markings is affected by material characteristics, traffic volume, weather, and location. Therefore, in the design of road markings, it is necessary to comprehensively take road conditions, traffic flow, traffic management and materials into account to conduct well design and deployment.

It is necessary to collect relevant data and to be more specialized in road marking design. For example, in terms of areas with more rain in southern regions, drainage gaps are needed to reduce the water blockage of road markings.

5.2　Provision principles

5.2.1　The design of road markings for general highway sections shall comply with the following provisions:

1　General highway sections of motorways and Class-1 highways shall be equipped with traveled way edge lines and lane lines. For Class-2 highway or below, except for the single lane highways, centerlines for opposing traffic shall be provided. Traveled way edge line shall be laid on the following sections of Class-2 highway or below:

1) Narrow bridges on highways and their upstream and downstream sections;

2) Curved sections to minimum highway design standard and their upstream and downstream sections;

3) Merging or diverging sections;

4) Highway sections with varying pavement width;

5) Highway sections where roadside obstacles are close to the traveled way;

6) Highway sections with frequent adverse weather conditions affecting traffic safety such as heavy fog;

7) Mixed traffic road section with high volume of non-motorized traffic or pedestrians.

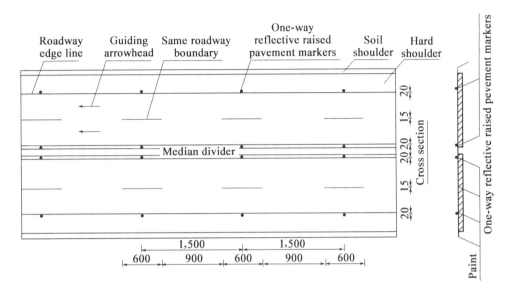

Figure 5.2.1　**Example of markings design of motorway basic sections with design speed of 100 km/h** (Unit: mm)

2　If there is a slow vehicle lane on a Class-2 highway, center lines, lane lines and traveled way edge lines shall be provided accordingly.

3　Traveled way edge lines shall be provided within the paved shoulders adjacent to the traveled way on both sides of the road. Traveled way edge lines for highways without paved shoulders shall be provided on both outer edges of the highway adjacent to the traveled way. Lane lines shall be provided between lanes with the same direction of travel.

4　The width of the road markings should comply with the provisions of Table 5.2.1.

Table 5.2.1　The width of road markings

Design speed (km/h)		Edge line (cm)	Lane line (cm)	Center line (cm)
120, 100		20	15	—
80, 60	Motorway, Class-1 highway	20	15	—
	Class-2 highway	15	10	15

continued

Design speed (km/h)		Edge line (cm)	Lane line (cm)	Center line (cm)
40, 30		15	10	15
20	Two-lane Two-way highway	10	—	10
	Single lane highway	10	—	—

Background:

The prevailing Road Traffic Signs and Markings (GB 5768) has a certain range of regulations on the centerlines, lane lines and edge lines. The Guidelines provides with some stipulation in Table 5.2.1 according to the design speeds.

5.2.2 The design of road markings for special sections shall comply with the following provisions:

1. For bridge sections with strong crosswinds, or with sharp curves and steep grades, tunnel portals, traveled way width transition sections, intersections and pedestrian crossings approaches, lane lines prohibiting passing across lanes shall be provided, and the line width shall be accorded with the center lines.

2. Where the road sections and bridge sections of Class-2 highways and below are as wide as the approach sections, the double solid yellow lines or single solid yellow lines shall be provided at the center lines on bridge sections, and the solid-dotted yellow lines shall be provided for a distance longer than 160 m at both ends of the bridge approaches, as shown in Figure 5.2.2-1 a). Where the section of highway and bridge is narrower than the roadway and the width is less than 6 m, the center lines shall not be provided within the bridge and the transitions at both ends, as shown in Figure 5.2.2-1 b).

3. The approaches of tunnels portals shall be taken as the independent design units. The design of the road markings shall be integrated with the devices such as the traffic signs, barriers, visual guiding devices and other devices in the design of the road markings, refer to Appendix A.

4. The road markings at climbing lanes shall be provided continuously. The broken line with the length of 100 cm and the clear spacing of 100 cm is set along the transitions on the left side of the travel direction. The solid line is provided in the normal section. The edge line is set along the right side of travel direction. Then it is transited to connect to the edge line of standard road section. The width of the broken line and the solid line is the same as that

of the edge line of the standard road section, as shown in Figure 5.2.2-2.

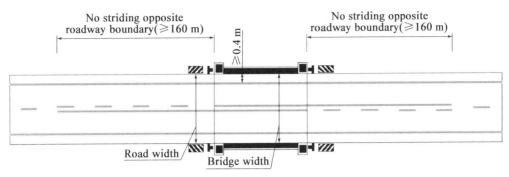

a) The provisions of traffic markings in bridge sections as wide as roadway

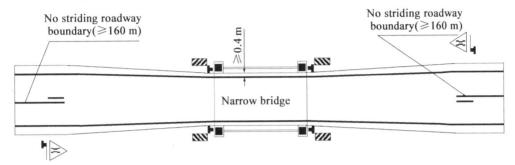

b) The provisions of traffic markings in the bridge sections which are narrower than the roadway and where width is less than 6 m

Figure 5.2.2-1 Example of markings at bridge sections of Class-2 highway and below

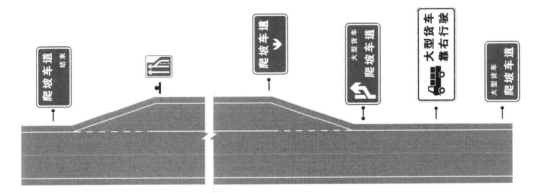

Figure 5.2.2-2 Example of markings at the climbing lane

5 Object markers shall be provided on the facades of overpass near the clearance profile of road, pier of aqueducts, end faces of the wing walls of tunnel portals, and facades of other obstacles. The facade is marked with alternating diagonal yellow and black strips with a width of 15 cm. Where installed, the downward inclined side shall face the traveled way and should be painted to a height of more than 2.5 m above the road pavement.

6 Bridge piers, central piers, toll islands, physical refuge islands or channelization islands, lamp bases, sign bases, and other solid facades that could pose a threat to safety within the clearance profile of a highway overpass shall be provided with object markers. The object

markers are with oblique lines of yellow and black with a line width of 15 cm. They are painted from the middle of the entity to the sides at an angle of 45°, and it should be painted to a height of 2.5 m above the road pavement.

7   If there are no pedestrian crossing facilities on the roads in front of schools, kindergartens, hospitals, and nursing homes, pedestrian crossings and indicative signs shall be provided refer to the current *Specifications for Layout of Road Traffic Facilities Around Primary and Secondary School* (GA/T 1215). The installation distance of the pedestrian crossing shall be determined according to the actual needs, but it should be more than 150 m. Where installed pedestrian crossings in the section without traffic signals, stop lines and advance signs of pedestrian crossing shall be installed on the pavement before reaching the pedestrian crossing, coordinated with pedestrian crossing indicative signs. If necessary, pedestrian crossing warning signs may also be installed.

The pedestrian crossings shall not be set under the following conditions:

1) Sections with poor sight distance, sharp curve, steep grade or other dangerous sections and transition sections where road width is changing;

2) Facilities for pedestrian to cross the road, such as pedestrian bridges and pedestrian under passes and road sections within a range of 200 m.

8   In the place where there is necessary to make vehicles slow down or remind drivers of safe driving, longitudinal or transverse speed reduction markings are necessary to be installed as required. Where installed speed reduction markings, attentions shall be paid to drainage and skid resistance. Transverse speed reduction markings may be used in the form of rumble stripes. Speed reduction markings should be installed in conjunction with speed limit signs or speed limit clearance signs.

9   Where speed hump facilities are installed on Class-2 highways and below, advance markings of speed hump shall be installed within 30 m before and after. Advance markings of speed humps warning shall be installed in coordination with the speed hump markings.

10 The word markings on highway pavement shall be arranged from far to near, and the number of words should not exceed three. The installation specification shall be in accordance with requirements specified in Table 5.2.2. The maximum speed limit value shall be treated as one word.

Table 5.2.2 Specification forword markings

Design speed (km/h)	Character height (cm)	Character width (cm)	Longitudinal clear spacing (cm)
120, 100	900	300	600
80, 60	600	200	400
40, 30, 20	300	100	200

***Background*:**

1 *The solid lane line is used to prohibit vehicle from lane change or passing. In general, the solid lane line should be placed simutaneously with the no passing signs.*

2 *This article is derived from the Road Marking Manual published by the Department of Transportation of British Columbia, Canada, in June 1994, and is applicable to the installation of road markings for Class-2 and below highway bridges.*

3 *Where the tunnel width of motorway, Class-1 highway with the design speed of 120 km/h or 100 km/h is narrower than the roadway, the zebra marking can be inclined toward the driving direction. It is installed in the right paved shoulder within 50 m in advance of the tunnel entrance portal; and as for other highways, it can be set within 30 m.*

5 *The setting of traffic markings at emergency lay by and bus stops can be found in the current Road Traffic Signs and Markings (GB 5768).*

8 *Speeding causes traffic crashes. The drivers may be the contributor of speeding, it is necessary for the highway management department to install some speed limit signs or warning signs on some road sections that call for the driver's attentions, such as steep grades or long tangents. The use of speed reduction markings is the method often adopted in the design. The specific installation principle can be found in the Background of the Clause 5.2.5 in this Guideline.*

10 *Road markings of highway pavement is the symbol that mainly use the literal of pavement to indicate or limit the vehicle driving, such as the speed limits, lane indications (such as quick lane, slow lane). Where the number of lanes in the same direction is greater than 2 or the traffic signs cannot be installed due to terrain constraints, the method of installation of literal symbols on pavement may be adopted. In order to increase the visual recognition, if condition permits, the uphill section may be selected. Considering the mutual influences among vehicles after the traffic volume increase, the article stipulates that the literal symbols on pavement shall be arranged from near to far.*

5.2.3 The design of road markings at the exits and entrances of interchanges, serving areas, and parking areas shall comply with the provisions as follows:

1 The road markings at the exits and entrances of interchanges, serving areas, and parking areas shall accurately reflect the organizational principles of traffic flows according to the type of interchanges, serving areas and parking areas.

2 Entrances and exits of interchanges shall be installed with direction arrows. The specification and iteration of the exit direction arrows may refer to the Table 5.2.3. The exit direction arrow shall be based on the gradient points of deceleration lanes, with space of 50 m. The entrance direction arrow shall be based on the starting point of the acceleration lanes. Depending on the length of acceleration lanes, three or two groups can be installed.

Table 5.2.3 Size and installation times of direction arrowhead

Design speed (km/h)	120, 100	80, 60	40, 30, 20
Length of direction arrows (m)	9	6	3
Iterations	≥3	3	≥2

3 In the field of serving areas and parking areas, the road markings like the parking space markings, division lines and direction arrows shall be installed according to the traffic organization design and function planning of the area.

5.2.4 The design of road markings at-grade intersections shall comply with the provisions as follows:

1 At-grade intersections between Class-3 or higher grade highway shall adopt channelization design, and channelization markings shall be installed. If allowed, channelization islands should be installed and the curb height should not exceed 10 cm. The at-grade intersections of other highways shall be equipped with stop and yield lines in coordination with the signs for stopping or slowing down to give way to pedestrians. The specifications and duplications of direction arrows may refer to the Table 5.2.3.

2 The channelized markings of at-grade intersections shall be designed and installed according to the actual situation of the at-grade intersections and the characteristics of traffic flow. If allowed, it is advisable to open up an exclusive left or right turning lane.

3 The scientific and reasonable channelization of at-grade intersections shall be based on the principle of reducing conflict points and making the vehicle pass quickly and safely.

4 The right-of-way shall be clarified before installation of traffic markings at at-grade intersections. The installation of stop and yield lines and other markings related to the right-of-way shall be improved, and the comprehensive installation of traffic signs and

markings shall be strengthened.

5 Complete safety facilities shall be installed up around the physical island of at-grade intersections.

Background:

3 The design of the channelization shall take into account both the safety and efficiency. They shall pay attention to the following aspects:

1) Fully reflect the forms of grade crossings and the characteristics of traffic arterial. Rationally allocate the main and minor roads, and clearly prioritize the right of way, so as to make the major roads or major traffic flow smooth, with less conflict points and small and scattered conflict zones.

2) Reduce the complexity of the drivers operation at-grade intersections and minimize the passing distance of at-grade intersections.

3) Make the vehicles reach the at-grade intersection more smoothly and reduce the speed differences between the vehicles.

4) Fully consider the needs of vulnerable groups, so that they can cross the at-grade intersection safely. The installation of pedestrian crossings shall consider the factors such as pedestrian flow, highway classification and traffic management mode.

4 The right-of-way management is the important content of the installation of road markings on at-grade intersections.

5 Large areas of channelization markings make it easier for drivers to violate traffic rules. Strengthening the application of physical islands can effectively change the situation. Because the physical island has certain impacts on safety, it is necessary to strengthen the safety devices around them.

5.2.5 The design of traffic markings at the toll plaza shall meet the following requirements:

1 Speed reduction markings and toll island markings shall be placed at the entrance of the toll plaza, and the spacing between speed reduction markings shall be calculated and determined according to the entry speed and the length of the plaza.

2 The lane lines may be installed on the toll plaza exit termination. Where the toll plaza space allows, the lane lines may be extended appropriately.

3 For the toll stations with ETC toll lanes shall be equipped with ETC related markings, including ETC lane edge lines, ETC lane speed limit markings, and ETC lane pavement literal markings.

4 For the toll plaza with more than 5 one-way toll lanes, the road markings shall be solely designed.

Background:
The distance between the horizontal speed reduction markings and the toll plaza shall be calculated according to the entry speed and the length of the plaza by using Newton's second law (the final velocity may be taken as the expected value). The control index is the same time for vehicles to pass through each speed hump marking, and as the space becomes closer and closer, the drivers would think they were faster and faster, so they take the initiative to slow down.

ETC toll lanes shall be marked with appropriate markings so that the vehicle can slow down to the appropriate speed before reaching the ETC lane, ensuring the vehicle safety. ETC toll lanes can make drivers to slow down by installed installation rumble stripes, pavement lettering markings, etc.

5.2.6 The design of road markings at the tunnel portals shall meet the following requirements:

1 Tunnel entrances shall be installed with object markings; channelization lines shall be installed on the right hard shoulders within the range of 30-50 m ahead of the tunnel entrance portal where width is narrower than that of the roadway or bridge; lane lines shall be placed 150 m ahead of the tunnel entrance portal, and the width of the line shall be same as that of the lane lines; raised pavement markers or colored anti-slip markings maybe used. See Appendix A.1.1.

2 Lane lines shall be 100 m after the exit of the tunnel, and the width of the lines shall be same as that of the lane line; a certain length of hard shoulder after the exit of the tunnel may be provided with a channelization line; color anti-skid markings may be installed as required. See Appendix A.1.2.

Background:
The tunnel portal is often the blackspots. The key point of installation the road markings of the tunnel portals is to ensure the safety. It mainly includes: make the tunnel portal more eye-catching by the object markings on the tunnel portal; prompting the drivers to follow the markings through channelization lines at the tunnel portals. For the road surface materials that is not uniform within 3 seconds of travel outside the tunnel portals, color anti-skid markings can be installed to minimize

the effect of uneven road surface materials on the drivers.

5.2.7 The design of road markings of the long downgrade shall meet the following requirements:

1 According to actual conditions, new types of road markings may be installed in road markings road sections with long downgrade, such as color anti-skid markings, horizontal or longitudinal speed reduction markings etc.

2 The road markings installed in road sections with long downgrade shall be in coordination with traffic signs.

3 The installation of road markings on long downgrade shall avoid adverse impact on the driving of drivers.

Background:
The road markings on long downgrade generally have two purposes. One is to urge the drivers to slow down. This type of markings mainly includes visual speed hump markings, lateral speed hump markings, etc. Another is to remind the drivers to pay attention. Such markings mainly include rumble speed hump markings and rumble driveway edge lines. Rumble speed hump markings are generally installed in front of the danger points to remind the drivers to watch out and avoid installed installation at danger points so as not to adversely affect the safe driving of the drivers.

5.2.8 The design of road markings within the service and rest areas shall meet the following requirements:

1 The installation of road markings in the service and rest areas shall be determined according to the plan and design of the relevant field in the house-building engineering.

2 The design of road markings in the service and rest areas shall match the traffic flow.

3 It shall be strengthened with the use of separation belts or separation facilities.

Background:
The installed installation of road markings in the service facility area is crucial for improving the road services. Before installed installation up the road markings in the service facility area, traffic flow and parking space planning shall be done. Based on this, road markings should be installed up.

The layout of traffic flow and parking space shall follow the following basic principles:

(1) Traffic flow planning shall be carried out on the basis of analyzing the needs of drivers.

(2) Different types of vehicles shall be provided with different parking spaces. The type of parking spaces shall be suitable for parking of vehicles.

(3) The traffic signs and markings in the service facilities area shall be designed according to the pedestrian guidance system and the vehicle guidance system respectively to meet the traffic guidelines of vehicles and pedestrians.

The main factors to consider in traffic flow planning include:

(1) Traffic flow planning shall fully consider the needs of drivers for fueling, resting, and catering.

(2) The traffic flow shall adopt the driving route consistent with the direction of the entrance and exit of the traffic, so as to avoid detour and retrace.

(3) Traffic flow such as people flow and traffic flow shall be clear, and the disturbance of people flow to the traffic stream shall be avoided.

(4) The traffic flow planning shall consider the technical requirements of different vehicles, such as the width of the driveway, the radius of the turn, etc.

(5) Avoid the impact of traffic flow on the exclusive lanes of logistics services.

The factors that need to be considered in parking planning include:

(1) The planning of parking spaces shall fully consider the driver's needs and the traffic volume, traffic composition and others.

(2) The installed installation of parking spaces shall be centralized and not be divided into multiple small parking spaces. The parking spaces for large and medium-sized vehicles shall be separated with that of small vehicles parking spaces for small vehicles and buses shall be located close to facilities such as restaurants and leisure facilities.

(3) The type of parking spaces shall be reasonably selected according to the width of the passageway, vehicle models, and traffic volume.

5.2.9 The installation of raised pavement markers shall meet the following requirements:

1 In the following cases, raised pavement markers should be installed on one side of the road marking and shall not intrude on the driveway:

1) On the edge lines of the motorway driveway;

2) On the edge lines of the driveway of the Class-1 highway interchanges, serving areas and parking areas;

3) Entrances and exits of interchanges ramps.

2 Raised pavement markers shall be installed on the division lines of the tunnel.

3 Raised pavement markers may be installed in the following cases:

1) On the lane lines of the motorway driveway;

2) On the edge lines and the division lines of the Class-1 highway;

3) On the longitudinal speed-limit markings;

4) On the dangerous sections such as diversion lines and small-radius flat curves, road narrowing, road obstacles, etc., of Class-2 and Class-3 highways.

4 Raised pavement markers may be individually installed on the edge lines and the division lines of the driveway.

5 Tunnel sections and fogy road section may be installed with active luminous raised pavement markers as required. Snowy road in winter may not be installed with raised pavement markers.

6 The color, position and spacing of the raised pavement markers shall comply with the provisions of the current *Road Traffic Signs and Markings* (GB 5768).

Background:
The raised pavement markers are reflective and non-reflective objects installed on the road surface to mark the boundaries of the driveway, the edge, the diverging and merging traffic, the curve, the dangerous road section, the change of the road width, and the position of the road obstacles.

Where the vehicle deviates from the driveway, the raised pavement markers can give the drivers a rumble alert to avoid traffic crashes. Reflective raised pavement markers can play a role of visual guiding at night. In the main text, according to different road conditions, the principle of installed installation up raised pavement markers is proposed. For example, the crashes of driving outside the road tend to happen on the motorways and first-class highways because of high operating speeds and the fatigue driving. Therefore, it is recommended that the raised pavement markers must be installed on edge lines of the motorways and the edge of the driveway of the first-class highway interchanges, etc. The active luminescence raised pavement markers on the fogy road sections and tunnel sections can be installed according to the need.

5.3 Material selection

5.3.1 Traffic marking paint can be divided into the type of liquid solvent, solid hot-melt, liquid two-component, and liquid water-based and skid resistance, and its technical specifications shall be consistent with the current requirements of *Pavement Marking Paint* (JT/T 280) and *Quality Requirement and Test Method For Road Road markings* (GB/T 16311).

5.3.2 The road markings shall be reflective. In the normal service life, the retro-reflection luminance coefficient of the white reflective markings shall not be lower than 80 mcd · m^2 · lx^{-1}. The retro-reflection luminance coefficient of the yellow reflective markings shall not be lower than 50 mcd · m^2 · lx^{-1}.

5.3.3 Where selecting the marking material, consideration shall be given to factors such as retro-reflection luminance coefficient, the value of skid resistance, stain-resistant performance, environmental protection performance, adhesion to the road surface, and cost performance of the marking material.

5.3.4 The thickness of the markings shall be selected from the Table 5.3.4 according to its type, location and construction process.

Table 5.3.4 Thickness range of markings (mm)

No.	Marking type		Thickness range of markings	Note
1	Solid hot-melt	Ordinary and reflective	0.7-2.5	Dry film
		Raised	3-7	Dry film. If there is a baseline, the thickness of baseline is 1-2
2	Two-component		0.4-2.5	Dry film
3	Water-based		0.3-0.8	Wet film
4	Resin anti-slide		4-5	Aggregate particle size is 2.0-3.3
5	Performing pavement marking tape		0.3-2.5	—

Background:

5.3.1-5.3.4 *Where selecting the material of markings, the following factors shall be considered:*

(1) The type of hot-melt spray (coating thickness: 0.7-1.0 mm) can be used on the roadway edge lines of motorways, zebra markings, etc., which can meet the requirements of reflection and has the highest cost performance.

(2) The durable marking paint can be used on division lines of the motorway, such as the type of hot-melt blade coating (the coating thickness is 1.5-2.5 mm).

(3) In order to improve the safety of driving at night, all roads, including ordinary roads, need to adopt reflective markings, and the brightness of road markings must meet the requirements of the minimum retro-reflection luminance coefficient within the normal service life.

(4) The resin anti-slide paint and hot-melt raised paint can be used on the blackspots.

(5) The hot-melt spray coating can be used on the cement pavement to increase the cost performance.

(6) The simulation experiment of the marking performance of the German BAST shows that the satisfaction rate of the marking performance with the two-component coating is the highest. This marking has excellent reflective performance and the longest service life. The disadvantages of this marking are high price and strict construction requirements.

(7) For roads with high requirements for environmental protection, the use of water-based paints will be the best choice. At the same time, the performance and price ratio of this kind of marking is good and the reflective performance is excellent.

5.3.5 The technical indicators of raised pavement markers shall comply with the requirements of the current in *Raised Pavement Markers* (GB/T 24725).

5.3.6 Where used in conjunction with paint markings, the raised pavement markers shall be directionally reflective, and the color shall be the same as the marking color. The double-sided reflective markings shall be used for the raised pavement markers installed on the division lines of the opposite-direction roadway or in the tunnel.

***Background*:**

In the events of crashes, fire or other emergencies, contraflow may be allowed, and double-sided reflective markings can be used.

6 Barriers and Railings

6.1 General

6.1.1 Barrier is a kind of obstacles. Where the width of actual clear zone is less than the effective clear zone width, and for vehicles driving out of the road, the consequences of collision with the barriers are lighter than those without the barriers, consideration shall be given to the installation of barriers. The installation of barriers shall also consider the economics of the project. The method for calculating the width of the clear zone is shown in Appendix B.

Background:

By rationalizing the design of highway projects, the effects of accidents due to driving out of the road will be minimized, and those that may have fatal consequences could be eliminated. Installation of barriers is only one of the ways or means reducing the consequences of driving out of the road. It does not mean that the more barriers or the higher the intensity would be the better, because the barrier itself is also an obstacle. Only where the consequence of the collision between the vehicle and the obstacle would be greater than the one between the vehicle and the barrier, installation of the barrier should be considered. The value of human life is priceless, but even in developed countries, whether a barrier is installed or not is based on the results of an engineering economic analysis.

It shall be pointed out that for road sections that meet the requirements for effective clear zone width, if there exists dangers such as cliffs, the safety still needs to be analyzed comprehensively according to the factors such as road alignment, traffic volume, vehicle types composition, and location of risk sources outside the effective clear zone width, to determine if a barrier needs to be installed. In addition, where there are high-speed railways and/or high-voltage transmission towers on the roadside, the installation of barriers also needs to comply with the relevant national laws and regulations.

6.1.2 The main purpose of installing the barriers is to keep the vehicle from collision whose impact energy is less than or equal to the design protection energy and to guide its direction of travel. The following factors shall be considered in the design:

1 Whether the width of the actual clear zone on the roadside or the median meets the requirements of effective clear zone width;

2 Where it cannot meet the requirements of effective clear zone width, the situation of obstacles on the roadside or medians shall be considered;

3 Where the requirements of effective clear zone width cannot be met, the following factors shall be considered such as the design traffic volume, design speed, the proportion of vehicles with the total mass greater than or equal to 25 tonnes, and the alignment conditions of the road sections, etc.;

4 Where the requirements of effective clear zone width are met, the following factors shall be considered such as whether or not there are dangerous terrain such as cliffs, deep valleys, deep ditch, etc. in the vicinity of the roadside, and whether or not the median barriers are designed with measures to prevent vehicles from entering the opposite-direction roadway;

5 Cost-effectiveness of barriers;

6 The coordination with the surrounding environment.

Background:
The factors considered in the design of the barriers are mainly required to estimate the risk of vehicles run-off-road accident. The risk of driving out of the road is related to the probability and the severity of the accident. Specifically, risk assessments of driving outside the road can be analyzed based on the existing conditions of roads and accidents; local risk assessment models and parameters can be gradually established and used.

6.1.3 The design process of barriers should meet the following requirements:

1 Collect data such as road horizontal and vertical alignment, cut-fill data, traffic volume and composition, operating speed and design speed;

2 Collect evaluation reports on safety of the project safety, and investigate the evaluation results of the alignment and its adjustment data;

3 Collect or investigate the distribution of various obstacles within the scope of highway effective clear zone width and materials about its intersection with other roads and railways, etc.

4 For the highway extension and reconstruction projects, collect relevant operation data for at least 3 years, such as traffic volume and composition, weather, and traffic accidents data;

5 Analyze the risk for vehicles of driving out of the road in accordance with the investigation results' analys is of roads with similar characteristics;

6 Determine whether to install the barriers, forms and levels of protection should be in accordance with the cost-benefit analysis;

7 The selected barrier structure shall pass the safety performance evaluation prescribed in the current *Safety Evaluation Standards for Highway Barriers* (JTG B05-01). See Appendix C for the general structure of some cable barriers, corrugated beam barrier guardrails, and concrete barriers.

6.2 Subgrade barriers

6.2.1 The various types of traffic obstacles in the range of effective clear zone width shall be handled in the following order:

1 Remove obstacles within the effective clear zone width;

2 Redesign obstacles so that they do not pose hazards;

3 Move the obstacles to a position where the vehicles cannot be easily collided into while driving out of the road;

4 Take measures to reduce accidental injuries, such as using dismantling energy dissipation structures;

5 In the event that the above measures cannot be implemented and the severity of accidents caused by vehicles driving out of the road is higher than the severity of collision to the barriers, consideration shall be given to install the barriers;

6 If the above measures cannot be implemented, the obstacles shall be warned and the traffic

shall be guided.

Background:

Since the barriers are also obstacles, based on the concept of inclusive design, it is best to ensure provision of the required width of the effective clear zone. Therefore, the first three measures are to ensure provision of the required width of the effective clear zone and the obstacles within the effective clear zone width do not cause damage to the pull-out vehicles; the fourth measure is to reduce the consequences of accidental injury. If these four measures cannot be implemented and the severity of accidents caused by vehicles leaving the road is higher than the severity of collision to the barriers, consideration shall be given to installation of barriers. If it is not feasible to install barriers, or barriers are not justified through economic analysis, drivers shall be warned of the obstacles, or visual guiding facilities shall be installed.

6.2.2 The installation of roadside barriers and the selection of the level of protection shall comply with the following provisions:

1 According to the current *Specifications for Design of Highway Safety Facilities* (JTG D81), the severity grades of accidents can be divided into three levels: high, middle and low. Roadside barriers and the level of protection shall be installed and selected according to the Table 6.2.2-1.

2 In following cases where road sections increase the likelihood of accidents or cause more serious consequences, the level of protection of the roadside barriers shall be increased by one grade in accordance with the Table 6.2.2-1.

Table 6.2.2-1 The principle of installing roadside barriers and the conditions for selecting the level of protection

The severity of the accidents and the principle of installing the barriers	There are the following conditions within the range of the effective clear zone width	Highway technical level and design speed (km/h)	Level of protection (code)
High, must be installed up	High-speed railways, motorway, high-voltage transmission towers, dangerous goods storage ware houses and other facilities	Motorway 120	Level 6-SS
		Highway, Class-1 highway 100, 80	Level 5-SA
		Class-1 highway 60	Level 4-SB
		Class-2 highway 80, 60	Level 4-SB
		Class-3 highway 40	Level 3-A
		Class-3, Class-4 highway 30, 20	Level 2-B

continued

The severity of the accidents and the principle of installing the barriers	There are the following conditions within the range of the effective clear zone width	Highway technical level and design speed (km/h)	Level of protection (code)
Middle, shall be installed up	1 Sections of Class-2 and above highway whose degree of side slope and embankment heights are within the shaded areas of Sections I and II of the Figure 6.2.2; sections of Class-3 and Class-4 highway whose road side is near cliffs, deep valleys, deep ditches with depths of more than 30 m; 2 Sections that have water areas with depth more than 1.5 m like rivers, streams, lakes, sea, and swamps; 3 Class-1 railways, Class-1 highways, etc.; 4 There are facilities like lighting, cameras, traffic signs, sound barriers, piers or abutments on bridges outside the motorway and Class-1 highway and these facilities cannot be safely crossed by vehicles	Highway, First-class highway 120, 100, 80	Level 4-SB
		First-class highway 60	Level 3-A
		Second-class highway 80, 60	Level 3-A
		Third-class highway 40	Level 2-B
		Third-class, IV highway 30, 20	Level 1-C
Low, should be installed up	1 Sections of Class-2 and above highway whose degree of side slope and embankment heights are within the shaded areas of Sections III of Figure 6.2.2; sections of Class-3 and Class-4 whose degree of side slope and embankment heights are within the shaded areas of Sections I of Figure 6.2.2; 2 Excavation sections with no cover plate on the road side ditch and vehicles that cannot safely cross in the Class-2 and above highway; 3 There are obstacles such as concrete foundations or large stones that are more than 30 cm high on the pavement or the excavation slope surface; 4 Obstacles in the triangle zone on the exit ramp	Highway, First-class highway 120, 100, 80	Level 3-A
		First-class highway 60	Level 2-B
		Second-class highway 80, 60	Level 2-B
		Third-class, forth-class highway 40, 30, 20	Level 1-C

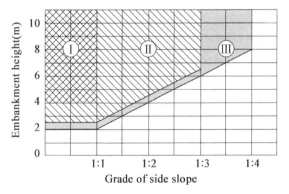

Figure 6.2.2 Relationship among slope, embankment height and barrier installation

1) The slopes of Class-2 and above highways equal to or close to the downslope section of the current maximum grade value specified in the *Technical Standards for Highway*

Engineering (JTG B01); the road round curve radius of Class-2 and above highways is equal to or close to the outside section with the minimum radius in the current *Technical Standards for Highway Engineering* (JTG B01).

2) In the design traffic volume, where the proportion of natural number of the vehicles with a total mass of 25 tonnes or more is greater than 20%.

3 For roads with Annual Average Daily Traffic (AADT) less than 2,000 minibuses and a design speed less than or equal to 60 km/h, safety and comprehensive economic analysis should be carried out to determine whether to install barriers and the level of protection of barriers. Where barriers need to be installed, the level of protection may be reduced by one grade on the basis of Table 6.2.2-1, but the minimum shall not be lower than the Level 1-C. For Class-4 single-lane highways with Annual Average Daily Traffic (AADT) less than 400 minibuses, measures of guidance and warning should be taken.

4 The end of the barrier facing the traffic flow shall be outreached or installed with facilities impact attenuator as follows:

1) The barrier shall be flared to the outside of the soft shoulder width and the flare rate shall not exceed the values specified in Table 6.2.2-2. Where the barrier is close to the edge line of the driveway, smaller values of flare angle should be adopted. Where feasble, the barrier shall be flared to the outside of the effective clear zone width.

Table 6.2.2-2 Flared angle of the upstream end of the barrier

Design speed (km/h)	Rigid barriers	Semi-rigid barriers
120	1:22	1:17
100	1:18	1:14
80	1:14	1:11
60	1:10	1:8

2) Where semi-rigid barriers are flared, their ends shall be subject to strengthening treatments.

3) Where the ends of the barrier are located at the boundary of filling and excavation, they shall be flared and buried in the soil that does not constitute an obstacle in the excavation section. Where a semi-rigid barrier is buried in the soil, it shall be extended and anchored into the soil.

4) Where it is unable to adopt flaring, crashworthy terminations shall be installed on

motorways, Class-1 highways and Class-2 highways serving as arterial highway in accordance with the provisions of the Clause 6.5.1 and 6.5.2, or be provided with crash cushions in front of the barrier terminations; Class-2 highways serving as the collector highway and the Class-3 and Class-4 highways shall adopt earth anchored terminations and warnings should be provided or facade markers should be installed.

5) For Class-2 highways serving as the arterial highways, if there are no barriers installed at the division of the driveway, the possibility of the collision of the vehicles against the downstream termination of the driveway barriers should be considered.

5   Barriers shall be designed for transition at the tunnel entrances and exits of motorways, Class-1 highways and Class-2 highways serving as the arterial highway; the barriers should be designed for transition at the tunnel entrances and exits of Class-2 highways serving as the distributed lines and Class-3 and Class-4 highways. Transitional design at the entrance shall meet the following requirements:

1) Tapered concrete barriers or concrete wing walls should be used to enter the tunnel portals.

2) The flare rate of the barriers entering the tunnel portal should not exceed the value specified in Table 6.2.2-2.

3) The traffic side of a concrete barrier or wing wall should be level with the inside surface of the maintainance walkway at the entrance of the tunnel.

4) Before the concrete barrier or wing wall enters the tunnel portal, its height may be gradually increased as needed. Their height at the tunnel portal shall not be lower than the height of the maintenance walkway.

6   For non-motorized and pedestrian-intensive sections of Class-1 and Class-2 highways serving as distributor roads, if a side separator belt has been installed and a barrier needs to be provided, the barrier should be installed on the side separator belt. Where no side separator belt is provided, the barrier should be installed on the soft shoulder.

7   Where the roadside barrier is installed on a slope, the following conditions should be noted:

1) The roadside barrier may be installed on slopes with gradients equal to or smoother than 1:6.

2) Under special circumstances, it may also be installed on slopes with gradients of 1:4 to 1:6. The height of the barrier from the road surface is constant, and the distance from the slope change point to the barrier collision surface shall not exceed 0.75 m. The earth pressure outside the barrier column shall be ensured.

3) The slope in front of the barrier collision is flat and there are no bulges.

Background:

1-2 *The severity of a run-off accident is related to roadside hazard levels and driving speeds. The more dangerous the roadside is and the higher the speed, the more severe the consequences of the accident would be.*

The factors related to the possibility of vehicle run-off-road accident mainly include:

1) Traffic volume and composition: Higher proportion of heavy vehicles in the traffic will result in higher possibility of accidents;

2) The unfavorable alignment combination mainly involves the outside horizontal curve. If the possibility of a vehicle running off is higher, especially under the combination of a long downward gradient and a sharp outside curve, it is more likely to lead to accidents.

The above factors quite often come together. For example, at ramps in multi-level interchange, highly environmentally sensitive areas, or key sections of motorways (important bridges or long tunnels on the national motorway network), the consequences of heavy vehicles passing through the barrier are serious. The likelihood of a vehicle driving out of the road and the severity of the accident will increase significantly under such situations.

The Guidelines is of a recommendation nature. According to provisions specified in the current Guidelines for Design of Highway Safety Facilities (JTG D81), designers can demonstrate and analyze the possibility of a vehicle driving out of the specific road section and the possible consequences of accidents according to the comprehensive analysis of safety or safety evaluation results combined with their experience, so as to consider installation of barrier reasonably and to select the appropriate level of protection.

3 *It is not economical to install barriers on a road with a very small annual average daily traffic. Australia's Roadside Design Handbook stipulates the following: in sections where the traffic volume is low and the speed is affected by road alignment (such as mountainous areas), although there are potential risks in the road clear zone, it is not considered justified, taking account of the actual situation, to continuously install expensive barriers.*

Norway's Roadside Design Manual stipulates that where the speed limit is less than or equal to 60 km/h and AADT is less than or equal to 12,000, or the speed limit is over or equal to 70 km/h and AADT is under or equal to 1,500, then barrier level shall use N1 (impact energy is 43.3 kJ).

The American Roadside Design Guide (2011 edition) suggests that where the hourly average traffic is less than or equal to 400, for a 1:1.5 side slope, barrier installation should be considered only where the filling height is higher than 15 m.

The Guidelines recommends: for highways with annual average daily design traffic less than 2,000 and a design speed of 60 km/h or less, it is advisable to specifically analyze the economy to determine whether or not to install a barrier. For first-class single-lane roads with Annual Average Daily Traffic (AADT) less than 400, measures of guidance and warning shall be taken instead.

4   *This revision requires the leading terminal of barriers to have the crashworthy performance in the first instance. In view of the fact that there are few crashworthy terminals developed in China and the application experience is limited, this revision draws lessons from foreign norms and provides some principles for the handling of barrier terminals for development and design reference.*

Barrier ends are flared through the transitional section according to the site situation on the road side. The flare can prevent the vehicle from hitting the terminal, but if the flare rate is large, the angle of vehicle hitting the barrier is also large, which is not conducive to protection. The flare rate given in the clause is the maximum rate.

The use and installation of barrier terminals complying with the level of protection shall be carried out according to the requirements developed by the supplier and in accordance with the treatment method developed and verified by the real vehicle collision test. Reinforcing treatment at the end of the flare can be achieved through the end posts, concrete bases or other methods.

5   *Entrances to tunnels are always considered to be blackspots, and improper handling of the opening is one of the reasons. Attention is required on installation of barriers at tunnel portals and design of transition from the at-grade barrier to the tunnel. Before motorways, first-class highways, or second-class highways as arterial highway enter a tunnel, the width of the subgrade is generally wider than that of the tunnel portal, and the entrance is a rigid structure. Proper transition from the at-grade barrier to the entrance is of critical importance. It shall be based on the principles of stiffness transition. Some principles are given in the Guidelines.*

6   *If a side divider is installed, whether to install the barrier is determined according to the traffic*

volume and composition, alignment, and speed. If the barrier needs to be installed, it shall be installed on the side divider. If there are no side dividers, the barriers shall be installed on the soft shoulders. There are two reasons for that. One is the requirement for building boundaries according to the Technical Standards of Highway Engineering, and the other is that if it is installed between the separation of MV and NMV, it occupies the lane and affects traffic when a vehicle breaks down. It is also not conducive to safety.

7 *For highways in China, especially in mountainous areas, there are more steep slopes on the fill slopes. If the width of the roadbed is insufficient, it is difficult to install barriers on the slopes. The Guidelines gives the conditions and treatment to be taken care of where the guardrail is installed on a relatively smooth slope.*

6.2.3 The installation of median barriers and the selection of the level of protection shall comply with the following provisions:

 1 If the width of integral section median is less than or equal to 12 m, or there are obstacles within the width range of 12 m on the motorways and the Class-1 highway serving as arterial highway, a median barrier must be provided. According to the conditions of the medians, the severity of the accidents may be divided into three levels: high, middle and low. The level of protection of the median barrier shall comply with the requirements of Table 6.2.3.

Table 6.2.3 Selection of level of protection for median barriers

Severity level of accidents	Conditions of medians	Technical level and design speed (km/h) for highways	Level of protection (code)
High	The width of the median barrier of motorways and Class-1 highways is less than 2.5 m with an integral barriers.	Motorway 120	Level 6-SSm
		Motorway, Class-1 highway 100, 80	Level 5-SAm
		Class-1 highway 60	Level 4-SBm
Middle	For two-way six-lane motorways or two-way eight-lane and above highways without paved shoulders on the left side, the width of the median barrier is less than 2.5 m with separate barriers, and the median barrier has obstacles that the vehicles cannot safely pass through.	Motorway 120, 100, 80	Level 4-SBm
	For two-way six-lane highways and above Class-1 highways, the width of the median barrier is less than 2.5 m in separate barriers, and the median barrier has obstacles that the vehicles cannot safely pass through.	Class-1 highway 100, 80	Level 4-SBm
		Class-1 highway 60	Level 3-Am

continued

Severity level of accidents	Conditions of medians	Technical level and design speed (km/h) for highways	Level of protection (code)
Low	Other road sections that do not meet the above conditions.	Motorway, Class-1 highway 120, 100, 80	Level 3-Am
		Class-1 highway 60	Level 2-Bm
		Class-2 highway 80, 60	Level 2-Bm

Note: 1. Obstacles refer to supporting structures of lights, cameras, and traffic signs, and piers on the bridge.
2. Class-1 highways with a design speed of 60 km/h are generally sections of distributor roads that is subject to terrain, geology, and other conditions. This table is applicable where it is necessary to install a median barrier.
3. Applicable to Class-2 highways where overtaking lanes are installed and separate facilities are not provided, and there is a possibility of traffic encroaching onto the opposite lanes.
4. The codes in the brackets show the protection levels of the barriers.

2 In the following cases, the level of protection of the median barriers shall be increased by one grade on the basis of requirements shown in Table 6.2.3:

1) Class-2 and above highways with longitudinal grade equal to or close to the downgrade section with the maximum grade value in the current *Technical Standards for Highway Engineering* (JTG B01); road right curve radius of Class-2 highways and above is equal to or close to the section with the minimum radius in the current *Technical Standards for Highway Engineering* (JTG B01).

2) In the design of traffic volume, where the proportion of natural number of the vehicles with a total mass of 25 tons or more is greater than 20%.

3 For Class-1 collector-distributor highways, the median of integral roadbed sections shall be provided with a divider for safe driving. According to the comprehensive analysis results of safety, consideration may be given to whether or not to install up a median barrier. The severity level of an accident may be selected with reference to the provisions of paragraph 1 of this clause.

4 For sections of Class-2 highways with an overtaking lane, the need to install median barriers or dividers may be based on the risk of encroachment onto opposing lanes and economic analysis. The severity level of an accident may be selected with reference to the provisions of paragraph 1 of this clause. Where median barriers are installed, the subgrade shall be widened as required; where dividers are installed, they shall not constitute a hazard to traffic safety.

5 Positioning of median barriers shall be based on factors such as the width, opening, topography of the median barrier, the utility ducts installed in the median, bridge piers, and structural columns of various facilities.

6 The terminations of medians on integral roadbed section should be combined with treatment of barrier at median openings; the left-hand side of the direction of travel on independent roadbeds shall be installed as roadside barriers.

7 The method of handling the median barrier at the entrance and exit of the tunnel is the same as the roadside barrier.

8 Where median barriers and greening facilities are installed at both ends of at-grade intersections of the Class-1 highway, the sight distance of the intervisibility triangle area shall not be affected.

Background:

1 *On the independent at-grade section of the highway, the requirement on selection of barriers level is same as the roadside barriers. For the integral roadbed section, it is also necessary to consider the possibility of accidents and the severity of accidents when the vehicle runs off the road and collides with the median barrier or crosses the median into the opposite lane. After installation of the integral median barrier, the vehicle is likely to lead to secondary accidents if crossing the median. The highest level of hazard is therefore used.*

4 *According to the experience of safety improvement of some Level 2 highways in China, collision can be effectively reduced by adding median barriers or separate facilities. Some second-class highways are designated subject to conditions, but even if some aspects of the collision avoidance performance of the median barriers do not reach the Level 2, it is still beneficial to reduce collision accidents. Therefore, this revision adds that the section of second-class highways with an overtaking lane can be justified for installation of a median barrier or separate facilities as needed.*

6.2.4 Where selecting the types of barriers, in addition to considering the protective performance, the following factors shall also be considered:

1 The degree of deformation of the barrier after collision shall be considered. The distance between the barrier surface of the roadside or median barrier and its obstacles shall be greater than the maximum transverse dynamic displacement value (W) of the barrier or the maximum dynamic incline equivalent value (VI_n) of the vehicle. Where the obstacle of protection is lower than the barrier, the maximum transverse dynamic displacement value

(W) of the barrier should be selected; where the obstacle is higher than the barrier, and the main driving model are large vehicles, maximum dynamic incline equivalent value (VI_n) of vehicles shall be selected.

2   Except for areas with heavy snow and strong wind in winter, concrete barriers should be used in the median barriers for roads with a large occupying proportion of large vehicles.

3   In areas with heavy snow and strong wind in winter, a form of barriers with less resistance to snow should be selected.

4   The transitional treatment of barriers, their terminations, and other forms of barriers should adopt standardized materials and products. The barriers specially needed for individual locations should be customized and processed.

5   The following factors shall be considered, namely initial cost of the barrier, the cost of maintenance after being put into use, including routine maintenance, crash maintenance, material reserves and maintenance convenience. An economically appropriate form in conjunction with the pavement maintenance method should be adopted and in advance the future demand for pavement maintenance should be considered.

6   Where selecting the form of barrier, factors such as the degree of environmental corrosion along the road line, climatic conditions and the impact of the barrier itself on the sight distance shall be taken into consideration, and aesthetic factors shall also be given proper consideration. For roads with special requirements for landscapes, a form of barriers that looks natural and integrates with the surroundings may be selected, but the level of protection of the barrier shall not be reduced.

Background:
When selecting the form of barriers, in addition to considering the protective performance and deformation factors of the barrier in the first instance, it is necessary to comprehensively consider the aspects listed in Table 6-1.

Table 6-1   Factors to consider when selecting the form of barriers

No.	Factors	Notes
1	Versatility	The form of barriers, the handling of their termination and the transitional treatment to different forms of barriers shall be standardized as far as possible. The coordination with other types of facilities (such as lampposts, signposts, and bridge piers) shall also be considered in the provision of median barriers. Barriers that are specially needed for individual locations need to be customized and manufactured. For example, in the area where the turning radius is very small, such as the outside of the plane intersection turning lane and the outside of the reverse loop, if a corrugated beam barrier guardrail is needed, it needs to be customized and specially made

continued

No.	Factors	Notes
2	Cost	In finalizing the design plan, the most likely consideration is the initial cost of various programs and future costs of maintenance. Under normal circumstances, the initial cost of the barrier will increase with the increase in the level of protection, but the maintenance costs will decrease. On the contrary, if the initial cost is low, the subsequent maintenance costs will increase significantly. After an accident, flexible or semi-rigid barriers require more care than rigid or high-strength barriers. In the sections with large traffic volume and frequent accident, the cost of crash maintenance will become the factors that must be taken into consideration. Rigid barriers are a better choice. Crash repairs: in general, flexible or semi-rigid barriers require more repairs than rigid ones after an accident. In areas of large traffic volume and high frequency of accidents, the cost of crash repairs (and the impact of accidents on traffic capacity) may become the most important factor to consider. This usually happens on roads near cities. In such situations, rigid barriers, such as concrete barriers, are often the option. Material reserves: the fewer the types, the less inventory categories and storage requirements are needed. Convenience: The simpler the design, the lower the cost, and the easier it is for on-site personnel to repair it. Pavement Maintenance: Some pavements do not have room for milling, which results in insufficient height of the barriers after road maintenance. This effect can be taken into account where new barriers are installed. Using barriers that have a variable height can reduce the influence brought by road maintenance
3	Aesthetic and environmental factors	Aesthetics is usually not a factor that can be controlled in the selection of a barrier. However, a tourist highway or a road with a high landscape requirement can be furnished with barriers that are natural in appearance, can be integrated with the surroundings, and have a corresponding level of protection. The selection of barrier also considers the degree of environmental corrosion along the line, the weather conditions and its effect on the sight distance, etc. For example, the convenience of removing snow needs to be considered in snow-covered areas. Because barrier installation has little effect on improving highway landscapes, tourist highways or highways with high landscape requirements shall try to seek measures that can replace the barriers, such as installing dish drain ditch or installing cover plate on road side channel. After verification, where barriers need to be installed, their appearance shall be simple and their colors shall be commensurate with the structures and the surroundings

According to the operating experience of already opened motorways and first-class highways in China, for road sections where large vehicles, especially large trucks, account for a large proportion, there have been frequent accidents of high severity caused by collisions of vehicles passing through the central separation zone with opposing vehicles. Therefore, this clause stipulates that 'sections with large proportion of large vehicles, except for those located in areas with heavy snow and strong wind in winter' are recommended to use concrete barriers. For road sections with heavy snow or strong wind, concrete barriers are not suitable because they could lead to road blockage due to snow.

As to whether integral or separate concrete barriers should be used, it is mainly determined by the types of facilities or structures needed protection in the median. For example, where there are obstacles such as piers, traffic signs, lighting poles, etc. in the median, or where it is necessary to make regular transitions to bridges or tunnels, or where it is difficult to coordinate with the communication pipelines, separate concrete barriers may be used (as shown in Figure 6-1 a); otherwise integral concrete barriers may be used (as shown in Figure 6-1 b).

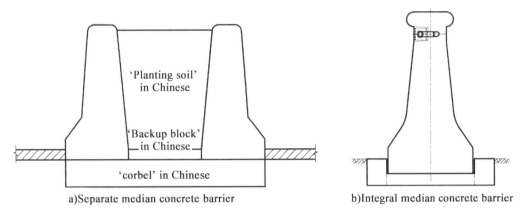

a) Separate median concrete barrier   b) Integral median concrete barrier

Figure 6-1 Example of median concrete barriers

The use of integral concrete barriers does not mean reducing the width of median barriers. From the perspective of safe driving and guaranteed sight distance, the concrete barriers shall preferably have a clear width of no less than 50 cm on both sides, or be able to meet the requirements of parking sight distance on the inner side of a flat curve section. The minimum sight distance needs to meet the requirements in the current Technical Standards for Highway Engineering (JTG B01) for the 'C' value of highway construction limits.

6.2.5 The minimum structural length of the barrier shall satisfy both the protection and structural requirements:

1. The minimum structural length playing the integral role of the barriers shall be in accordance with the provisions of Table 6.2.5 of the current *Specifications for Design of Highway Safety Facilities* (JTG D81), or shall be determined according to the instruction manual of the barriers.

2. The minimum protection length of the barrier shall be determined according to the trajectory of the vehicle out of the driveway and the position and width of the obstacles in the effective clear zone width, as shown in Figure 6.2.5. The barrier protection length is divided into five parts: a_1, b_1, b_2, c_1 and c_2. Among them, a_1 is the length of the obstacle; b_1 and b_2 are the extended length to avoid the pull-out vehicle colliding obstacles; c_1 and c_2 are the terminations of the barrier, including the anchoring part. The

value of each part is recommended as follows:

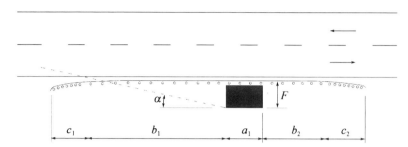

Figure 6.2.5 Diagram of the barrier protection length

1) b_1 and b_2 are related to speed and pull-out angle α. The pull-out angle maybe obtained based on investigations of accident on roads with similar situations, and may also be prudently selected as 5°; the speed maybe design speed, operating speed or speed limit; F is the distance from the barrier to the outer edge of the obstacle, and is width of obstacle in the effective clear zone width.

2) b_1 may also be selected with reference to Table 6.2.5.

Table 6.2.5 Values of b_1

Speed (km/h)	b_1 (m)	
	Common cases	Cases of higher severity of accident
≤40	8	25
50	30	40
60	40	55
70	50	70
80	60	85
90	75	100
100	90	120
≥110	110	150

3) Where the obstacles outside the road are traffic signs, lighting pillars, piers, etc., if the side ditch does not act as an obstacle and the degree of side slope is less than 1 : 4, the value can be simplified, $b_1 = 10F$. Other calculation methods may also be used under special circumstances.

4) For two-lane highway, $b_2 = b_1$; for four-lane highway and above, $b_2 = 0.5\ b_1$.

3 The minimum structural length of the barrier shall be the maximum of the above two values.

4 Where the distance between two adjacent barriers is less than the minimum structural length

of the barrier, they shall be installed continuously.

5 The sum of the lengths of the two types of barriers connected by the transitional sections shall not be less than the maximum value of the minimum structural length of the two types of barriers.

Background:

This revision refers to the requirements for the minimum length of the barrier in the United States, Canada, Australia, and Norway, supplements the requirements for the 'length of barriers,' and gives the diagrams and calculation formulas. These are obtained based on the situation of roadside obstacles.

The minimum length of the barrier given in the previous edition is the length of the barrier structure, mainly considering the length of the barrier structure of the overall function. This revision reserves it, and it is stipulated that the minimum length of the barrier installation is the larger value between the two. If the barrier structure provided by the suppliers is verified by the actual vehicle crash testing, and its structure length is less than the minimum structure length as specified in the text, the length can be installed according to the length of barrier protection and its structure length.

6.2.6 The cable barrier is the main representative form of the flexible barrier. It consists of the end structure, the intermediate end structure, the intermediate column, bracket, cable and cable end ground tackles and other components. The general structure of roadside Level 1-C, Level 2-B and Level 3-A cable barriers is shown in Appendix C.1. Where designing a cable barrier, the following requirements shall be met:

1 The end structure consists of a triangular frame, a base plate and a concrete base. The structure and dimensions of the various parts of the end structure shall comply with the requirements of Table 6.2.6-1. The road side Level 1-C to Level 3-A end structures are shown in Figure 6.2.6-1 to Figure 6.2.6-3.

Table 6.2.6-1 Structures and dimensions of the end structures of cable barriers

Level of protection	End column				Concrete bases				The height of the lowest cable (cm)	Maximum column distance (cm) (in soil/concrete)
	Specifications (mm)	Height above ground (cm)	Buried depth (cm)	Form	Depth (cm)	Length (cm)	Width (cm)	Volume (cm^3)		
Level 1-C	$\phi 114 \times 4.5$	74	40	Triangle	100	300	60	1.8	43	700/400
Level 2-B	$\phi 114 \times 4.5$	87	45	Triangle	120	330	70	2.8	43	700/400
Level 3-A	$\phi 114 \times 5$	100	50	Triangle	150	420	70	4.4	43	700/400

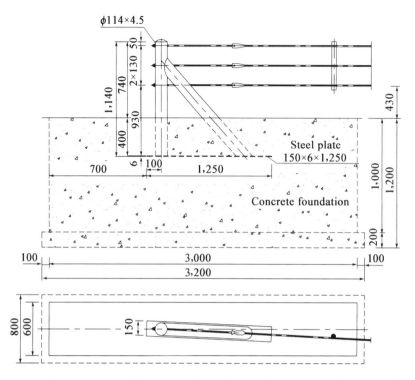

Figure 6.2.6-1 Roadside first-class (C) end structure (Unit: mm)

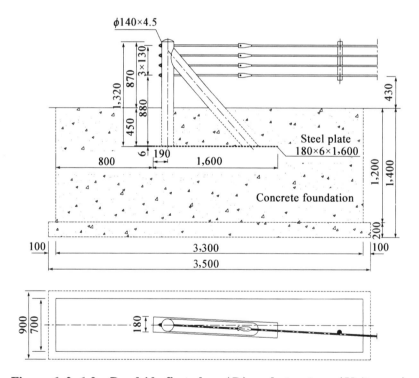

Figure 6.2.6-2 Roadside first-class (B) end structure (Unit: mm)

2 The intermediate end structure consists of a triangular frame, a base plate and a concrete base. Each structure and dimension is same to the end column. The intermediate end structure shall be installed where the following conditions are met:

1) With the mechanical construction method and the length of the roadside cable barrier is more than 500 m.

2) With the manual construction method and the length of the roadside cable barrier is more than 300 m.

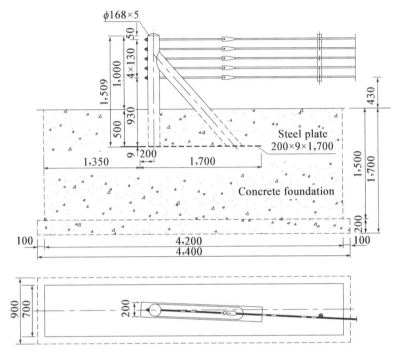

Figure 6.2.6-3 Roadside third-class (A) end structure (Unit: mm)

3　The structure and dimensions of the middle column shall comply with the requirements of Table 6.2.6-2. Figure 6.2.6-4-Figure 6.3.4-6 are the structural diagrams of the roadside First-class (C) to Third-class (A) middle columns of the cable barriers. The distance between the middle columns in the soil should not be larger than 6 m/7 m, and the distance between the middle columns installed in the concrete should not be larger than 4 m. The space between columns of cable barriers installed in the curve sections shall be adjusted according to Table 6.2.6-3. In sections that cannot be entered like small bridges, passages, and open culverts, and sections of underground pipelines or other sections that cannot reach the prescribed depth of embedment, the middle columns maybe installed in the concrete bases.

Table 6.2.6-2 Structures and dimensions of the middle columns of cable barriers

Level of protection	Middle column					Maximum column distance (cm)
	Buried method	Buried depth (cm)	Height above ground (cm)	Outside diameter (mm)	Wall thickness (mm)	
Level 1-C	In soil	140	74	$\phi 114$	4.5	700
	In concrete	40				400

continued

Level of protection	Middle column					Maximum column distance (cm)
	Buried method	Buried depth (cm)	Height above ground (cm)	Outside diameter (mm)	Wall thickness (mm)	
Level 2-B	In soil	165	87	φ114	4.5	700
	In concrete	40				400
Level 3-A	In soil	165	100	φ140	4.5	700
	In concrete	40				400

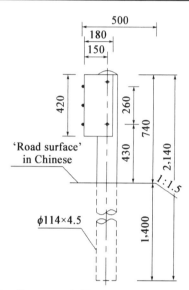

Figure 6.2.6-4 Structural diagrams of the middle column of Level 1-C cable barrier (Unit: mm)

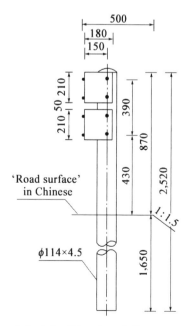

Figure 6.2.6-5 Structural diagrams of the middle column of Level 2-B cable barrier (Unit: mm)

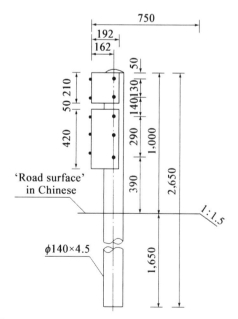

Figure 6.2.6-6 Structural diagrams of the middle column of Level 3-A cable barrier (Unit: mm)

Table 6.2.6-3 Column spacing in curve part

Level of protection	Column distance (m)	4	5	6
Level 1-C, Level 2-B, Level 3-A	Curve radius R (m)	$120 \leq R \leq 200$	$200 < R \leq 300$	$R > 300$

4 The structure and dimensions of the bracket are shown in Appendix C Figure C.1.1 to Figure C.1.3.

5 The cable and cable end ground tackle shall meet the requirements of Table 6.2.6-4.

Table 6.2.6-4 Cable and cable end ground tackles for cable barriers

Level of protection (code)	Cable			Cable end ground tackle and wire rope breaking force (kN)
	Initial tension (kN)	Cable diameter (mm)	Cable distance (mm)	
Level 1-C, 2-B, 3-A	20	18	130	170

6 The roadside cable barriers shall be located in the highway soft shoulders. The barrier surface may overlap with the left edge line of the soft shoulder or the left side of the kerbstone. The thickness of the outer soft shoulder protective layer shall not be less than 25 cm; the horizontal position of the median cable barrier should be determined based on the distribution of structures and underground pipelines; any part of the barrier shall not intrude into the road construction limit.

7 Where the soil compactness within the buried depth range of roadside and medians is less than 90%, or where the thickness of the protective layer outside the roadside barrier soft shoulders is less than 25 cm, it may be processed in accordance with Appendix C.4 of the *Guidelines*.

Background:

In the past decade, there have been some experiences and demands for the application of cable barriers on motorways, first-class to third-class highways and medians. The state, the Ministry of Transport, and some provinces have also conducted some research and actual vehicle crash testings. Based on these achievements, this revision has made corresponding changes to the provisions of the structure of the cable barrier.

1 *The end columns of the cable barrier are the main structures that bear the tension of the cable and the impact force of the colliding vehicle. They consist of a triangular support, a base plate and a concrete base. Cable barrier assembling is shown in Figure 6-2; the column ends are shown in Figure 6-3; the structure and size of the various parts of the text are shown in Table 6.2.6-1.*

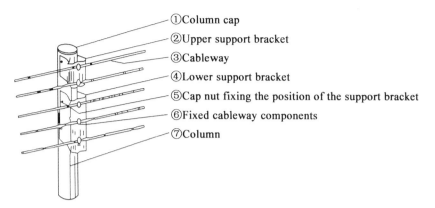

Figure 6-2 Assembly drawing of cable barriers (illustrated)

① Column cap
② Upper support bracket
③ Cableway
④ Lower support bracket
⑤ Cap nut fixing the position of the support bracket
⑥ Fixed cableway components
⑦ Column

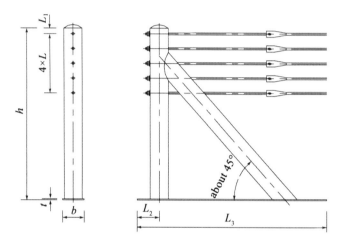

Figure 6-3 Structure diagram of the end structures of cable barriers

Note: h, L_3 are determined based on the height above ground of the end structure.

The height of the cables and brackets above the ground mainly considers the location of the collision with vehicles. The cable shall in the height that could not cause the large vehicles to go out of the road, but also prevent the small vehicles from entering the underside of the cables. During the interaction between the collision vehicle and the cable barrier, it is expected that the collision vehicle will gradually return to the normal driving direction through the energy absorption and guidance of the barrier. The distance from the column surface to the outer surface of the cable is guaranteed by the width of the bracket. The role of the bracket is firstly to fix the position of the cable, and secondly to suspend the cable from the vertical surface by a certain distance to prevent the collision vehicle from blocking at the column. The distance from the column to the outer edge of the cable is determined to be 110 mm after considering above factors.

The distance between two cables is mainly decided from the perspective of even distribution of the impact force. According to the vehicle model, impact angle and other factors, it is necessary to fix the cables at certain heights to prevent the vehicle from going out and in between the cables, and allow as many cables as possible to interact simultaneously with the impact force to avoid over-concentration of impact forces on a few cables. Therefore, a cable height separation of 130 mm is appropriate.

2. *Two types of buried and assembled structures can be adopted for the ends. The buried end structure is integrated with the concrete bases. The buried depth of the end columns varies from 400 m to 500 mm depending on the type. The inclined column of the triangular support is at an angle of 45° with the ground. A steel plate is welded on the bottom. On one hand, it could form a stable frame with the triangular support. On the other hand, the steel plate at the bottom can greatly increase the cohesive force with the base concrete and easily control the position of the elevation. The assembled end structure is integrated with the concrete bases through the embedded parts. The embedded parts of the end structure are different due to different structures and categories. Considering the convenience of construction and the actual application effect, the embedded end structure is recommended. In order to reduce the collision of the vehicle to end columns, it is necessary to flare the end columns as far as possible.*

The end structure is installed at the end of cable barriers. In order to maintain the initial tension of the cable and to simplify the tensioning equipment during installation, to maintain a certain degree of cable levelness and prevent the occurrence of deflection, the installation length of the cable is generally from 300 m to 500 m, which means that the length of each cable shall not exceed 500 m. The factors of facilitating maintenance are also considered here.

3. *The installation length of cable barriers is limited by cable handling, construction, maintenance, etc. The cable length can reach 500 m during mechanical construction and 300 m during manual construction. Where the installation length of the barrier exceeds the range of 300 m to 500 m, the intermediate end structure shall be adopted in the design.*

1) *The intermediate end structure is triangular and requires a paired installation. That is, starting from installing the cable barrier from the beginning end structure, the cable is extended out span by span via intermediate columns until the intermediate end structure is reached at the other end of the cable length (300-500 m). Since the length of the cable barrier continues to extend, as another cable's starting point, the other pair of intermediate end structures needs to be installed back by 12 m to 21 m (three spans). In this way, the two sections of the cable barriers are alternated by the intermediate end structures, and two intermediate columns are provided between the two intermediate end structures. The arched intermediate end structure is suitable for cable barriers protecting non-motorized transportation devices and pedestrians, so there is no need for paired installations. That is, the two-section cable barriers can be connected by an arched intermediate end structure. Therefore, the intermediate end structure can be used as an intermediate transition structure extending along the length of the barrier. Once installed, the function of the intermediate*

end structure is the same as that of the end column, and it bears the initial tension of the cable and the impact force of the colliding vehicle. Therefore, it is also very important to ensure its strength and stability. The intermediate columns can be welded steel pipes. The columns are buried in the soil or concrete in different depths due to their different conditions. Because the columns buried in the soil are close to the edge of the road, the earth pressure near the slope is relatively small. To ensure the strength of the cable barrier, a certain buried depth is needed. In the column buried in the concrete, the buried depth is 40 cm in consideration of the locking effect of the concrete structure on the columns. The bracket installed on the column is positioned with bolts through the through hole, and the uppermost hole shall be no less than 50 mm from the top of the column.

2) The column distance is closely related to the number of cables, the diameter of the columns, and the buried depth. Although larger distance would be more economical, from the perspective of the performance effects, column distance of Level1 and 2 (code C, B) cable barrier is installed to a maximum of 6 m, and Level 3-A cable barrier to a maximum of 7 m. However, if the column is buried in concrete, the maximum value of 4 m can be used like the corrugated beam barrier guardrails. If the cable barrier is installed in the curve part, in order to ensure a smooth transition of the cable in the curve part, and that the curve section barrier functions normally, the distance between the columns is determined by the radius of the road curve and the category of the cable barrier.

The intermediate column of the cable barrier is a support structure between the end columns or the middle end columns. In addition to the installation buried in the soil and the concrete, there is also a telescoping structure that could be easily removed and installed, and is suitable for cold and snowy area to remove snow.

5 Cable and cable end ground tackles are important parts of barriers. The cable is made of galvanized steel wire with certain rigidity and excellent corrosion resistance. The construction is 3×7 right-handed and the outer diameter of the cable is 18 mm due to the strength requirement. The outer diameter of the cable refers to the diameter of the circumscribed circle of the cross section.

The cable end ground tackle is a component of the cable that is connected to the end column (or intermediate end column) and includes anchor heads, stay bolts and fasteners. First, the cable shall be fixed in the anchor head. The methods used include the alloy-injection and the wedge-fixing, which can be selected according to the construction conditions. Then, it can be fixed on the column with stay bolts. The exposed part of the end column stay bolts in the direction of travel shall not be too long, and appropriate safety precautions must be taken.

In order to maintain the initial tension of the cable after installation of the cable barrier, it is possible to use a method of releasing and then tensioning before pulling. After the cable barrier is put into use, the tension of the cable needs to be tested at regular intervals. Where the cable barrier does not meet the requirements, it needs to be adjusted in time to avoid the failure of the cable barrier due to the lack of tension.

6 *Specific clauses on the location of the roadside cable barriers are the same as that of clause 6.2.7, paragraph 3. Where the median needs to install cable barrier, it is better to adopt separate barriers when considering the strength, convenience of transport and maintenance, and the installation of greening and underground pipelines. Considering the need of aesthetics, it is generally appropriate to arrange in symmetrical way. The distance from the outer edge surface of the cable to the edge of the median barrier must meet the requirements of the highway construction limit.*

7 *For details, see the clause 6.2.7, paragraph 10.*

6.2.7 The corrugated beam barrier guardrail is the main representative form of the semi-rigid barriers. For the general structure of the roadside barriers and median barriers with partial level of protection, see Appendix C.2. Where designing a corrugated beam barrier guardrail, the following requirements shall be met:

1 Where designing a corrugated beam barrier guardrail, the following provisions shall be complied with Table 6.2.7-1 and Figure 6.2.7-1.

Table 6.2.7-1 Structure and dimensions of some corrugated beam barrier guardrail structures

Level of protection	Code	Beam slab (mm)	Column (mm)	Bracket/ Anti-obstruction block (mm)	Crossbeam (mm)	Beam height[1] (mm)	Column depth (mm)	Column distance (mm)
1	C	310×85×2.5	ϕ114×4.5	300×70×4.5		600	1,400	4,000/2,000
2	B	310×85×3	ϕ114×4.5	300×70×4.5		600	1,400	2,000/1,000
3	A	506×85×3	ϕ140×4.5	196×178×400×4.5		697	1,400	4,000/2,000
3	A	506×85×4	ϕ114×4.5	300×270×35×6		697	1,650	4,000/2,000
4	SB	506×85×4	□130×130×6	300×200×290×4.5		697	1,650	2,000/1,000
5	SA	506×85×4	□130×130×6 and ϕ102×4.5	300×200×290×4.5	ϕ89×5.5	697	1,650	3,000/1,500

continued

Level of protection	Code	Beam slab (mm)	Column (mm)	Bracket/ Anti-obstruction block (mm)	Crossbeam (mm)	Beam height[1] (mm)	Column depth (mm)	Column distance (mm)
6	SS	506 × 85 × 4	□130 × 130 × 6 and φ102 × 4.5	350 × 200 × 290 × 4.5	φ89 × 5.5	697	1,650	2,000/1,000
7	HB	506 × 85 × 4	□130 × 130 × 6 and φ102 × 4.5	400 × 200 × 290 × 4.5	φ89 × 5.5	697	1,650	2,000/1,000

Note: 1) The beam height refers to the height of the barrier center from the design base line, and the intersection line between the barrier face and the road surface is the design base line. If there is a kerbstone near the road center line in the side of the roadside barrier, and the left elevation of the kerbstone does not overlap with the barrier surface, the beam height shall also increase the height of the kerbstone.

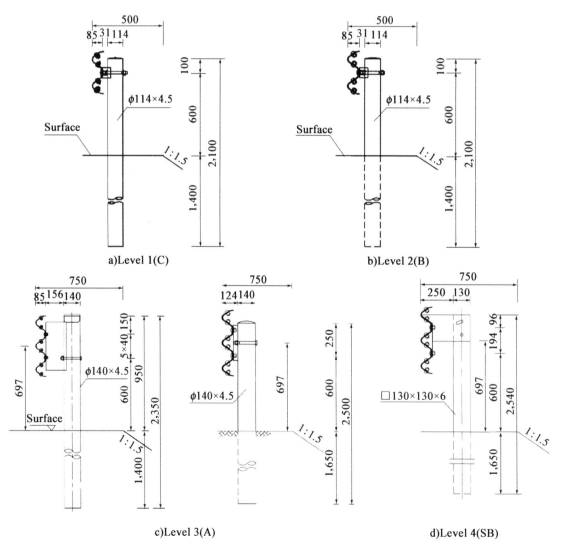

Figure 6.2.7-1

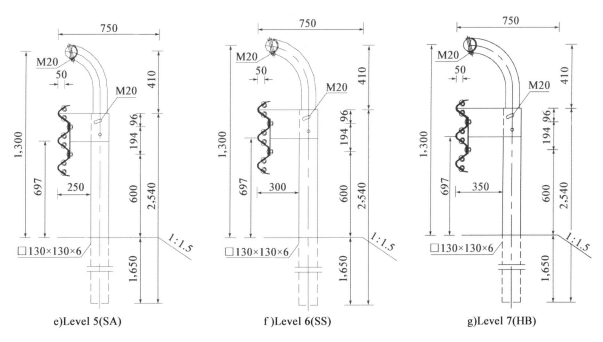

Figure 6.2.7-1 Cross-section layout of roadside corrugated beam barrier guardrail (Unit: mm)

2　The types of combination and separation, which are adopted in some of the median corrugated beam barrier guardrails, may be determined based on the width of the median barrier, the distribution of structures and pipelines:

1) The specifications and dimensions of separated corrugated beam barrier guardrails shall comply with the requirements of Table 6.2.7-1. The cross-section layout is shown in Figure 6.2.7-2.

2) The specifications and dimensions of the combined corrugated beam barrier guardrail shall comply with the requirements of Table 6.2.7-2. The cross-section layout is shown in Figure 6.2.7-3.

Table 6.2.7-2　Construction and dimensions of the median corrugated beam barrier

Level of protection	Code	Beam slab (mm)	Column (mm)	Diaphragms (mm)	Beam height[1] (mm)	Column depth (mm)	Column distance (soil/concrete)
3	Am	2(310×85×4)	φ140×4.5	480×200×50×4.5	600	1,400	200/100

Note: 1) The beam height refers to the height of the barrier center from the design base line, and the intersection line between the barrier face and the road surface is the design base line. If the barrier surface is close to the kerbstone in the direction of the road on the right side, and the right elevation of the kerbstone does no to verlap with the barrier surface, the beam height shall also increase the height of the kerbstone.

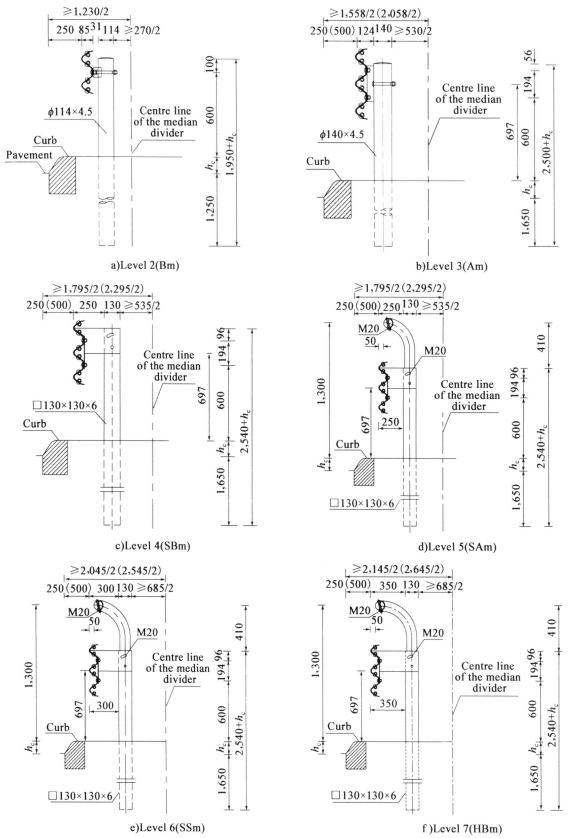

Figure 6.2.7-2 Cross-section layout of separated median corrugated beam barrier guardrails (Unit: mm)

Note: h_c is the height of the curb.

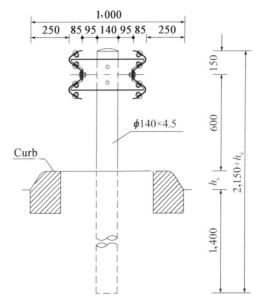

Figure 6.2.7-3 Cross-section layout of third-class (Am) median corrugated beam barriers (Unit: mm)

Note: h_c is the height of the curb.

3 The position of the corrugated beam barrier guardrail along the cross-section of the road shall meet the following requirements:

1) The roadside corrugated beam barrier guardrails shall be located in the highway soft shoulder. The barrier surface shall overlap with the left edge line of the soft shoulder or the left side of the kerbstone. The thickness of the outer soft shoulder protective layer shall not be less than 25 cm.

2) Where there are structures and underground pipelines in the medians, the horizontal position of the barrier can be properly adjusted or the type maybe changed.

3) Any part of the barrier shall not intrude into the road construction limit.

4 Based on the line of intersection between the barrier surface and the road surface, the height of the corrugated beam barrier guardrail center shall meet the following requirements:

1) The height of the bi-beam center is 600 mm;

2) The height of the tri-beam center is 697 mm;

3) The kerbstone surface near the traffic flow direction should be located behind the barrier surface; otherwise the beam height shall also increase the height of the kerbstone.

5 Calculated from the pavement, the burial depth of the column of corrugated beam barrier guardrail shall meet the following requirements:

   1) For the corrugated beam barrier guardrail installed in the soil foundation, the buried depth of the column shall not be less than that specified in Table 6.2.7-1 and Table 6.2.7-2. Where there is a kerbstone, the overall height shall also contain the height of the kerbstone which is above the pavement;

   2) Corrugated beam barrier guardrails installed in the reinforced concrete bases such as bridges, passageways, and open culverts, the buried depth of the columns shall not be less than 30 cm;

   3) Corrugated beam barrier guardrails installed in the reinforced concrete bases of road sections such as stones and underground pipelines, the buried depth of the columns shall not be less than 40 cm.

6 Termination processing shall be carried out at the starting point of the road side corrugated beam barrier guardrails and meet the following requirements:

   1) The upstream termination of the driving direction shall be installed as the types like outreach round-head, outreach buried or energy-absorbing. See Appendix C, Figure C.2.13. A transition section shall be provided between the termination section and the barrier standard section.

   2) The downstream termination of the driving direction may use round head type, Appendix C Figure C.2.1-Figure C.2.7, and maybe installed in line with the standard section barrier. Considering the possibility of cars driving outside the road and getting collisions, Class-2 highways may also be installed up as outreach round head.

   3) The position of the starting point of the barrier at the junction of the cut-fill subgrade shall extend from the zero point of cut-fill section to a certain length into a soil that does not constitute an obstacle and then be anchored.

   4) Where the width of the protective soft shoulder on the outside of the barrier column is insufficient, the columns may be reinforced according to the provisions of Appendix C.4 of the *Guidelines*.

7 The termination processing of the barriers installed at the median's start and end part and median opening shall meet the following requirements:

1) In the case of separated corrugated beam barrier guardrails on standard road sections, the round terminations and the transition section alignment shall be consistent with the median barrier. The column spacing shall be half of the standard section spacing. See Appendix C, Figure C.2.14.

2) Where a combined corrugated beam barrier guardrail is used on the standard road section, the round head termination maybe used in the start or end parts, see Appendix C, Figure C.2.8 b), but the termination shall be provided with cushioning facilities or object markings in accordance with the provisions of the *Guidelines*.

8 The termination treatment of the corrugated beam barrier guardrail in the triangular zone of the traffic diversion shall meet the following requirements:

1) The barriers at the triangular zone of the traffic diversion shall be constructed in accordance with the roadside corrugated beam barrier guardrail, and be laid out according to the alignment and topography of the triangular zone, of which the distance between columns shall be halved within 8 m near the main road of the highway and 8 m near the ramp, and the barriers on both sides of the triangle zone shall be connected with round terminations, as shown in Appendix C, Figure C.2.15.

2) In the dangerous triangle zone facing the direction of traffic flow, if there is a large traffic sign, a impact attenuator shall be provided in the triangle zone. If there is a small traffic sign column, it shall be installed as dismantling energy and dissipation structures, otherwise the impact attenuator facilities shall be installed in the triangle zone. For the selection of the level of protection of the impact attenuator, see section 6.5 of this clause.

9 The termination treatment of the corrugated beam barrier guardrail at the entrance and exit of the tunnel shall meet the following requirements:

1) The roadside corrugated beam barrier guardrail at the entrance of the tunnel shall be gradually extended toward the tunnel, and a transitional wing wall matching the overhauling road section shall be installed at the tunnel portal, as shown in Appendix C Figure C.2.16.

2) The roadside corrugated beam barrier guardrail at the exit of the tunnel can adopt the method of overlapping with the tunnel wall. The end barrier shall be handled with scarf welding.

10 Where the soil compactness within the buried depth range of roadside and medians is less than 90%, or where the thickness of the protective layer outside the roadside barrier soft shoulders is less than 25 cm, the columns may be reinforced in accordance with Appendix C.4 ofthe *Guidelines*.

***Background**:*

The commonly used roadside corrugated beam barrier guardrails mainly have eight levels (codes: C, B, A, SB, SA, SS, HB, HA). There are no corresponding corrugated beam barrier guardrails for the Level 8-HA. According to the current Technical Standards for Highway Engineering (JTG B01), intermediate are required for integral sections of motorways and first-class highways. According to the degree of danger of the median, commonly used levels of protection of median barriers can be divided into seven levels: two-eight (codes: Bm, Am, SBm, SAm, SSm, HBm, HAm). The barrier located on the inside of the separated section is treated as a roadside barrier.

1 *How to select the corrugated beam barrier guardrail structure that suits the characteristics of China's highways according to the new barrier impact conditions is the focus of the revision of the Guidelines. The working group considered the following factors when determining the barrier structure:*

1) With a view to adopting foreign mature forms of barrier structure as reference standards as far as possible, the research team has collected the latest barrier standard design drawings from developed countries such as Japan, the United States, and Germany.

2) Taking full consideration of highway conditions and vehicle conditions in China, the research team determined the geometric parameters of the highway based on the current Technical Standards for Highway Engineering (JTG B01).

3) Learning from the latest scientific research results, such as the characteristics of the loose soil in the median and the treatment of the barrier columns.

4) The results of full-scale crash testing of Chinese barriers.

5) Based on the existing survey results on the use of barriers, improving some of the original improper designs.

6) Economic conditions.

Most foreign developed countries determine the structure of barriers based on the results of full-

scale crash testing. The Guidelines, on the one hand, is revised according to the 'Eleventh Five-Year Plan' National Science and Technology Support Project: 'Study and Demonstration Project of Mountain Road Network Safety Assurance Technical System', the Ministry of Transport's 2013 Construction Science and Technology Project: 'Research on Improvement Technology of Highway corrugated beam barrier guardrail Collision Avoidance Capability' and Guangdong Provincial Department of Transport 2014 Research Project: 'Level A corrugated beam barrier guardrail Protection Performance Analysis and New Product R & D' to carry out real vehicle crash test validation and to improve results; on the other hand, refers to the Japanese Vehicle Barrier Standard Diagrams & Background (January 2008) whose road conditions are similar to China, and determines China's structure of the corrugated beam barrier guardrails after considering China's road conditions, material specifications and other factors.

1) The impact energy at the Level 1-C of the roadside corrugated beam barrier guardrail is 40 kJ, which is equivalent to that of the Japanese Level C. The Japanese Level C barrier consists of double beams (350 mm × 50 mm × 2.3 mm), columns (114 mm × 4.5 mm), and brackets (300 mm × 70 mm × 4.5 mm). The column distance is 4E/2B. Compared with Japan, the Level I (C) barrier structure used in the Guidelines is changed as follows: the bi-beam is used (310 mm × 85 mm × 2.5 mm); according to Chinese national standard of steel plate, the standard items with 2.5 mm thickness are adopted.

2) The impact energy that can be absorbed at the Level 2-B of the roadside corrugated beam barrier barrier is 70 kJ. Its structure is based on the roadside barriers (1994 version) with the weakest Level A anti-obstruction block and the 114 mm/4.5 mm columns. The Guidelines stipulates that Level 2-B barriers are mainly applicable to second-class-first-class highways and some first-class highways. However, in ascertaining the barrier cross-section layout, the current Technical Standards for Highway Engineering (JTG B01) stipulates that 'the lateral width of Level 2, 3 and 4 highways is the width of the shoulder minus 0.25 m'. Therefore, if the barrier is installed, the width of the shoulder shall be minus 25 cm, so as not to invade the existing road construction limit.

3) The impact energy that can be absorbed at the Level 3-A of the roadside corrugated beam barrier guardrail is 160 kJ, which is equivalent to the Japanese Level SC (160 kJ) barrier energy. The Japanese Level SC barrier consists of three-corrugated beam barriers (500 mm × 85 mm × 4 mm), columns (140 mm × 4.5 mm), and brackets (300 mm × 270 mm × 35 mm × 6 mm). The column distance is 4E/2B. The Guidelines provides two types of barrier structures at Level 3-A:

One is the three-corrugated beam barrier adopting the form in compliance with the national standard Corrugated sheet beams for road guardrail—Part 2: Tri-beam barrier (GB/T 31439.2), and the specification is 506 mm × 85 mm × 3 mm; the column adopts φ140 mm × 4.5 mm; anti-obstruction block adopts 196 mm × 178 mm × 400 mm × 4.5 mm.

The other is the tri-beam adopting the form in compliance with the national standard Corrugated sheet beams for road guardrail—Part 2: Tri-beam barrier (GB/T 31439.2), and the specification is 506 mm × 85 mm × 4 mm; the column adopts 140 mm × 4.5 mm; bracket adopts 300 mm × 270 mm × 35 mm × 6 mm.

4) The impact energy that can be absorbed at the Level 4-SB of the roadside corrugated beam barrier guardrail is 280 kJ, which is equivalent to the Japanese Level SB (280 kJ) barrier energy. Japan's Level SB barrier consists of a tri-beam of 500 mm × 85 mm × 4 mm, an anti-obstruction block of 300 mm × 200 mm × 290 mm × 4.5 mm and a square pipe column of 125 mm × 125 mm × 6 mm. Compared with Japan, the Level 4-SB barrier structure used in the Guidelines has the changes as follows:

①The tri-beam adopts the form in compliance with the national standard Corrugated sheet beams for road guardrail—Part 2: Tri-beam barrier (GB/T 31439.2), and the specification is 506 mm × 85 mm × 4 mm.

②The column adopts 130 mm × 130 mm × 6 mm, which conforms to the current provisions of Cold Formed Steel Hollow Sections for General Structure's Dimensions, Shapes, Weight and Permissible Deviations (GB/T 6728) (China has no specifications of 125 mm × 125 mm × 6 mm in GB/T 6728 standard).

③The anti-obstruction block is 300 mm × 200 mm × 290 mm × 4.5 mm, which is appropriately adjusted according to the tri-beam barrier and column used.

5) The impact energy that can be absorbed at the Level 5-SA of the roadside corrugated beam barrier is 400 kJ, which is equivalent to that of the Japanese Level SA (420 kJ). Japan's Level SA barrier consists of a tri-beam of 500 mm × 85 mm × 4 mm, a beam of 89.1 mm × 5.5 mm, an anti-obstruction block of 300 mm × 200 mm × 290 mm × 4.5 mm, a square pipe column of 125 mm × 125 mm × 6 mm and a round pipe column of 101.6 mm × 4.2 mm. Compared with Japan, the Level 5-SA barrier structure used in the Guidelines has the following changes:

①The tri-beam adopts the form in compliance with the national standard Corrugated sheet beams for road guardrail—Part 2: Tri-beam barrier (GB/T 31439.2), and the specification is 506 mm × 85 mm × 4 mm.

②Beams and casings are made of hot-rolled seamless pipes of 89 mm × 5.5 mm and 73 mm × 6.0 mm as specified in the standards of China, and the upper columns are made of ordinary carbon structural welded steel pipes of 102 mm × 4.5 mm.

③The lower column adopts 130 mm × 130 mm × 6 mm, which conforms to the current provisions of Cold Formed Steel Hollow Sections for General Structure's Dimensions, Shapes, Weight and Permissible Deviations (GB/T 6728) (China has no specifications of 125 mm × 125 mm × 6 mm in GB/T 6728 standard).

④The anti-obstruction block is 300 mm × 200 mm × 290 mm × 4.5 mm, which is appropriately adjusted according to the tri-beam barrier and column used.

6) The impact energy that can be absorbed at the Level 6-SS of the roadside corrugated beam barrier guardrail is 520 kJ, which is about 1/4 lower than the impact energy (650 kJ) of Japanese Level SS barriers. Japan's Level SS barrier consists of a tri-beam of 500 mm × 85 mm × 4 mm, a beam of 89.1 mm × 5.5 mm, an anti-obstruction block of 400 mm × 200 mm × 290 mm × 4.5 mm, a square pipe column of 125 mm × 125 mm × 6 mm and a round pipe column of 101.6 mm × 4.2 mm. Compared with Japan, the Level 6-SS barrier structure used in the Guidelines has the following changes:

①The Tri-beam adopts the form in compliance with the national standard Corrugated sheet beams for road guardrail—Part 2: Tri-beam barrier (GB/T 31439.2), and the specification is 506 mm × 85 mm × 4 mm.

②Beams and casings are made of hot-rolled seamless pipes of 89 mm × 5.5 mm and 73 mm × 6.0 mm as specified in the standards of China, and the upper columns are made of ordinary carbon structural welded steel pipes of 102 mm × 4.5 mm.

③The column adopts 130 mm × 130 mm × 6 mm, which conforms to the current provisions of Cold Formed Steel Hollow Sections for General Structure's Dimensions, Shapes, Weight and Permissible Deviations (GB/T 6728) (China has no specifications of 125 mm × 125 mm × 6 mm in GB/T 6728 standard).

④The anti-obstruction block is 350 mm × 200 mm × 290 mm × 4.5 mm, and the length is 50 mm shorter than that of the Japanese standard. Factors such as the impact energy, the width of road shoulders in China's highways, and the forms of tri-beam barriers and columns have been adjusted accordingly.

7) The impact energy that can be absorbed at the Level 7-HB of the roadside corrugated beam barrier guardrail is 640 kJ, which is equivalent to that of the Japanese Level SS (650 kJ).

8) The deformation values of some tested corrugated beam barrier guardrails are shown in Table 6-2

for reference.

Table 6-2 Deformation value of some corrugated beam barrier guardrail structures

Barrier form	Test items	Vehicle model	Test results
Level 1-C corrugated beam barrier beam	Maximum lateral dynamic displacement value of barrier W, m	Minibus	0.23
		Medium bus	0.25
		Medium truck	0.56
	Maximum dynamic incline equivalent value of vehicle VI_n, m	Medium bus	0.19
		Medium truck	0.91
Level 2-B corrugated beam barrier beam	Maximum lateral dynamic displacement value of barrier W, m	Minibus	0.79
		Medium bus	0.64
		Medium truck	—
	Maximum dynamic incline equivalent value of vehicle VI_n, m	Medium bus	1.15
		Medium truck	—
Level 3-A corrugated beam barrier beam[1]	Maximum lateral dynamic displacement value of barrier W, m	Minibus	1.10
		Medium bus	1.15
		Medium truck	1.35
	Maximum dynamic incline equivalent value of vehicle VI_n, m	Medium bus	1.55
		Medium truck	2.73
Level 4-SB corrugated beam barrier beam	Maximum lateral dynamic displacement value of barrier W, m	Minibus	0.85
		Medium bus	1.34
		Medium truck	—
	Maximum dynamic incline equivalent value of vehicle VI_n, m	Medium bus	2.27
		Medium truck	—
Level 4(Am) combination corrugated beam barrier beam[2]	Maximum lateral dynamic displacement value of barrier W, m	Minibus	0.88
		Medium bus	1.32
		Medium truck	—
	Maximum dynamic incline equivalent value of vehicle VI_n, m	Medium bus	1.88
		Medium truck	—

Note: 1) The Level A structure is similar to Appendix C, Figure C.2.3 a), and the height of the column is slightly shorter.
2) The Level Am combined corrugated beam barrier structure is inconsistent with Figure 6.2.7-3, for reference. The specifications of the test barriers here are: the wall thickness of the barrier is 4 mm; the diameter of the column is ϕ140 mm; the embedded depth is 1,400 mm, and the width of the diaphragm is 500 mm.

2 *The median corrugated beam barrier guardrail can be divided into two types: separate and combined. If the width of the median is greater than or equal to 2 meters, and there are many structures in it or pipelines buried under it, then the type of separate barriers can be used. If the width of the median is less than 2 meters, and there are few structures in it or pipelines buried under*

it, combined barriers should be used.

Types of separate median barriers with level of protection from 2 to 7 (codes: Bm, Am, SBm, SAm, SSm, HBm) and roadside barriers with level of protection from 2 to 7 (codes: B, A, SB, SA, SS, HB) are basically the same. The combined corrugated beam barrier guardrail is applicable to a road section with a median width less than 2m, and the guardrails on the two sides of the barriers are connected by a diaphragm. The main type of combined barrier is Level 3 (code Am) and so on.

3 *The installed position of the corrugated beam barrier guardrail in the cross-section of the road shall meet the following requirements:*

(1) *The determination of the location of the roadside barrier in the cross-section of the highway mainly considers two factors: ①The roadside barriers shall not invade the existing road construction limits as specified in the Technical Standards for Highway Engineering (JTG B01); ② It is necessary to take into account the range of deformation of the guardrail post after impact, so that outer wheel of the vehicle can stop within the soft shoulder. Based on the above two considerations, this article provides that the barrier surface can coincide with the left edge line of the soft shoulder or the left side of the kerb. For reasons such as the road alignment, the lateral position of the barrier can be properly shifted outwards, but the outside soft shoulder protective layer of the column shall be wider than 25 cm. If the transition to the bridge barrier or the use of termination flared terminal is needed, the overall strength of the barrier may be enhanced by installing concrete bases, deepening the uprights, or adopting other measures.*

(2) *The cross-section layout of the median corrugated beam barrier guardrails is generally determined first according to the width of the median and the laying position of underground pipelines. In the Technical Standards for Highway Engineering (JTG B01—2014), the median width shall be determined according to the functions. Taking into account the strength, maintenance convenience and the installation of greening and underground pipelines, the median width should be wider than normal for the separate median barriers. For the combined barrier or other forms of barriers, such as integral concrete barriers, the median width should be lower than normal.*

The median barriers are generally arranged symmetrically. The distance from the outer edge of the corrugated beam barrier guardrail face to the edge of the median must meet the requirements of the highway construction limit.

The combined corrugated beam barrier guardrails shall be laid along the center line of the road in principle. Where there are structures and underground pipelines in the center line of the road, the center line of the barrier column may be installed to one side, or change the combined type into a separate one so as to avoid obstructing the structure at the center line position.

4 *Once the vehicle collides with the barrier, it is desirable that the barrier can act on the effective part of the vehicle, neither making the vehicle out of the barrier nor allowing the vehicle to drive under the barrier. The ideal situation is to force the vehicle to steer steadily through the entire action of the barrier and then return to the normal driving direction. However, the quality of vehicles in the world today varies from large-tonnage heavy trucks to very small mini-vehicles, and the mass of vehicles varies greatly. Modern cars have a tendency toward miniaturization, and their mass has become lighter and lighter. In order to reduce air resistance, the front cover is more streamlined and low. Where such vehicle collides with the barrier, it is easy to drive under the barrier leading to serious consequences. Another situation is that the tonnage of vehicles is getting larger and larger, that is, vehicles are becoming larger and heavier. This large vehicle may cause jumping problems when colliding with the barrier. In particular, when colliding with the corrugated beam barrier barrier, the bumper of the vehicle may be twisted and beveled because it bumps against the top of the corrugated beam barrier guardrail. This situation is particularly serious at wide impact angles and is more dangerous when the vehicle is at high speeds.*

Once this happens, it is possible to tilt the bumper back and forth. Under the effect of the car's impact force, it is easy to slip onto the slope of the barrier, and an accident that the vehicle jumps out of the barrier occurs. The two situations mentioned above, that the vehicle drives under the barrier or the vehicle runs out of the barrier, are of course undesirable. This requires a proper study to determine the reasonable height of the barrier.

The determination of the height of barrier in the 1994 edition mainly refers to the experience of the United States: 1) According to the full-scale collision test of vehicles and barriers with different center-of-gravity heights; 2) Investigation data of the collision accidents of the barriers in use; 3) Geometrical characteristics analysis of modern vehicles. The installation height of barriers is determined through these three aspects.

The determination of the installation height of the barrier is actually related to the effective protection of most vehicle collision points. Therefore, the installation height of the barrier cannot be arbitrarily changed without being fully tested and verified. According to the specific conditions on the road side for design of the installation height of the barrier, the collision center point, which is the height of the connecting bolt hole center from the road surface, is controlled to be 600 mm. If the roadside or median is separated by a kerbstone, and the faces of the kerbstone and the barrier are not in alignment, the height of the collision center point shall be calculated from the top of the kerbstone. For the tri-beam steel barrier, the beam center height of the lowest bi-beam is also controlled to be 600 mm, which can more effectively protect large vehicles. For Level 5 (SA, SAm) and Level 6-SS barriers, due to the high impact energy required to be resisted, a beam is added to the top of the tri-beam barrier, which can effectively prevent large vehicles from crossing the barrier, and can increase the guide effect. The clear distance between this beam and the corrugated beam barrier or tri-beam is 305.5 mm, which increases the transparency of the barrier and improves the appearance of the barrier.

5 *The strength of the corrugated beam barrier guardrail is mainly determined by the rigidity of the column, the bearing capacity of the soil and the tensile strength of the beam. In particular, the relationship between the horizontal bearing capacity of the column and the displacement is an important factor in determining the strength of the column. To this end, Japan Public Works Research Institute and other organizations conducted a special test on the strength of the barrier column. The barrier column for the test is a round steel tube with a diameter of $\phi 114.3 \times 4.5$ mm, $\phi 139.8 \times 4.5$ mm, and column lengths of 1,200 mm, 1,500 mm, and 1,800 mm. The burial conditions are divided into: in soil, concrete sealing, ground anchors adding, tar asphalt filling, asphalt paving. Two loading methods were used, namely: static load - loading with a 25 t bulldozer, lever-type chain tensioner; and dynamic load - loading with a 20 t truck, traveling at 27 km/h.*

1) Results of static load test in Baizi District, Changyi Highway

—*Relationship between load and displacement: Columns that buried in soil, its bending position after loading is not related to the diameter and depth of the column. It is located approximately 40 cm below the ground surface, which is just above the surface of the upper road surface.*

According to the load-displacement curve, about 5cm before the displacement is, it is the stage where the subgrade reaction works. The displacement is in the range of 5 to 50 cm, which is exactly the bending stage of the column. The curve is gentle and the displacement increases rapidly.

—*The relationship between the size and strength of the column: the strength of the column is significantly affected by the diameter of the column. Where the displacement is between 5 cm and 50 cm, the column continues to bend, and the reaction deformation increases. The difference in column section coefficient is reflected in the strength. On the contrary, if the depth of the buried column is different, there is no difference in strength. In three cases, the maximum bending moment of the column occurred at 40 cm below the ground, regardless of the buried depth. This shows that the experimental columns are all buried in the lower subgrade with sufficient strength and have sufficient embedded depth for the column.*

—*The strength of the column after adding the concrete seal depends on the section coefficient.*

—*The columns with concrete seals have their maximum moments at the ground surface. The columns buried in the soil have their maximum moments 40 cm below the ground.*

2) Test results of Japan Public Works Research Institute

—Static load test: According to the load-displacement curve, where the column depth is 1.8 m, before the displacement of 10 cm, the bearing capacity of the foundation will work; where the displacement is 10 cm to 80 cm, the column is bent, and its horizontal bearing capacity depends on the section coefficient of the steel pipe. Where the column depth is 1.5 m, the column is not bent, which is caused by the yield of the foundation. This shows that the horizontal bearing capacity of the column is closely related to the compactness of the foundation, that is, the bearing capacity of the foundation.

—Dynamic load test: In the initial stage of loading, the load displacement curve is steep, and the maximum horizontal bearing capacity is also larger than the static load. In addition, the dynamic load increases the strain rate of the steel and the yield point of the steel, and reduces the bearing capacity of the column.

The Texas Transit College and the State Department of Highways and Public Transportation jointly conducted a series of column static tests to determine the performance of barrier wood columns and steel I-beams buried in 18, 24, 30, and 38 in(45.72 cm,60.96 cm,76.20 cm,96.52 cm)ches and two different types of soil. The results showed that: Steel columns absorb less energy than wood columns. At burial depths of 18 inches(45.72 cm) and 24 inches(60.96 cm), clayed soils consume more energy than sandy soils. Sandy soils absorb more energy in buried depths of 30 inches(76.20 cm) and 38 inches(96.52 cm).

The Guidelines, by referring to the barrier standards of Japan, the United States and other countries, stipulates that the buried depth of the second-class (B) columns of the bi-beam barrier shall not be less than 125 cm, and the buried depth of the third-class (A, Am) columns shall not be less than 140 cm. The buried depth of Level 4-(SB, SBm), Level 5-(SA, SAm), and Level 6-SS columns of corrugated beam barrier barrier shall not be less than 165 cm. In the presence of kerbs, the depth of the columns shall also allow for the height of the kerbs. The determination of the above data fully takes into account factors such as the narrower soft shoulders in China, the decrease of the lateral earth pressure of the columns, and the degree of compaction of the soft shoulder filling.

Where an underground pipeline is installed below a barrier column, or a stone road section is encountered, or under other special conditions, the column shall be installed in the concrete bases. Where the column is placed in a concrete base, its buried depth shall not be less than 40 cm. According to the results of the Japanese test of adding concrete seals to the columns and anchor, it was found that the columns buried in the concrete seal layer all bend at the ground surface, that is, the maximum bending moment occurs at the surface. The so-called adding concrete seal is to bury the columns in the earth and spread a concrete layer on the ground surface. The so-called anchoring method is to use concrete seals plus 13 mm 400 mm round steel anchoring. Where the method of burying with concrete seals and anchoring is used, the tested column is subjected to a pull-out force, and cracks occurred in the concrete seal. But the load displacement curves of the two types of tests are almost the same. It can be seen that the maximum bending moment of the column in the concrete seal is generated on the ground surface, and the strength of the column depends on the section coefficient. Therefore, it is entirely reasonable that the Guidelines stipulates that the buried depth in the concrete shall not be less than 40 cm. In the section where the concrete base is installed, greening and beautification can be carried out through the soil layer between the top of the foundation and the top surface of the soft shoulder to improve the road capacity. It shall be pointed out that due to the structure of the retaining wall and the types of materials used, the barrier bases on the retaining wall section needs to be specially designed.

Where barrier columns are installed on road sections that cannot be excavated, such as bridges, passages, and culverts, two methods can be used: one is to pre-bury a sleeve in concrete and seal it with mortar or concrete; the other is to pre-bury foot anchor bolts in concrete through flange connection.

6. The terminal of the roadside corrugated beam barrier guardrail at the downstream end, that is, the trailing end of the barrier installation, is generally handled as the round head termination beam. The upstream end of the roadside barrier, that is, the leading end of the barrier, can be handled in three ways: one is the use of a flared anchoring type, which is gradually extended to the ground through a diagonal beam and anchored at the end with a concrete foundation. If the anchor end hits the front of the vehicle, the vehicle will climb along the inclined beam and dissipate the energy, which avoids the barrier breaking the compartment. The second type is flared round end. According to the results of the real car crash test of the Mountain Highway Network Security Assurance Technical System Research and Demonstration Project, the round-headed end has a greater risk of injury to the passengers of the collided vehicle. The improvement requires flare to the width of the soft shoulder or outside the effective clear zone width, to end either at the boundary of the filling or excavation, and be buried in the soil and anchored. The third is the use of energy absorption terminal to protect the passengers.

7. For barriers installed at the median, both the leading and trailing ends shall be furnished with crashworthy treatment. Otherwise, if the vehicle is hit, it may cause the end-beam to pierce the car compartment and cause serious casualties.

In the event of a frontal collision of the vehicle, the crash barriers cannot be barbed, arched or roll over the car. The acceleration of the vehicle during the collision cannot exceed the required limit.

Where the vehicle collides with the barrier at between its end and standard section, the terminal structure should have the same performance of redirecting the vehicle as the median barrier standard section does.

The terminal form specified in the Guidelines is tailored for both separate and combined types barriers. Basically, the two sides of the barrier are connected by a round head. The dismantling energy device and dissipation column or sliding base are not adopted, and no design like energy absorption or displacement is used. Therefore, the energy absorption effect of the termination will not be very good, but this structure is easy to manufacture and install with lower cost.

8 The triangular areas of the motorway, exits and entrances of first-class highway, interchange cross roads, rest areas and parking areas shall be specially designed in accordance with the conditions for installation of barriers. The barrier structure on individual sites shall be consistent with the roadside corrugated beam barrier guardrail. Where it is laid, within 8 m of one side of the main line of the highway and first-class highway, and within 8 m from the side of the ramp, the column spacing shall be doubled. At the apex of triangle areas, the simplest way to tackle is connecting the side barriers with curved guardrails.

The rules of the previous edition stipulate that ' cushioning facilities shall be provided in the dangerous triangle area facing the direction of traffic flow. ' There are always guide signs in the area of the dangerous triangle facing the direction of traffic. If the highway is designed with a high speed, the British regulation recommends that where the diameter of the column exceeds 90 mm and the wall thickness exceeds 3.2 mm and the vehicle collides, it will cause injury to the passengers. The provisions of the Guidelines provide that in the dangerous triangle area facing the direction of traffic flow, cushioning facilities shall be provided if there are large group signs. This effectively absorbs impact energy and reduces the speed of frontal collisions with the vehicle. In the event of a side collision, the impact angle of the vehicle can be changed to guide the vehicle into the correct direction. The cushioning facilities can be widely used in the dangerous triangle area of traffic diversion, the front face of the overpass piers, and the leading end of the median concrete barriers. The cushioning facilities provided must have corresponding protection capabilities. If it is a small sign, it can be installed as a dismantling energy dissipation structure. If it is not installed as dismantling energy dissipation structure, it is recommended to install cushioning facilities.

9 *Tunnel entrances and exits, due to the great difference in road width and brightness between the inside and outside of the tunnel, often become black-spot sections. Therefore, it is necessary to properly handle the barriers at the entrance and exit of the tunnel. If conditions allow, cushioning facilities can be installed at the entrance side of the tunnel as required.*

10 *At present, the presence of planting soil and backfill soil in the median of Chinese motorways and first-class highways has affected the full use of the bearing capacity of the barrier columns. The roadside sometimes has this kind of situation, especially where the roadside guardrail flares, the required thickness of the soil shoulder protective layer cannot be reached, affecting the functioning of the guardrail. Appendix C.4 provides some ways to change. This revision has deleted the method of welded steel pipe on the side of the column because this method has encountered difficulties in construction whereas successful experience on application in engineering is limited.*

6.2.8 The concrete strength level, reinforcement amount and foundation installation of the concrete barrier shall be determined by design calculation. The concrete strength level of highways and Class-1 highways shall not be lower than C30. Where designing a concrete barrier, the following requirements shall be met:

1 The roadway concrete barriers may be divided into F-type and single slope type according to the structure, and it shall be selected in accordance with the road side situation, the proportion of the vehicle composition and the long-term pavement maintenance plan and other factors:

1) The requirements for the construction of the F-shaped concrete barrier are shown in Figure 6.2.8-1 and Table 6.2.8-1. According to the need, a climbing resistant ridge may be installed at the top of the barrier, as shown in Figure 6.2.8-2. The structural requirements are the same as that specified in the Table 6.2.8-1 except that H_1 minus 20 cm.

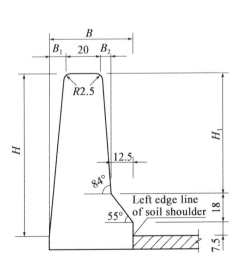

Figure 6.2.8-1   F-type concrete barriers (Unit: cm)

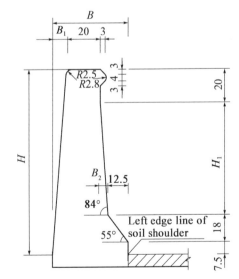

Figure 6.2.8-2   Reinforced concrete barriers (Unit: cm)

Note: H and B in the picture should meet the requirements of Table 6.2.8-1.

Table 6.2.8-1 Construction requirements of F-type concrete barriers (Unit: cm)

Level of protection	Code	H	H_1	B	B_1	B_2
3	A	81	55.5(35.5)	46.4(44.3)	8.1	5.8(3.7)
4	SB	90	64.5(44.5)	48.3(46.2)	9	6.8(4.7)
5	SA	100	74.5(54.5)	50.3(48.2)	10	7.8(5.7)
6	SS	110	84.5(64.5)	52.5(50.3)	11	8.9(6.8)
7	HB	120	94.5(74.5)	54.5(52.3)	12	9.9(7.8)
8	HA	130	104.5(84.5)	56.5(54.4)	13	10.9(8.9)

Note: The data in the brakets are for the F-type concrete barriers with the climbing resistant ridge.

2) The requirements for the construction of the single slope roadside concrete barrier are shown in Figure 6.2.8-3 and Table 6.2.8-2.

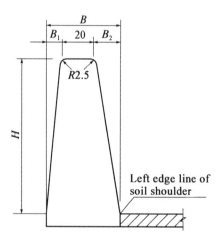

Figure 6.2.8-3 Single slope concrete barriers (Unit: cm)

Table 6.2.8-2 Structural requirements for single slope concrete barriers (Unit: cm)

Level of protection	Code	H	H_1	B	B_1	B_2
3	A	81	42.1	8.1	14.0	A
4	SB	90	44.5	9	15.5	SB
5	SA	100	47.2	10	17.2	SA
6	SS	110	49.9	11	18.9	SS
7	HB	120	52.6	12	20.6	HB
8	HA	130	55.5	13	22.5	HA

3) The roadside concrete barrier may adopt seat and underpinning methods:

The seat mode is to lock the base of the barrier in the road surface structure, and touse the resistance of the pavement structure to the displacement of the basic leg to improve the stability against overturning of the barrier, as shown in Figure 6.2.8-4 and Figure 6.2.8-5. The bearing capacity of the foundation shall not be less than 150 kN/m². The foundation shall be configured with appropriate amount of structural reinforcement and firmly welded with the barrier steel bar. The strength of basic concrete is the same as that of the barrier.

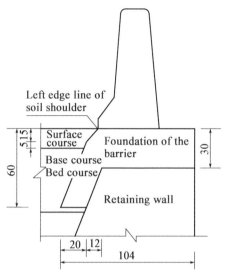

Figure 6.2.8-4 Seat foundation on retaining walls (Unit: cm)

Note: this figure is suitable for the protection level of third grade(A) of concrete barrier foundation.

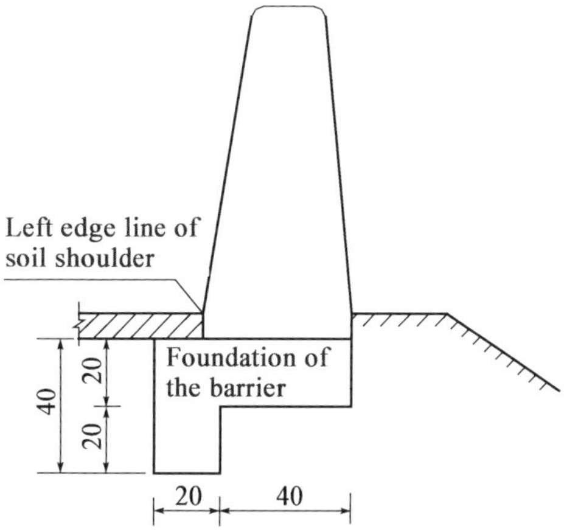

Figure 6.2.8-5 Seat foundation on soil foundation (Unit: cm)

Note: this figure is suitable for the protection level of third grade(A) of concrete barrier foundation.

The underpinning method is to drive steel pipe piles before the cast-in-place roadside concrete barrier, as shown in Figure 6.2.8-6. The specifications of steel pipe pile are ϕ140 mm × 4.5 mm, with length of 90-120 cm, and longitudinal spacing is 100 cm. Steel pipe piles must be firmly buried in the base and integrated with the concrete barrier. The bearing capacity of the foundation shall not be less than 150 kN/m².

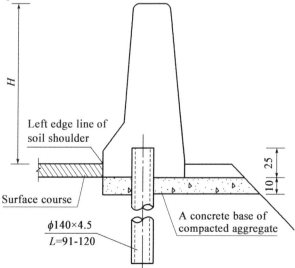

Figure 6.2.8-6 The foundation mode of underpinning (Unit: cm)

4) For the general structure of Level 1-C and Level 2-B concrete barriers, see Appendix C.3. For cross-section requirements, see Figure 6.2.8-7 and Figure 6.2.8-8.

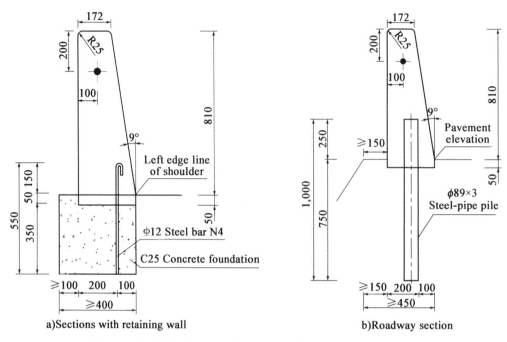

a) Sections with retaining wall   b) Roadway section

Figure 6.2.8-7 Level 1-C concrete barriers (Unit: mm)

2 Some of the median corrugated beam barrier barriers may adopt separated or integral types and maybe determined based on the width of the median barrier, the distribution of structures and pipelines. Integral or separated concrete barriers maybe divided into F-type and single slope type according to the structure:

1) The requirements for the construction of the integral F-shaped median concrete barrier are shown in Figure 6.2.8-9 and Table 6.2.8-3. Road sections with higher level of protection may be provided with climbing resistant ridge at the top of the barrier as required.

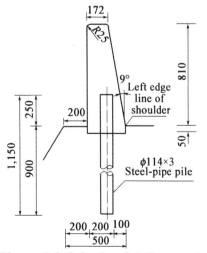

Figure 6.2.8-8 Level 2-B concrete barriers (Unit: mm)

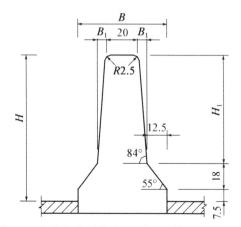

Figure 6.2.8-9 F-shaped median concrete barriers (Unit: cm)

Table 6.2.8-3 Construction requirements for F-type median concrete barriers (Unit: cm)

Level of protection	Code	H	H_1	B	B_1
3	Am	81	55.5	56.6	5.8
4	SBm	90	64.5	58.6	6.8
5	SAm	100	74.5	60.6	7.8
6	SSm	110	84.5	62.8	8.9
7	HBm	120	94.5	64.8	9.9
8	HAm	130	104.5	66.8	10.9

2) The requirements for the construction of the integral single-slope median concrete barrier are shown in Figure 6.2.8-10 and Table 6.2.8-4.

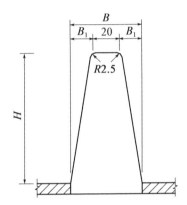

Figure 6.2.8-10 Single slope median concrete barriers (Unit: mm)

Table 6.2.8-4 Structural requirements for single slope median concrete barriers (Unit: cm)

Level of protection	Code	H	B	B_1
3	Am	81	48	14.0
4	SBm	90	51	15.5
5	SAm	100	54.5	17.2
6	SSm	110	57.8	18.9
7	HBm	120	61.2	20.6
8	HAm	130	65	22.5

3) The cross-sections of F-shaped and single slope separate concrete barriers shall be the same as the corresponding roadside concrete barriers. A reinforced concrete support block with width of 40 cm and thickness of 10 cm shall be installed every 2 meters in the back of the concrete barriers, and middle space can be filled with planting soil for greening, as shown in Figure 6.2.8-11. The distance between the tops of separate concrete barriers shall not be less than 40 cm, and the remaining width C value shall meet the provisions in the current *Technical Standards for Highway Engineering* (JTG

B01). The water in the middle of the separate concrete barriers may be discharged through the vertical blind ditch and then the horizontal drain. Where the degree of foundation compactness is less than 90%, a 40 cm-wide and 10 cm-thick reinforced concrete sleeper beam shall be installed every 4 meters.

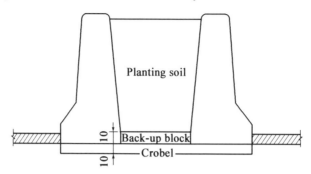

Figure 6.2.8-11　Structure diagram of median separation concrete barriers

4) Where the median concrete barriers needs protective piers, signposts, lighting poles and other facilities, cast-in-place concrete barriers maybe used to surround the structures at the construction site, but the widened sections shall not intrude into the road construction limits. Between the widened section and the standard section, a transition section shall be installed. The side shape of the widened section and the transition section shall be consistent with that of the standard section. The length of the widened section shall not be less than 20 times the width of the widened section, and the angle of the transition section shall not be greater than 2°, as shown in Figure 6.2.8-12.

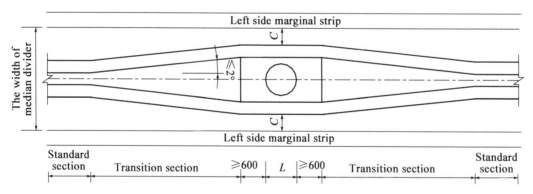

Figure 6.2.8-12　Widened section of median concrete barriers (Unit: mm)

5) The foundation of the median concrete barrier may be used in the following two ways: the base of the integral concrete barrier may be directly supported on the soil foundation and the bearing capacity of the soil foundation shall not be less than 150 kN/m². The concrete barrier is locked in the foundation and the buried depth is generally 10-20 cm. Both sides of the concrete barrier shall be paved with road surface materials with the same or higher strength than that of the driveway; sleeper beams shall be installed below the separate concrete barrier, and support blocks shall be provided between the barriers,

as shown in Figure 6.2.8-11.

6) Termination treatment shall be carried out at the start, end and opening of the median barrier with concrete barriers. The structure of concrete terminations is shown in Figure 6.2.8-13 and Figure 6.2.8-14. The basic treatment method of the termination shall be consistent with that of its connected concrete barriers. The section shape of the junction part of termination and concrete barriers in the standard section shall be uniform.

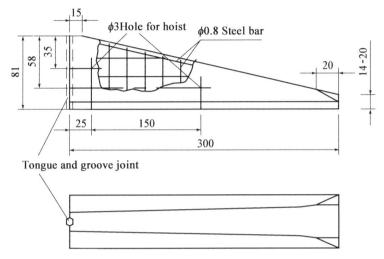

Figure 6.2.8-13　Termination structure of concrete barriers (Unit: cm)

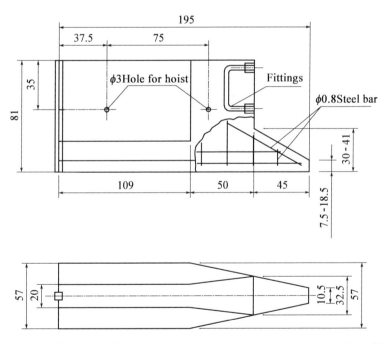

Figure 6.2.8-14　Diagram of termination structure of concrete barriers (Unit: cm)

3　Where the concrete barrier is installed on the super-elevation sections, special design shall be made according to the size of the super-elevation rate and curve radius. The section shape and the center height of the barrier shall be kept constant, and the barrier maybe installed in the manner of its vertical central axis perpendicular to the horizontal plane or the super-elevation plane. The pavement drainage on the super elevation road sections shall be discharged to the collecting well through a longitudinal drainage hole provided on the side of the central divider guardrail, and then discharged horizontally, or may be discharged through a drainage hole with certain spacing at the bottom of the concrete barrier.

4 Where the concrete barrier and the anti-glare facilities are installed at the same time, the road sections that may have an impact on stopping distance shall be checked. Where the delineators are attached to the concrete barrier, the delineators may be installed on the side wall or the top of the concrete barrier.

5 The construction types of concrete barriers on the same highway should be consistent.

6 The longitudinal length of each section of the concrete barrier shall be longer where the conditions of cast-in-place and lifting allow. The length of pre-cast concrete barriers shall be 4-6 m; the longitudinal length of cast-in-place concrete barriers shall be determined according to the requirements of lateral expansion joints, generally, as 15-30 m. A dummy joint shall be installed for cast-in-place concrete barriers every 3-4 m.

7 The reinforcing steel bar of pre-cast concrete barriers shall meet the requirements of protection degree. The influence of the length of the pre-cast blocks and the way of lifting shall also be considered. Cast-in-place concrete barriers maybe equipped with stress or structural reinforcing steel bar according to the requirements of the level of protection.

8 The longitudinal connection between the cast-in-place concrete barrier blocks maybe handled by butt junctions and transmission reinforcing steel bar.

9 The longitudinal connection between pre-cast concrete barrier blocks shall be handled as follows:

　　1) Longitudinal tongue and groove joint connection: suitable for roadside barriers of Level 3-A and median barriers of Level 3-Am, as shown in Figure 6.2.8-15.

　　2) Longitudinal connecting bolts: vertically pre-cast the connection bolt blocks in the upper half of the termination of the concrete barrier. After the two concrete barriers are aligned and in position, insert the I-shaped connecting bolts to connect the concrete barrier as a whole, as shown in Figure 6.2.8-16. This connection method is suitable for other concrete barriers of high level protection except for the Level 3-A and Level 3-Am.

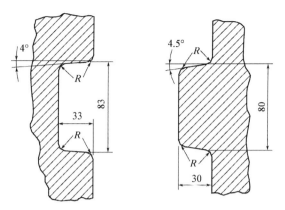

Figure 6.2.8-15 Longitudinal tongue and groove joint connection (Unit: mm)

Note: $R = 5$.

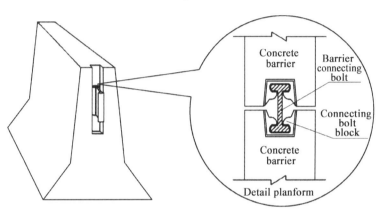

Figure 6.2.8-16 Longitudinal connection bolts method

3) Longitudinal connection reinforcement method: reserve steel casing in the concrete barrier, and connect the concrete barrier by inserting the reinforcing steel bar into the casing. The spacing of the steel casing shall not be longer than 35 cm. As shown in Figure 6.2.8-17 is Level 3-A pre-cast concrete barrier.

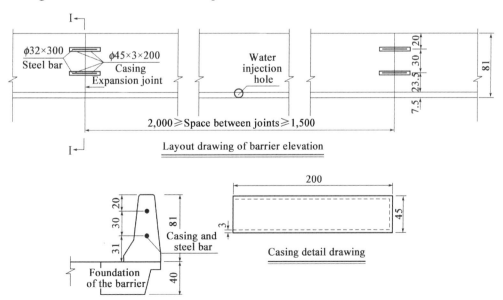

Figure 6.2.8-17 Longitudinal connection reinforcement method

10 The concrete barriers at the entrance of the tunnel shall be extended to the tunnel according to the outreach rate specified in Table 6.2.2-2. Transitional wing walls matching the maintaining driveway section shall be installed at the entrance of the tunnel, as shown in Appendix C.2.16. The concrete barriers at the exit of the tunnel may be treated as a normal alignment extension to the tunnel portal.

Backgrounds:

1 *The United States has conducted a large number of real vehicle crash tests on types of concrete barrier structure in the mid-1970s and the end of the 1990s. The advantages and disadvantages of NJ-shaped and F-shaped concrete barriers have been compared and the single slope concrete barriers have been developed. The research results have been widely adopted in European and American countries as well as Japan. The research results are summarized as follows:*

1) *The United States conducted a real vehicle crash test on the F-shaped concrete barrier. The evaluated results showed that the F-shaped barrier has better vehicle stability than the NJ-shaped for the collision vehicle.*

2) *The height of the concrete barrier is an important factor in determining its protection level.*

3) *According to the comparative test on the cross-section shape of concrete barriers, among the tests between NJ-shaped, F-shaped, single slope type and straight-wall type, the latter section shapes of barriers are better for vehicle stability, but the immediate responding acceleration to the passengers tends to be unfavorable.*

4) *The comprehensive evaluation of the single slope concrete barrier from the aspects of vehicle stability and passenger damage indicates that it is superior to concrete barriers of other section shapes.*

5) *The single slope concrete barriers have been evaluated by the real vehicle crash test of Level 4 (8 t, 82 km/h and 10°) in Report No. 350 of the United States NCHRP, and have been incorporated into the standards in the United States and Japan.*

6) *The Japanese specification has canceled the NJ barriers.*

Based on foreign research achievements and domestic implement experience, the 2006 version specification has eliminated the NJ-shaped barriers. Many useful experimental researches have also been conducted on concrete barriers. For example, Beijing Shenhuada Traffic Engineering Test

Co., Ltd. has carried out researches on roadside reinforced barriers. Several types of concrete barrier structures are identified, such as F-shaped, single slope type, and reinforced type, mainly by referring to the research results of the United States, Japan, and China, along with the Japanese Vehicle Barrier Standard Diagrams & Background (March 2004).

1)-2) The structures of the F-shaped and single slope concrete barrier are determined based on the results of the United States computer simulation and the full-scale crash test, and by referring to the Japanese Vehicle Barrier Standard Diagrams & Background (March 2004) combining the width of Chinese earth shoulders.

The reinforced concrete barrier in the previous edition is based on the F-shaped barrier. A climbing resistant ridge is deployed at the top of the barrier, which has a certain effect on restraining the large vehicle from climbing up the concrete barrier. Considering that the F-shaped barrier can meet the impact test conditions of the same protection level, in order to facilitate the construction, the climbing resistant feature is listed as an option in this revision, that is, a climbing resistant ridge may be equiped at the top of the barrier for the needs of a higher level of protection.

3) When designing the foundation of the road side concrete barrier, the size of the foundation concrete shall be determined by checking the anti-overturning stability of the barrier. According to the position of the roadside concrete barrier, embankment forms and construction procedures, the following two construction forms can be used for the foundation of the roadside concrete barrier:

①Seat form: According to the results of the 'Research on Development of Highway Cliff Barriers' (Western Transportation Construction Science and Technology Project) led by the Ministry of Transport in 2001, the safety of the barriers built on high retaining walls and high embankments depends mainly on the stability of the barrier bases. Through the theoretical analysis and the model test results, the basic part of the seat form is selected after the optimization of the plans. The seat foundation legs extend into the base course of pavement and make use of the resistance caused by the displacement between the base course of pavement and the base legs to improve the anti-overturning stability of the barrier. The force-bearing form is appropriate, as shown in Figure 6.5.5-1 and Figure 6.5.5-2. The bearing capacity of the foundation shall be no less than 150 kN/m^2. The foundation shall be furnished with appropriate amount of structural reinforcements and the main reinforcement shall be firmly welded with the barrier bar. The strength classification of base concrete shall be the same as that of the barriers.

②Underpinning form: The underpinning form can be used for high-filling embankment sections. Steel pipe piles should be inserted before constructing the cast-in-place roadside concrete barrier, or holes should be drilled to insert steel pipe piles. The steel pipe piles may also be inserted by *excavate and fill method. The bearing capacity of the foundation shall not be less than 150 kN/m^2. The specifications of steel pipe piles are ϕ140 × 4.5 and the length shall range from 90 cm to120 cm. The spacing of steel pipe piles is 100cm. Steel pipe piles shall be firmly fixed in the base and integrated with the concrete barrier.*

4) According to the results of the 'Key Technologies and Demonstration for the Prevention and Control of low-grade Highways' of Project in the National Science & Technology Pillar Program during the Twelfth Five-Year Plan Period, First-class (C) concrete barriers suitable for Third-class and IV highways has been developed. The structure is shown in Figure 6.2.8-7. The barrier has passed the verification of the real vehicle crash test of The Specification of Safety Performance Evaluation for Highway Barriers (JTG B05-01—2013).

2 *The concrete median barrier can be divided into two types in terms of its structure: the integral ones and the separate ones. The former can be used for the sections with narrow medians or where there are few communication and power lines in the median; the latter can be adopted for wide medians equipped with monitoring, communication, power lines and other facilities.*

1)-2) Based on the results of the computer simulation and full-scale collision tests of the United States and The Standard Diagram and Background of Safety Fences for Vehicles issued in Japan in March, 2004, and the actual conditions of the medians in China, structures of concrete median barriers are determined as F-shape and single-slope respectively presented in Figure 6.2.8-7 and Figure 6.2.8-8 in the text. The longitudinal center line of the concrete median barrier shall be in alignment with or properly offset from the center line of the median, but the offset longitudinal center line shall not reach the boundary line of highway construction.

3) The separate concrete median barrier of F-shape or single-slope can be used to solve the problems in the installation of monitoring, communication, power lines and other facilities in the median. The separate barrier is applicable where the median is more than 2-meter in width. Due to its high cost and poor transparency, caution must be exercised where the separate concrete median barrier is adopted. In addition, in the design, it is necessary to check the calculation of its strength and stability. The separation width can be calculated by the width of the median. The value of the spacing between the tops of the barrier recommended in the article is a minimum one, and the value needed in practice can be designed according to specific conditions.

Regarding the calculation of the lateral clearance value of the concrete barrier, in the regulations of some countries, the calculation shall be made by using the slope change point of the concrete barrier as the boundary. However, due to the frequent use of the single-slope concrete barrier in recent years, the C value of the lateral clearance shall be calculated by using the point at which the concrete barrier intersects the road.

The plain concrete bolsters shall be provided at the position of both the expansion joint and the false joint, and their labels should be the same as those of the concrete barrier.

*4) Where there are piers, signposts, lighting poles or other facilities in the median, the concrete barrier shall be specially designed. The shape of the barrier's side facing the roadway shall remain unchanged. The width of the barrier shall be determined on the basis of the size and features of the structure and shall meet the requirement of the boundary line of highway construction. In order to prevent the impact force caused by the vehicle colliding with the concrete barrier from getting transmitted to the structures in the median, and to guarantee the need for the deformation of the concrete barrier, the concrete barrier and the structures in the median shall not be concreted as a whole. In order to make the barrier transit smoothly to reduce the impact on the vehicle, a transition section shall be installed between the standard section of the barrier and the section housing the bridge pier, sign post, lighting poles and other facilities. In addition, the angle of direction change of the transition section should meet the requirement shown in Figure 6.2.6-10 in the text, and under such circumstance, it shall be calculated by the following formula (taken from the standard diagram of concrete barriers published in 1999 in Oregon, USA, numbered RD535):
$\alpha = \arctan(1.667/v)$, and in this formula, v refers to the design speed in km/h.*

5) The concrete median barrier placed on the base, relying on self-weight, tends to get displaced under the effect of the vehicle impact force and may even endanger the safety of vehicles on the opposite roadway. By referring to the provisions of the Japanese standard of barriers and domestic research results, this article demands that for the integral concrete barrier, the base bearing capacity of the barrier shall reach 150 kN/m^2 or more, and the barrier shall be interlocked under the base, which implies that the concrete barrier shall be embedded in the underlying base. Under the concrete base, there shall be a semi-rigid base whose thickness shall be no less than 20 cm and can be adjusted in accordance with the relevant provisions of the roadbed construction specifications. Above the concrete base, there shall be a further concrete base or grading macadam base with a thickness ranging from 10 cm to 20 cm. During construction, the concrete base or grading macadam base can be laid to the prescribed elevation at first, and then the hoisted or cast-in-place concrete barriers can be installed. For separate concrete barriers, there shall be bolsters under the barriers with support blocks between the barriers, shown in Figure 6.2.8-11 in the text.

6) The barrier terminal is a special zone. Due to the fact that where the car collides with the barrier terminal, it is almost a right-angle frontal collision, an appropriate design shall be conducive for the climbing of the colliding vehicle to absorb the impact energy so as to reduce the damage of the vehicle and passengers in the vehicle. It follows that the barrier terminal is a special structure which shall be specially designed. The two forms proposed in the article are the two ones that are widely used and relatively more effective worldwide at present which are obtained by extensive studies and constant improvement through practical applications. Therefore, the two forms are adopted in this detailed regulation.

Both of the two forms of the concrete barrier terminals are applicable at the beginning, ending and opening positions of the concrete median barrier. The structure shown in Figure 6.2.8-13 in the text of this detailed regulation is the sloped concrete barrier terminal with which the colliding vehicles can climb the terminal to absorb the energy in the collision; The other structure shown in Figure 6.2.8-14 is the pointed terminal which the vehicle frontally collides with cannot climb up the terminal, but the vehicle colliding with its side can be better guided into the heading direction, so this form of terminal can be used on the basis of its installation location.

3 *In the super-elevation section of roads, the installation of concrete median barrier may affect the drainage to a certain degree which mainly depends on the position of the reference point (the rotating axis) where the cross fall changes. If the median is not affected by the rotation of the cross fall, the barrier can be installed with the same form used for the linear section of the road. If the median is affected, there are two barrier-placement forms, in which the sectional central axis of the barrier is perpendicular to the horizontal plane or the super-elevation plane. The appropriate form can be used in accordance with the requirements of the horizontal drainage, aesthetics, etc, but the barrier must be functionally effective with the height of its center and the shape of the cross section unchanged.*

The central median shall be designed with drainage facilities. Where the central divider is drained in the longitudinal direction, drainage ditches are generally placed on one side of the barrier; while in the lateral direction, drainage openings can be provided at the lower margin of the barrier. Because of the widely varying rainfall and different geometric conditions of highways in different areas on the vast land of China, there is no detailed provision in the article on the size and spacing of drainage openings which can be ascertained by combining the requirements of the highway drainage design and the local conditions of the rainfall and highway in the area.

4 *The height of concrete median barriers generally ranges from 81 cm to 100 cm, which is insufficient for anti-glare purpose. Therefore, on any road section where anti-glare facilities shall be installed, there should be embedded connections in the appropriate position on the top of the barrier, while their positions and quantities shall correspond with the structure of anti-glare facilities. For road sections where the facilities can affect the stopping sight distance of drivers, it is necessary to check its calculation. If it fails to meet the regulatory requirements, corresponding measures shall be taken such as moving anti-glare facilities inwards and installing speed limits.*

In attaching delineators to the concrete barrier, the height, spacing, and type of the delineator shall be considered to determine the method of the attachment.

5 *Taking account of aesthetic requirements and the convenience of formwork construction, this article demands that the same concrete barrier structure shall be used on the same road.*

6 *The concrete barrier can be constructed by precast or cast-in-place methods. For precast concrete barriers, the length of each block is mainly restricted by the hoisting equipment and the radius of curvature on the curved road section. From the perspective of increasing the overall strength and stability of the barrier, the precast block is required to be as long as possible; but for the convenience of casting, installation and the requirements of expansion joint, the length would have a certain limitation. Therefore, the length from 4 meters to 6 meters of each block is prescribed in the article. This is based on the current hoisting condition in China, and given that with the increase of its protection level, the concrete barrier mainly relies on the self-weight to stop vehicles from crossing the road, and accordingly a too-short precast block may increase the difficulty of longitudinal anchorage. The Japanese standard of the barrier prescribes that the minimum length of precast blocks shall be 5 m. On the basis of the local conditions, the precast blocks in different areas shall be as long as possible but remains an appropriate length within the specified range. The longitudinal length of the cast-in-place concrete barrier is proposed according to the requirement of the transverse joint whose design shall be produced by referring to the clear specification of the current Code for the Design of Highway Reinforced Concrete and Prestressed Concrete Bridges and Culverts (JTG D62—2004). In order to reduce the inhomogeneous cracking of concrete, a fake joint shall be installed every 3 meters to 4 meters with reference to Figure 6-4.*

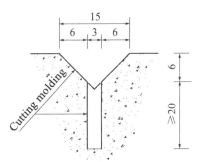

Figure 6-4 The reference of the fake joint specifications (Unit: mm)

7 *Reinforcement design for concrete barriers shall be conducted based on the requirements of protection level, hoisting condition, temperature stress and deformation, and basic connection*

methods. Reinforcement design for concrete barriers installed on roadside structures shall be prepared on the basis of cantilever beams; a certain quantity of steel reinforcement is necessary for the concrete median barrier no matter the barrier is precast or cast-in-place. The precast barrier block has to be placed by hoisting which is an important stage in the construction. Therefore, for the safe, convenient and quick hoisting, positions of hoisting holes shall be designed appropriately. Holes are normally provided at the point about 1/4 of the length of the barrier block on both ends of the precast block. For a relatively long block, the calculation of hoisting stress shall be conducted to determine the position of hoisting holes. The cast-in-place barrier can be reinforced by nominal steel bars or structural steel bars based on the protection level.

9 *On some highways in China, the terminals of the concrete barrier blocks are blunt, and the barriers have no connection with adjacent ones. Consequently, they have very poor longitudinal integrity. Under the effect of the car's impact force, the barrier blocks will be disengaged and misaligned, which cannot redirect the colliding vehicle into the appropriate trajectory. Accordingly, the barrier loses its function which it is supposed to perform. In order to overcome the mentioned deficiencies, there are three longitudinal connection methods for precast barriers based on the protection level:*

1) *The longitudinal notch/bezel connection method: it is applicable to the barrier of protection Level 3-(A and Am). The grooves are precast according to Figure 6.2.8-15 in the text so that after the installation, successive barrier blocks can come to occlusion and bear the force together. The groove shall be made from the very top to the bottom of barrier block. The contact surface of the notch connections shall be designed with a certain number of steel bars to resist the shearing and torsion generated during the collision;*

2) *The longitudinal bolt connection method is for the barrier of other protection levels except Level 3-(A and Am) as shown in Figure 6.2.8-16. In the detailed design, other connection methods with which the overall strength can be guaranteed such that the collided barrier would not have excessive deformation can also be employed.*

3) *Steel sleeves are inserted at the both terminals of precast concrete barrier, and steel bars are added in the steel sleeves. In Figure 6.2.8-17 presents the precast concrete barrier of protection Level 3-A. The spacing between steel sleeves of the barrier which is designed above Level 3-A should be no longer than 35 cm.*

6.3 Bridge railings and railings

6.3.1 Bridge Railings and railings shall be installed according to the following principles:

1 Bridges of highways of all classification shall be installed with roadside barriers.

2 Motorways and Class-1 highway bridges as secondary arterials shall be installed with median barriers, and Class-1 highway bridges as main collective roads shall be installed with median barriers.

3 On the bridge with the sidewalk, the sidewalk and the lane maybe separated by kerbor barriers:

   1) On the highway bridges with a designed speed of 60 km/h or less, the sidewalk (the bicycle lane) and the lane maybe separated by kerbs. Moreover, the kerb and the sidewalk may be combined, and the combined type barrier which meets the demand of the protection of vehicles and the passing of pedestrians (bike) shall be adopted under this circumstance. This design is shown in Figure 6.3.1 a).

   2) On the highway bridges with a designed speed of over 60 km/h, the combined type barrier which meets the need of the protection of vehicles and the passing of pedestrians, and the railing shall be used on the roadside. This design can be found in Figure 6.3.1 b).

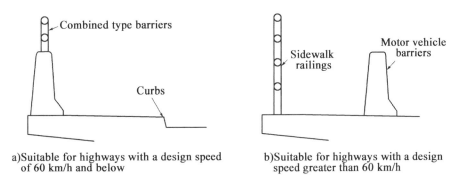

a) Suitable for highways with a design speed of 60 km/h and below

b) Suitable for highways with a design speed greater than 60 km/h

Figure 6.3.1 A schematic diagram of the barrier and railing for the bridges with a sidewalk

   3) Where there are motorways and Class-1 highways both with sidewalks (bicycle lanes) that have to take load of a large number of pedestrians or have many factors of danger, the pedestrian overpass should be installed independently.

Background:
Generally, the roadside of bridges is subject to more hazards than at-grade roads because vehicles overrunning out of the bridge often cause serious traffic accidents in that vehicles are crashed and people in the vehicles get killed. Therefore, by taking account of factors including speed, traffic volume and cost needed to be invested, the provisions of the article are made on the basis of the

function and technical grades of highways as well as the requirement of the current Technical Standards for Highway Engineering (JTG B01).

For highways with sidewalks, it is generally believed that it may not be necessary to consider the possibility of vehicles falling from bridges, and that on highways with a relatively low designed speed, kerbs can be installed to protect pedestrians (as shown in Figure 6.3.1 a). However, given that vehicles and pedestrians on the highway bridge with the sidewalk (the bicycle lane) are on the same plane, severity of accidents of vehicles colliding with pedestrians and bike (non-motorized vehicles) would be largely increased, especially for the sections with the large traffic volumes and high traffic speeds. In order to prevent secondary accidents caused by vehicles falling from bridges, and to separate motorized vehicles from bicycles (non-motorized vehicles) to improve the safety of vehicles and pedestrians (non-motorized vehicles), it is reasonable to install combined type barrier at the boundary between the sidewalk and the lane (bicycle lane), as shown in Figure 6.3.1 b), so as to protect vehicles and pedestrians (non-motorized vehicles).

The combined type barrier separating the sidewalk (bicycle lane) and its adjacent lane can also be used as the railing of the sidewalk (bicycle lane). Where the total height of the combined type barrieris unable to reach the minimum height requirement of the sidewalk (bicycle lane) railing, it can be considered to install additional members, such as metal railings, on the top of the combined type barrier, which shall be designed according to the appropriate design load of the sidewalk or bicycle lane.

6.3.2 Based on the severity grades of the traffic accidents that can be caused by vehicle driving off the bridge or into the opposite lane, the protection grade shall be selected according to the provision in Table 6.3.2, and the selection shall comply with the following provisions:

Table 6.3.2 Selection of the protection grade of bridge railings

Classes of highway	Design speed (km/h)	Severity grades of the traffic accident that can be caused by vehicles driving off the bridge or into the opposite lane	
		High: bridges crossing over sections of highways, railways, or the Class-1 conservations of city drinking water source	Middle: other bridges
Motorway	120	Level 6-SS and SSm	Level 5-SA and SAm
	100 and 80	Level 5-SA and SAm	Level 4-SB and SBm
Class-1 highway	60	Level 4-SB and SBm	Level 3-A and Am
Class-2 highway	80 and 60	Level 4-SB	Level 3-A
Class-3 highway	40 and 30	Level 3-A	Level 2-B
Class-4 Highway	20		

Note: The code for the protection grade of the barrier is marked in the parenthesis.

1 The barrier's anti-collision grades of foot bridges, passageways and culverts on the Class-2 and higher class highway should be the same as that of the adjacent subgrade barrier.

2 Where the highway bridge adopts a monolithic superstructure, the protection grade of the median barrier maybe decided based on the condition of the subgrade's median barrier.

3 Under the following circumstances, according to comprehensive justification, the protection level of the barrier may be increased by one or more grades on the basis of Table 6.3.2:

1) The barrier is located on the continuous long down slopes; the median barrier is on the road section where the radius of the right-turning horizontal curve is close to or equal to the minimum radius value provided in the current *Technical Standards for Highway Engineering* (JTG B01); the roadside barrier is on the outer side of road section where, the radius of the left-turning horizontal curve is close to or equal to the minimum radius value.

2) The height of the bridge is over 30 meters.

3) In the design traffic volume, the proportion of vehicles with a total mass exceeding 25 tonnes is higher than 20%.

4 The protection level of the barrier on the bridges crossing over the large-scale Class-1 conservation zones of drinking water source and highways as well as the cable load-bearing bridge such as the super-large suspension bridge and cable-stayed bridge should be determined as Level 8-HA.

6.3.3 Where selecting the form of the bridge barrier, the following factors shall be taken into account:

1 The protection performance of the bridge barrier. The selected barrier's form must be able to effectively absorb designed impact energy in strength to prevent the vehicle whose energy is less than the designed collision energy from driving out of the bridge or into the opposite lane, and to make the vehicle turn to the right running direction.

2 The degree of collided barrier deformation. After the collision, the maximum dynamic displacement extension (W) of the barrier or the maximum dynamic incline equivalent value (VI_n) of large and medium-sized vehicles shall not exceed the distance between collision-facing surface of the barrier and the protected obstacle. The maximum dynamic

displacement extension (W) or the maximum dynamic incline equivalent (VI_n) may be selected referring to the following factors:

1) Where minibus is the main vehicle passing across the bridge, the maximum dynamic displacement value (W) of the minibus may be selected as the deformation control index in spite of the height of obstacles outside the bridge.

2) Where there are obstacles on the outer side of the bridge which are higher than its barrier, the maximum value of the maximum dynamic incline equivalent value (VI_n) of all the tested vehicles shall be used as the deformation control index.

3) Where there are obstacles on the outer side of the bridge which are lower than or in the same height as its barrier, the maximum value of the maximum dynamic displacement extension (W) of all the tested vehicles shall be used as the deformation control index.

3 Requirements for environment and landscape include:

1) On steel bridges, metal beam guardrails should be adopted.

2) On bridges with specific requirements for landscape, metal beam guardrails or the combined type Bridge Railings should be installed.

3) In regions with severe snow deposit, metal beam guardrails or combined type bridge barriers should be adopted.

4) The form of barriers for footbridges, passageways and culverts on Class-2 and higher class highways should be the same as that of the adjacent subgrade barriers.

4 Requirements for the structure. Where the self-weight of the bridge and the influence of the vehicle's impact load on the bridge's deck plate need to be reduced, metal beam guardrails should be used.

5 Full life cycle cost of barriers. Besides the initial construction cost of barrier, the maintenance cost after bringing into use including regular maintenance, accident maintenance, material reservation and convenience of maintenance shall be taken into consideration.

Background:
The common structural forms of the bridge barrier include the rigid barrier, the semi-rigid barrier

and the combined type barrier. The rigid barrier includes the F-shaped concrete barrier, the single-slope concrete barrier, the metal beam guardrail, etc. Among them, due to low frequency of use, the form of the reinforced beam-column concrete barrier is abandoned in this revision. In the semi-rigid barrier, the most commonly used type is the metal beam guardrail for its pleasing appearance, transparency, high strength, and little deformation. However, there is still controversy in China on whether the corrugated beam barrier barrier and thrie-beam barrier can be used as the barrier of the medium-scale and above bridges. The opposite opinion lies in that the deformation of these two types of barriers is too large to guarantee safety. The supportive side believes that as long as they are verified to be fulfilling the function of containing, buffering and redirecting by passing the test of the corresponding level, they can be used as the bridge barrier. In addition, the current corrugated beam barrier barrier can reach Grade 7 (HB), so there is no problem in its strength. The designer must reasonably select the bridge barrier based on its specific requirements. The combined type barrier, which is not only as rigid as the concrete barrier, but also as flexible and transparent as the semi-rigid barrier, is more widely used in large and medium bridges.

In the selection of the bridge barrier form, some national, industrial and provincial regulations, such as the stipulation that ' the highway crossing the railway overpass shall be installed with the reinforced wall-type concrete barrier and protective screenings' given in the Notice of the Issues Related to the Construction and Maintenance Management of Barriers on the Road Section of the Highway and Railway Overpass and the Parallel Road Sections of the Highway and Railway (Railway Transportation [2012] No. 139) jointly issued by the former Ministry of Railways and Ministry of Transport, shall also be taken into account. The above-mentioned regulation shall be taken into consideration in deciding the barrier form of the bridge crossing over railways.

6.3.4 In selecting the material of the bridge barrier, factors such as ultimate strength, durability, maintenance frequency, replacement convenience, and long-term performance shall be considered. The materials of the barrier such as steel bars, concrete, steels, timber and aluminum alloys shall be used in accordance with provisions in the current *Code for Design of Highway Reinforced Concrete and Prestressed Concrete Bridges and Culverts* (JTG D62), *Code for Design of Highway Masonry Bridge and Culvert* (JTG D61), and *Specifications for Design of the Highway Steel Bridge* (JTG D64), etc. The use of special materials shall in accordance with the requirements of relevant national and industrial standards.

Background:
Bridge barriers are made of materials such as steel bars, concrete, steels, timbers and aluminum alloys and so on, which means the quality, variety, specification, property, economy and color of these materials, to a large extent, can directly affect or even determine the structural form, function, applicability, robustness, durability, economy and aesthetics of the bridge barrier, and

to a certain degree, influences the transportation, storage, constructing technology and maintenance frequency of the barriers.

In order to make the bridge barrier fulfill the basic requirements of applicability, robustness and aestheticis, the selection of materials shall comply with certain principles; this article proposes the factors to be considered and technical specifications to be followed in material selection.

6.3.5 The structure of the bridge barrier shall conform to the following provisions:

    1 The structure of the metal beam guardrails shall meet the following rules:

        1) The collision-facing surface of the barrier shall be accommodating, smooth and continuous without sharp corners.

        2) The positional relationship between the vehicle and the barrier is shown in Figure 6.3.5-1. The height of the barriers of all protection grades shall meet the following requirements:

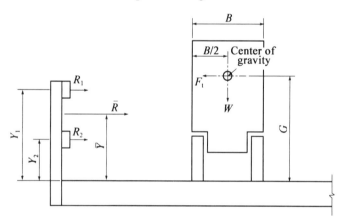

Figure 6.3.5-1 Position relationship between vehicles and barriers

Note: The calculation baselines for Y and Y_i are: the intersection of the barrier surface with the deck surface. If there is a curb, it should be the intersection of the parapet and the curb top.

        ①The weighted average height $\overline{Y}$ from the transverse load bearing capacity of all beams from the decks shall not be less than the value specified in Table 6.3.5-1. $\overline{Y}$ is calculated by the Equation (6.3.5) below.

$$\overline{Y} = \frac{\Sigma(R_i Y_i)}{\overline{R}} \quad (6.3.5)$$

Where:

    R_i—The transverse load bearing capacity of the ith beam (kN);

    Y_i—The height of the ith beam from the bridge deck (m).

Table 6.3.5-1 The weighted average height of the metal beam guardrails from its beam's transverse load bearing capacity to the deck

Protection grade	Minimum height (cm)	Protection grade	Minimum height (cm)
2nd (B)	60	6th (SS)	90
3rd (A)	60	7th (HB)	100
4th (SB)	70	8th (HA)	110
5th (SA)	80		

② The total height of the metal beam guardrail with the protection grade of Grade 4 (SB) and below shall not be less than 1.00 m; The total height of the metal beam guardrail with the protection grade of Grade 5 (SA) shall not be less than 1.25 m; The total height of the barrier of Grade 6 (SS) and above shall not be less than 1.5 m.

3) The total height of the beams shall not be less than 25% of that of the barrier. The net distance between the beams which corresponds to the retreat distance of the column should be within or below the shadow area shown in Figure 6.3.5-2 a), and the ratio between the sum of the total height of the beams which correspond to the retreat distance of the column and the column height should be within or above the shadow area shown in Figure 6.3.5-2 b).

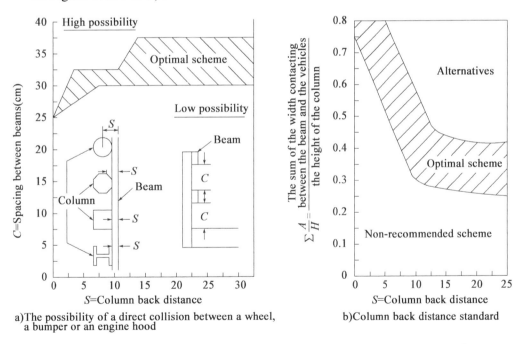

a) The possibility of a direct collision between a wheel, a bumper or an engine hood

b) Column back distance standard

Figure 6.3.5-2 Selection criteria for specification and layout design of bridge barrier components

4) The section thickness of barrier components shall be determined according to calculation and no less than the minimum value in Table 6.3.5-2.

Table 6.3.5-2 Section minimal thickness of metal barrier

Materials	Section types	The minimal thickness (mm)			
		Major longitudinal effective components	Longitudinal ineffective members and secondary longitudinal effective components	Subplots, rods and nets	Anchor ears and secondary components
Steel	Hollow sections	3	3	3	3
	Other sections	4	3	3	3
Aluminum alloy	All sections	3	1.2	3	1.2
Stainless steel	All sections	2	1.0	2	0.5

5) The design of beam connection shall meet the following requirements.

①The length of connection sleeve shall be larger than or equal to the twice of the beam width and shall not be less than 30 cm, as shown in Figure 6.3.5-3.

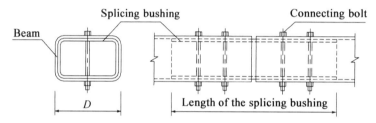

Figure 6.3.5-3 Beam connection

②The module of bending section of connection sleeve shall not be lower than that of beams, and the bolt shall meet the requirements of shear strength.

③There may be bulges or invaginations on the beam connection parts of the barrier collision-facing side. The bulges or invaginations shall not exceed the section thickness of beams or 1 cm.

6) Bridges of motorways and first class highways should not installed kerbs. Where it is necessary to installed kerbs for reducing the influence on bridge decks caused by collision, its height should range from 5 cm to 10 cm. The interior side of kerbs should keep in the same plane with the beam collision-facing side or lay a suitable place between columns and beams.

7) The pedestrian path (bikeway) with kerbs shall only be designed on the second (B) protection level bridges with the design speed less than or equal to 60 km/h. And the kerb height should be 15 cm and should not be over 20 cm. The structure of typical pedestrian path is shown in Figure 6.3.5-4. Where the heights of subgrade kerbs and

bridge kerbs are not the same, their altitude interception shall be transited among the range of 20 times or above. On the bridges with the design speed greater than 60 km/h, the barriers should be installed between pedestrian path (bikeway) and roadway to protect pedestrians.

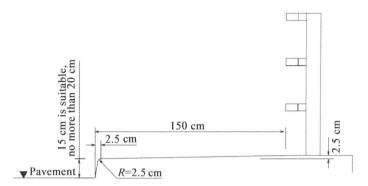

Figure 6.3.5-4 Schematic diagram of a typical combined type of kerbs and pedestrian paths

2 The structures of concrete barriers and combined type barriers shall meet the following requirements:

1) The concrete barriers can be divided into F-type, single-slope type and reinforced type according to the structure. The concrete parts of combined type barriers should adopt F-type, see Figure 6.3.5-5 a)-c). Without the experimental verification, section shapes of the collision-facing side and connection ways of barriers must not be changed optionally, but the reverse side may adopt suitable shapes according to the actual conditions. Sections with higher protection level may install resistance climbing ridges on the top of barriers as required. See Figure 6.3.5-5 d).

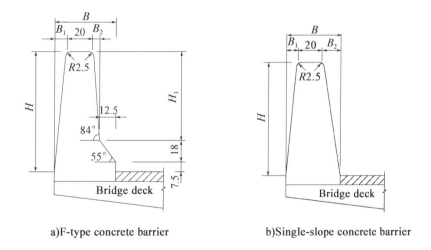

a) F-type concrete barrier   b) Single-slope concrete barrier

Figure 6.3.5-5

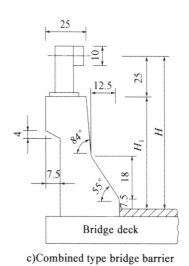
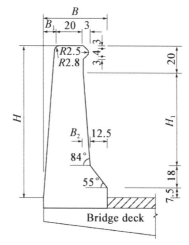

c) Combined type bridge barrier

d) Concrete barriers with resistance climbing ridge

Figure 6.3.5-5 General construction examples of concrete and combined barrier (Unit: cm)

Note: a)-d) figure, B, B_1, B_2, H, H_1 and other parameters are calculated according to the total height of the fence.

2) The height of concrete barriers of each protection level shall not be less than the specified values in Table 6.3.5-3.

Table 6.3.5-3 Height of concrete barriers

Protection level	Height (cm)	Protection level	Height (cm)
2-B	70	6-SS	110
3-A	81	7-HB	120
4-SB	90	8-HA	130
5-SA	100		

Note: Baseline of the height of concrete barriers is the intersecting line between the interior side and the pavement.

The heights of combined barriers of each protection level may be 10 cm higher than the heights mentioned above.

The vertical section of 7.5 cm in the interior side of F-type concrete barriers may be used for pavement overlay. Where the thickness of pavement overlay is over 7.5 cm, the height of concrete barriers shall be adjusted or the protection performance of concrete barriers shall be evaluated.

3) The thickness of reinforced protective layer of barrier collision-facing side section shall not be less than 4.5 cm.

4) The quantity of reinforcement cross section of barriers is determined according to calculation and shall meet the regulations for the minimal reinforcement ratio in *Code for Design of Highway Reinforced Concrete and Prestressed Concrete Bridges and*

Culverts (JTG D62).

3 Expansion joints shall be installed on Bridge Railings based on major structures according to the following regulations.

1) Metal beam guardrail

①Where the total displacement of vertical design of expansion joints is less than or equal to 5 cm, the expansion joints shall be able to transit 60% of the tensile strength of beams and all the design maximum bending moment. The length of connection sleeve of expansion joints shall be larger than or equal to 3 times of beam width. See Figure 6.3.5-6.

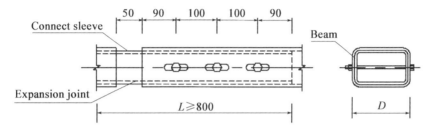

Figure 6.3.5-6　Expansion joint design with displacement less than 5 cm (Unit: mm)

Note: D is the beam width.

②Where the vertical design displacement of expansion joints is larger than 5 cm, the expansion joints shall transit all design maximum bending moment. The top supports shall be installed at both sides of expansion joints and the center-to-center spacing shall not be larger than 2.0 meters. The length of connection sleeve of expansion joints shall be no less than or equal to 3 times of beam width. See Figure 6.3.5-7.

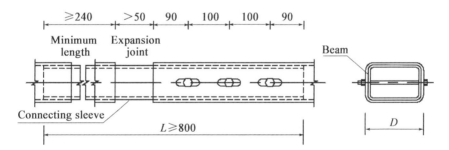

Figure 6.3.5-7　Expansion joint design with displacement larger than 5 cm (Unit: mm)

Note: D is the beam width.

③Where vertical or transverse complex displacement occurs in expansion joints, Bridge Railings in expansion joints may be disconnected. But columns shall be installed at both ends of expansion joints. And the center-to-center spacing shall not be larger than 2.0 meters. The gap between the two beam ends shall not be larger than the design displacement of expansion joints with a plus of 2.5 cm. The ends of beams shall not cause any risk to the crashed vehicles. See Figure 6.3.5-8.

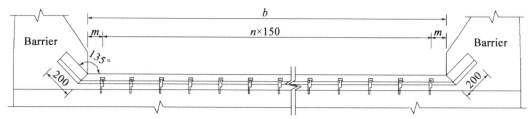

Figure 6.3.5-8 Example of cross section of the retractor device

2) Rigid barriers

The expansion joints of bridge decks shall be disconnected and the gap shall not be larger than the design displacement of expansion joints of bridge decks. The mounting holes of expansion joints on bridges shall be reserved on the rigid barriers of bridge expansion joints. The size of mounting holes shall be determined according to the size and bending height of expansion joints.

3) Combined barriers

The concrete parts shall meet the requirements of expansion joints of concrete barriers. And the mental structure parts shall meet the requirements of expansion joints of metal beam guardrails.

4 Bridge Railings may be installed with secondary components for different requirements, apart from bearing components for vehicle impact loads. And it shall also comply with the following provisions:

1) General requirements of secondary components design:

①All secondary components shall be firmly connected with bearing components of Bridge Railings.

②The secondary components shall not intrude into the limit of highway constructions. And the plane projection shall not exceed the projection range of main bearing components. See Figure 6.3.5-9.

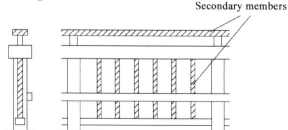

Figure 6.3.5-9 Secondary components installation example

2) The design of secondary components shall meet the following requirements:

①Vertical bars shall be installed in equidistance between longitudinal effective components and firmly connected with longitudinal effective components. In the joints between longitudinal effective components and vertical bars, longitudinal effective components shall be partly bending or in deformation where vertical secondary bars are bearing loads.

②Metal mesh may be installed respectively according to the design requirements of netting for falling objects and fencing based on their functions. Before installation, metal mesh shall be burred and rolled, so as to make the edges stay in the same plane.

③The surface of solid plates shall be smooth and the connection joints between two plates shall not be larger than 3 mm. And the minimal thickness shall meet the requirements in Table 6.3.5-2. The maximal thickness should not surpass the minimal thickness with a plus of 1.0 mm. Where solid plates are used in vignettes or to block dazzle of subtending vehicles, the maximal thickness should not be larger than the minimal thickness with a plus of 2.0 mm. Where solid plates are used as secondary components, the effects of wind load on Bridge Railings shall be considered.

④Where the soundproof facilities and Bridge Railings are installed cooperatively, the effect of soundproof facilities on safety shall be considered.

5　The sealing and drainage of metal components shall meet the following requirements

1) The hollow section components shall be placed with drainage holes or have all the joints completely sealed.

2) The diameter of galvanized holes and the drainage hole shall be no more than 1/12 of the hollow section's circumference. The drainage hole of the component shall not be shorter than 8 mm (non-galvanized component shall not be less than 6 mm) and not longer than 15 mm before galvanization. The galvanized holes and the drainage holes shall be spaced out at least 70 cm apart. The galvanized holes and drainage holes shall be properly placed.

Background:
The foundation of the corrugated beam barrier barrier and Thrie-beam barrier which belong to semi-rigid barrier shall be firmly connected to the main body structure of the bridge, while other structural requirements of the corrugated beam barrier barrier and Thrie-beam barrier shall

conform to those of the at-grade barrier.

This article stipulates structural requirements for the types of semi-rigid barriers, namely the metal beam column barrier, the concrete barrier, and the combined barrier.

As the columns and other components of noise insulation facilities will have large impact on vehicles during collision, installation of noise insulation facilities on bridge barriers is not preferred. If this is unavoidable, necessary measures have to be employed to eliminate the impact of the noise insulation facilities on road safety.

6.3.6 The structure of the Bridge Railings installed on the pedestrian path shall meet the following requirements:

1 The minimal height of the barriers shall be 110 cm from the top of the pedestrian path.

2 The maximal clear spacing between two barrier components shall not be more than 14 cm, and horizontal bars barriers should not be recommended. The reticular opening shall not be greater than 5 cm where using metal mesh barriers.

3 The design of the barrier structure must be safe and reliable, with anchor bars placed at its base. Stress conditions of anchor bars shall meet the provisions of *the General Specifications for Design of Highway Bridges and Culverts* (JTG D60) and of the article 3.5.3 of the *Guidelines*.

4 The connections between the pedestrian barrier components shall be able to effectively avoid injuries and disassemble conveniently.

5 The combined barriers which functions as the bridge barrier as well as the pedestrian barrier shall meet the structural requirements of pedestrian barriers and Bridge Railings.

6.3.7 The structure of barriers for bicycle lanes on the bridge shall meet the following requirements:

1 The minimal height of barriers for the bicycle lane shall be 140 cm from the top of the bicycle lane.

2 The spacing among the barriers, the connection of the components, the fixation of the foundation and the combined barriers shall meet the provisions of article 6.3.6 herein.

3 A friction beam of a certain width may be attached to the barriers at 110 cm above the top of the bicycle lane if required.

6.3.8 Bridge Railings and bridge deck shall be firmly connected. The method of connection between Bridge Railings and the bridge deck maybe chosen from the methods stated below according to the level of protection, the structure and the form of the barrier and the strength calculation results:

1 The guard rail posts of the metal beam barrier maybe directly embedded or anchor bolted to the bridge deck. Condition permitting, replaceable barrier foundation with a special pedestal may also be adopted.

1) Direct embedded connection is applicable to the bridge whose thickness of the edge is over 30 cm. Where pouring concrete over the structure, sleeves shall be reserved for column installation. The diameter of the sleeves shall be 4-10 cm wider than the diameter of the column or the length of its hypotenuse. The structures around the sleeve shall be reinforced with rib. See Figure 6.3.8-1.

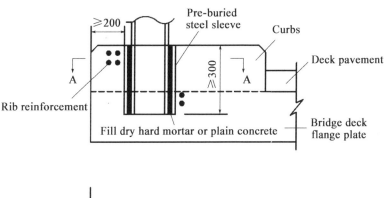

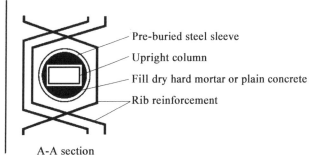

Figure 6.3.8-1 Direct embedded connection (Unit: mm)

2) The anchor bolted connection is applicable where the embedment depth of the column is less than 30 cm. Bay bolts of specified length shall be embedded into the concrete structure in advance. The plate stiffener and the flange plate shall be welded at the bottom of the column, and shall be connected to the bay bolts. See Figure. 6.3.8-2.

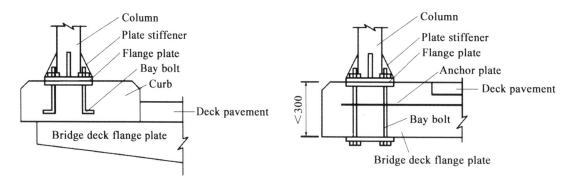

Figure 6.3.8-2　Anchor bolt connection mode (Unit: mm)

2　The connection between the concrete barrier and the bridge deck shall meet the following requirements:

1) Where the cast-in-place method is adopted in the construction, the barrier and the bridge deck shall be connected by pre-embedded reinforcing bars to form a whole.

2) Where prefabricated parts are adopted during the construction, the bridge structure and the barrier shall be connected together by connecting facilities such as anchor bolts to form a whole. The vertical connection shall be in compliance with the relevant provisions in Section 6.2 of the *Guidelines*.

3　Where connecting combined barriers, the method of connecting concrete barriers to the bridge deck shall be adopted.

6.3.9　The design of the ends and transition sections shall meet the following requirements:

1　For bridges with design speed greater than 60 km/h, if barriers are not installed on the adjacent subgrade sections, the bridge barrier shall be moderately flared outward or another section of barrier shall be added as a transition section on the subgrade to avoid the vehicle's crash into the ends or running out of the bridge. For highways with design speed no more than 60 km/h, the bridge shall be equipped with impact attenuator facilities or visual facilities.

2　A transition section shall be included in the design, if the structural form of the highway Bridge Railings is different from that of subgrade barriers and the speed limit of the highway is greater than 60 km/h. The transition section should be included in the design where the structural form of the highway Bridge Railings is different from that of subgrade barriers and the speed limit of the highway is less than or equal to 60 km/h. The design of the transition section shall meet the following requirements:

1) The transition section shall adopt the method of installing end-wing wall or connecting the semi-rigid barrier to the rigid barriers. The end wing wall or the semi-rigid barrier shall overlap the rigid barrier in the transition section.

2) The end wing wall maybe placed at the end of the bridge and transformed from the Bridge Railings or may be independently installed in the subgrade section. Pre-embedded parts shall be installed in the end wing wall in accordance with the requirements of the subgrade barriers. See Appendix C Figure C.2.17 a).

3) If lap joint is adopted, the barriers on the subgrade section shall be strengthened, and the length of the barriers shall not be shorter than 10 meters. See Appendix C Figure C.2.17 b).

4) If rigid barriers are adopted in both Bridge Railings and subgrade barriers, the rigid barriers shall be disconnected at the abutment expansion joints while the other barrier forms shall not be disconnected in the transition sections, yet a beam with extension parts shall be adopted. For the design sample of the transition section of metal beam barriers and subgrade corrugated beam barriers barriers, see Figure 6.3.9.

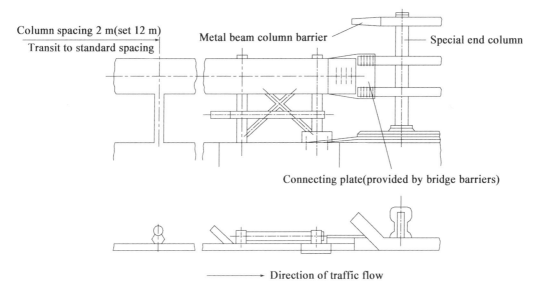

Figure 6.3.9 Design sample of the transition section of corrugated beam barrier and metal beam barrier

5) The drainage facilities at the ends of the bridge shall be designed as a part of the barrier transition section.

3 The design of the transition section of the Bridge Railings at the connection parts between the bridge and the tunnel of the motorway, Class-1 highway and Class-2 highway as

arterials shall refer to the provisions in article 6.2.2 and 6.2.3 of the *Guidelines*. While the design of the transition section of the Bridge Railings at the connection parts between the bridge and the tunnel of the collector Class-2 highway and Class-3 and Class-4 highway shall refer to the provisions of article 6.2.2 of the *Guidelines*.

6.3.10 The design of the test pieces of the newtyped Bridge Railings shall meet the following requirements:

1 The design of the test pieces of the new typed Bridge Railings shall be in line with the ultimate limit state of load-carrying method. All kinds of standard values of loads for Bridge Railings are recorded in chapter 3 of the *Guidelines*. The coefficients of loads in parts and combination shall be in accordance with the provisions in the current *General Specifications for Design of Highway Bridges and Culverts* (JTG D60).

2 In Appendix D, the design process and method for the test pieces of the new typed Bridge Railings based on the yield line theory is provided. If the predicted failure mode of the test pieces is different from that described in Appendix D, an effective yield line solution shall be established or the finite element method shall be adopted. If the Bridge Railings are installed on the rigid structures such as the retaining wall or the spread foundation and thus failure mode of the Bridge Railings extends to the support foundation, the method of Appendix D shall not be adopted

Background:

2 The design process and method of the test pieces of the new Bridge Railings based on yield line theory mainly make reference to the American AASHTO LRFD Bridge Design Specifications (2012 edition). The yield line theory is a method for ultimate limit state analysis. A yield line is a crack on the reinforced concrete slab. The reinforcement across this crack has yielded and experienced plastic rotation. The load-carrying capacity of the component in the vicinity of the crack can be calculated according to the yield line theory. The theory can be applied in many kinds of slab components.

As shown in Figure 6-5, a square plate is supported on its four sides. The plate will bear the averagely distributed load, which will gradually increase until the slab is broken.

At the beginning, the plate's response to the load is elastic. The stress of the steel reinforcement is at its maximum, and the deformation occurs at the center of the plate. At this stage, very fine fracture will appear at the bottom of the plate, and the flexural tensile strength of the concrete at the center of the span has been exceeded.

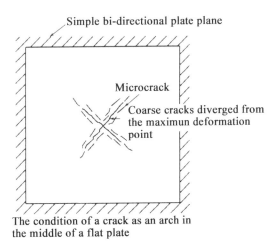

Figure 6-5 Bottom reinforcing bar begins to yield at the point of maximum deformation in the two-way slab with simple support

Increasing the load will accelerate the formation of the fine cracks. Further increase of the load will enlarge the size of the fracture, and ultimately the steel reinforcement will yield. Large cracks will radiate from the largest deformation point. As the load increases, the cracks will move toward the free edge of the plate, and then all the reinforcing bars that pass the yield line will yield.

The plate will be damaged under this limit state. As shown in Figure 6-6, the plate is divided into four rigid plane areas: A, B, C and D. The yield lines form the boundary of these areas, which will rotate about the yield lines. These areas will also rotate about the axis of the supporting lines, leading to the movement of the supporting load. At the junction point, the work done by the hinge of the rotating yield line is equal to the work consumed by the load on the moving region. That's the yield line theory.

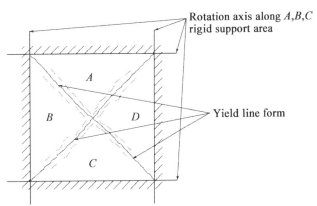

Figure 6-6 The mechanism of yield of steel reinforcement along the yield line at the bottom of bi-directional slab supported by simple support

According to this theory, elastic deformation can be ignored. All deformation is assumed to concentrate at the yield line. For convenience, the unified value is determined at the maximum deformation.

Appendix D provides the design process of the testing samples for achieving a certain level of protection. This method is based on the application of yield line theory. For situations different from those stated in the predicted failure mode as in testing samples in Figures C.3.1-1 and Figure C.3.1-2, a strict yield line or finite element solution shall be established. The method of Appendix D does not apply to barriers mounted on rigid structures, such as the retaining wall or the spread foundation, because in that case, cracks will extend to supporting components.

The functions of the Bridge Railings do not need to be the same as those on the at-grade section. The design of the new Bridge Railings needs to meet the demands on-site and conform to the Highway Guardrail Safety Performance Evaluation Standard (JTG B05-01).

Bridge Railings of which protection levels have already been verified need not be retested. Due to limitation of resources, it is not reasonable to replace all existing Bridge Railings to meet the new requirements once a new standard is implemented. Many existing barriers are proven to be functioning well, and only need to be replaced when the bridge is widened.

6.4　Median opening barrier

6.4.1　Median opening barrier shall meet the following requirements:

1　Median opening barrier must be installed at the median opening of the highway.

2　A median opening barrier may be installed at the median opening of the Class-1 highway, serving as the secondary arterial highway where U-turning is prohibited.

3　A median opening barrier should be installed at the center line of the highway, with a length that should adequately close the median opening

4　The height of the median opening barrier shall be the same as the height of the median barrier.

5　A delineator or reflector shall be installed at the upper part of the median opening barrier. The reflectors should not be smaller than 4 cm long and 18 cm wide and maybe made by reflective sheeting or reflective film from III to V types. The color and the height should be consistent with those of the median.

6 Anti-glare facility should be installed on the median opening barrier if it is required on a highway section.

Background:
The reflector specifications specified in this article (4 cm × 18 cm) are in line with the post delineator. Only reflective materials that meet or exceed these specifications can be correctly identified by the driver under high-speed driving conditions.

6.4.2 The level of protection about the median opening barrier shall be consistent with that of adjacent sections. For those sections with good highway alignment, the level of protection maybe one to two grades lower than that of the adjacent ones after justification, but the median opening barrier on the motorway shall not be lower than Level 3-Am.

6.4.3 The form of the median opening barrier shall meet the following requirements:

1 Non-emergency vehicles shall be effectively stopped at the median opening.

2 The median opening barrier shall be easy to open and close and shall be movable. It should be able to open up at least 10 m within 10 minutes.

3 A transition section shall be added between adjacent median barriers.

4 The fixed ends of the movable median opening barriers shall be firmly installed and its connection parts shall have anti-theft function.

5 Where collision occurs, the components of the median opening barriers shall not shatter or scatter and damage or harm the impact vehicles, pedestrians and vehicles nearby.

Background:
2 *The highway barrier of median opening is a movable facility that is installed at median openings to allow the transit of special vehicles such as traffic accident handling vehicles and ambulances, and to allow vehicles to pass through when the other side of the highway is closed or under construction. The highway barrier of median opening shall be movable, and easy to open and close. It should be able to open up at least 10 m within 10 minutes.*

3 *The highway barrier of median opening usually has its structure and rigidity varied from the standard section of the median barrier. A reasonable structure and rigidity transition section is needed between the highway barrier of median opening and the standard section of the median barrier, for snagging is likely to occur once vehicles collide at the connection if the ends of the*

highway barrier of median opening do not have safe transition arrangement. The connected width of the standard section of the median barrier in the real-vehicle full-scale crash test shall be no less than that in the actual project when selecting the form of the highway barrier of median opening.

6.5 Impact attenuator facilities

6.5.1 Impact attenuator facilities shall meet the following requirements:

1 For roadside barrier which is located within the clear zone width and without safety treatment, its upper end shall be equipped with crash cushions or crashworthy terminals.

2 Crash cushions and crashworthy terminals shall be placed at the diverging end of the main line and the ramp of motorways as well as the entrance of tunnels. Crash cushions need not be installed if there is a barrier transition section at the entrance of the tunnel connecting to the barrier outside the tunnel.

3 On motorways and the Class-1 highways serving as arterial roads, redirective crash cushions should be installed at the leading terminals of median barriers and terminals of the middle pier of overpasses crossing the motorway.

4 Non-redirective crash cushions may be used at the terminal of channelization island of toll booths.

5 Redirective or non-redirective crash cushions shall be installed if there are dangerous obstacles of special forms within the clear zone along the motorway roadside and if no other safety protection methods can be implemented.

7 Visual Guiding Devices

7.1 General

7.1.1 The design of visual guiding devices shall comply with the following provisions:

1 The reflector of the visual guiding devices shall maintain a constant, adequate brightness with the normal incident angle and viewing angle and shall be recognizable and confirmed by both large vehicles and small vehicles with both low beam and high beam headlights.

2 The supporting structure of the visual guiding devices shall be able to support the reflectors, and shall minimize damage from errant vehicles and provide for the safety of occupants.

3 The spacing and height of different visual guiding devices should be coordinated to ensure the consistency and continuity of sight on road sections with various visual guiding devices.

4 Visual guiding devices shall consistently function in adverse weather conditions such as periods of rain and snow.

7.1.2 The design of visual guiding devices may be conducted in the following order:

1 Collect information about road sections for visual guiding, including information on the various barriers, the frequency of bridge and tunnel structures, and the placement of small at-grade intersections along the route.

2 Identify the types of visual guiding devices.

3 Determine the parameters such as the form of visual guiding devices and their spacing.

7.1.3 New types of visual guiding devices shall be promoted and utilized on the basis of comprehensive analysis of implementation effectiveness, the results of technical and economic comparison studies, durability analyses, etc.

***Background*:**

Visual guiding devices actively mark the highway alignment along the route, the structures, roads sections with potential safety hazard, and the distributions of small intersections to the drivers. Devices that provide visual cues include delineators, traffic merge warning signs, chevron alignment signs, tunnel outline belts, warning posts, warning blocks, and intersection marker posts. The visual guiding devices can actively guide the driver through retroreflective materials or the active luminance system even at night, which are with highly cost effective Conditions permitting, the visual guiding devices may be used with higher frequency to represent their energy-saving and cost effectiveness advantages.

There are a variety of new visual guiding devices in the market. This Guideline hereby encourages promotion and application of new types of visual guiding devices based on a comprehensive analysis of implementation effectiveness and technical and economic comparisons and durability analyses. However, the products shall initially be safe and functional.

7.2 Installation principles

7.2.1 The application of delineators shall comply with the following provisions:

1 For motorways and Class-1 highways, delineators shall be placed continuously along the entire length of the mainline segment as well as along the ramps and connecting roads of interchanges, rest areas, parking areas, and escape ramps, and they shall be continuously installed at median openings. For Class-2 highways or below, delineators should be placed on sections with limited sight distances, sections with design speed greater than or equal to 60 km/h, sections with varying lane numbers or lane widths, and sections with continuous sharp curves or steep grades. For other sections, delineators may be placed as needed.

2 Bidirectional delineators shall be placed along tunnel sidewalls. If there is a safety walk in the tunnel, additional delineators shall be mounted above the end of the safety walk adjacent to the approach traffic lane or along the sidewall of the safety walk, as shown in Figure 7.2.1-1.

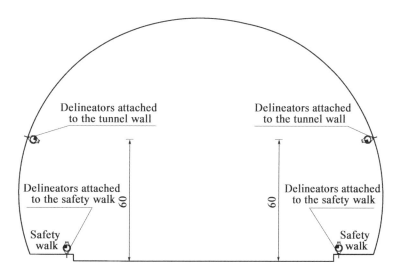

Figure 7.2.1-1 Example of delineator placement in tunnel (Unit: cm)

3 Delineators shall be installed symmetrically along the left and right sides of the travelway direction. For motorways and Class-1 highways, delineators with white reflectors shall beplaced on the right-hand side of the roadway in the direction of travel, and delineators with yellow reflectors shall be placed in the median. For Class-2 highways or below, white delineators for both directions are used. Delineators along escape ramps are red in color. Delineators for tunnels or Class-2 highways or below should be reflective on both sides.

4 The spacing between adjacent delineators shall not exceed 50 m for tangent sections. For curves, such spacing shall not exceed the provisions as shown in Table 7.2.1. For sections with varying roadway width and lane numbers, or sections with vertical curves, such spacing maybe reduced as appropriate.

Table 7.2.1 Spacing between adjacent delineators for curves

Radius (m)	≤89	90-179	180-274	275-374	375-999	1,000-1,999	≥2,000
Spacing (m)	8	12	16	24	32	40	48

The spacing of delineators from the start to the end of curves are shown in Figure 7.2.1-2. 'S' indicates the spacing of delineators on curves. If the value of $2S$ or $3S$ is greater than 50 m, 50 m will be adopted.

5 Delineators placed on the safety walk in a tunnel shall be mounted at the same height. For other sections, the center of the reflector should be 60-75 cm high. Others heights may be adopted based on further analysis as needed in special circumstances.

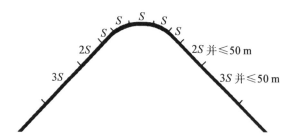

Figure 7.2.1-2 Example of spacing between delineators on curves

Note: In the figure, 'S' indicates the spacing of delineators on curves. Where $2S$ (or $3S$) >50 m, 50 m is the maximum spacing.

Background:

5 The centerline of corrugated beam barriers shall be approximately 60 cm above the pavement elevation. The centerline of the reflectors shall be 60-75 cm above the pavement as a baseline. If the road pavement is commonly covered with very thick snow, the reflector heights shall be adjusted accordingly. In addition, designers should take into account the effects of landscaping when considering and adjusting heights in this Clause.

As for 'If needed, other heights may be adopted after justification', which is taken the actual placement effects and costs into consideration. If the delineator is installed under the barrier plate of a post, its height shall be consistent with vertical intersection points of concrete barriers or safety walks, and its reflective effect shall be acceptable. Due to its proximity to the pavement, protuberant road signs are not necessary. This placement method maximizes effectiveness in areas where snow removal is required in winter. Figure 7-1 shows the delineators of the Shin Tomei motorway in Japan, which are installed on corrugated beam posts, concrete barrier, and tunnel safety walks. This placement method does not necessarily apply to areas with more rainfall and lush vegetation, because of the work involved in pruning and maintaining the vegetation.

Figure 7-1 Delineators of the Shin Tomei motorway in Japan

7.2.2 Traffic merge warning signs shall conform to provisions in Chapter 4 of the *Guidelines* and provisions in the prevailing *Specification for Layout of Highway Traffic Signs and Markings* (JTG D82).

7.2.3 Alignment chevron signs shall conform to relevant provisions in Chapter 4 of the Specification and provisions in the prevailing *Specification for Layout of Highway Traffic Signs and Markings* (JTG D82).

7.2.4 Tunnel outline belts shall conform to the following provisions:

1 Outline belts may be placed at a spacing of 500 m for all long tunnels. For special tunnel sections such as those with limited sight distance, designers should reduce the spacing of outline belts as appropriate.

2 For tunnels on Class-2 highways or below without lighting, outline belts may be placed as needed.

3 Tunnel outline belts should be mounted at a suitable location in advance of an emergency lay by.

4 Tunnel outline belts shall not produce glare.

7.2.5 For those sections with certain safety hazards that do not meet the standard for installing barriers, the shadowed section in area II may be provided as is shown in Figure 6.2.4 of Class-3 or Class-4 highways, on devices such as warning posts, warning blocks, etc. The warning pier shall be provided with a foundation.

7.2.6 For small intersections along a highway without corresponding guide signs or warning signs, intersection marker posts shall be placed on both sides of the intersection.

***Background*:**
Crossing warning sign posts shall be placed on both sides of small intersections along the road to remind the mainline driver to be alert and to prevent crashes caused by vehicles entering the main line.

The placement principles and construction specifications for crossing warning sign posts shall comply with part of the regulations of Road Traffic Signs and Markings (GB 5768), and the color of the crossing warning sign posts shall be red and white.

7.3 Placement

7.3.1 Delineator reflectors shall face oncoming traffic, and the intersection angle between the surface normal line and the centerline of the highway shall be 0°-25°. Delineators for tunnel safety walk locations shall be placed on the top face of the safety walk.

Background:

Reflectors shall be perpendicular to driver line of sight, whether on tangents or curves. The rule that the intersection angle between the surface normal line and the centerline of the highway shall be 25° is primarily applicable to the post delineators.

7.3.2 The placement of the merging warning signs and chevrons shall meet the relevant provisions in the Chapter 4 of this *Guideline* and the current regulations contained in *Specifications for Layout of Highway Traffic Signs and Markings* (JTG D82).

7.3.3 The position of the tunnel outline belt shall be perpendicular to the travel direction.

7.3.4 The color of the warning posts and the warning blocks shall alternate yellow and black in color, as shown in Figure 7.3.4.

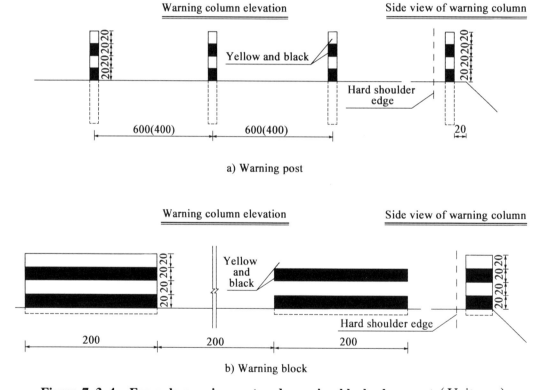

Figure 7.3.4 Example warning post and warning block placement (Unit: cm)

Note: The distances shown inside and outside the parentheses in the figure are applicable to the curves and the tangents, respectively.

7.3.5 The color of crossing sign post shall be red and white, and the placement is shown in Figure 7.3.5.

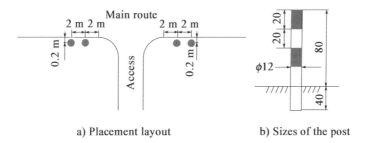

Figure 7.3.5 An example of the placement of crossing sign posts (Unit: cm)

7.4 Delineator types

7.4.1 In selecting the type of delineator, the following factors shall be considered:

1. The delineators can be placed as post delineators or attached delineator according to the application, as shown in Figure 7.4.1. Post delineators can be further divided into normal post delineator and elastic post delineator. The selection shall be based on practical conditions.

2. Based on the different types of roadside barriers and the placement of structures, delineators can be attached on corrugated beam barriers, concrete barriers, tunnel side walls, and cable barriers. Post delineators may be placed on road sections without barriers, except for road sections with warning posts or warning blocks.

3. Other outlining warning devices may be added to the delineators, such as attaching retro-reflective sheets to the barrier post.

4. If delineators are needed on both sides of two-way highways and tunnels, the bidirectional reflector delineators shall be installed.

5. The delineators with high retroreflective performance and larger size shall be installed on road sections with complex alignment conditions.

6. Flexible material shall be used for post delineators.

7.4.2 Tunnel outline belt should be of white color, and the width should be 15-20 cm. Tunnel outline belts shall not protrude into the clearance profile.

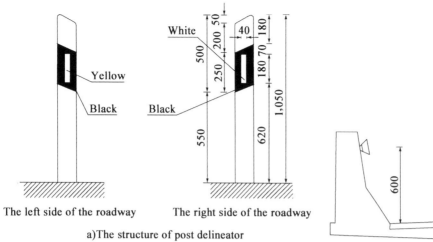

a) The structure of post delineator

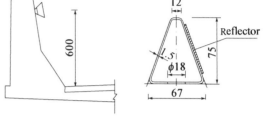

c) Delineators attached on concrete barriers

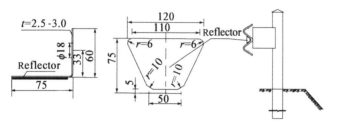

(a) Delineators attached on the grooves of corrugated beam barriers

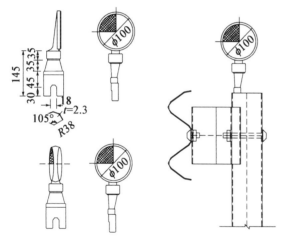

(b) Delineators attached on the post of corrugated beam barrier barriers

d) Delineators attached on tunnel side walls

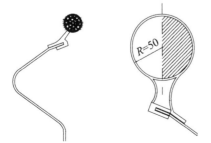

e) Delineators attached on cable barriers

b) Delineators attached on the barrier board of corrugated beam barriers

Figure 7.4.1　Examples of delineators (Unit: mm)

7.4.3 Self-luminous visual guiding devices should be used in road sections with frequent adverse weather or greater safety hazards. Self-luminous products can be divided into solar energy self-luminous products and external power self-luminous products. If self-luminous products are to be continuously placed on the same road sections, the products must remain bright or flash. If the self-luminous products flash, the frequency should be between 40-60 flashes/min and the frequency shall be adjustable.

***Background*:**

Delineators with higher reflective performance and larger size can be adopted to provide delineation in areas with adverse weather conditions such as fog, sandstorms, rain and snow, or with complex alignment conditions. Self-luminous products may be chosen for sections with greater safety hazards.

7.5 Structural requirements

7.5.1 Delineator structural requirements shall meet the regulations contained in the current version of *Delineators* (GB/T 24970).

8 Fencing

8.1 General

8.1.1 The design of fencing shall meet the general provisions as follows:

1 Fencing shall be capable of effectively deterring pedestrians and animals from inadvertently entering an access-controlled highway.

2 The distance from the top of the fence to the ground should be 1.5-1.8 m. For highway sections close to urban areas, the highest value may be taken; while in the sparsely populated desert areas where animals are under 50 cm tall, the height of the fences can be reduced to 1.3-1.5 m in conjunction with comprehensive traffic safety analyses.

3 The design of fences shall adapt to the region terrain, climate, and environmental characteristics. In areas where the climate has a corrosive effect on metal fencing, anti-corrosion coatings should be applied to the surface of the metal.

4 The strength and rigidity of the fences shall be guaranteed under the design wind load. The fences do not provide any protective features. The structural design of fences can follow the relevant regulations on traffic signs.

Background:
3 *The corrosion of metals in industrial areas, urban areas, or coastal areas is relatively high. Therefore, fencing should have high corrosion resistance capability.*

4 *The structures of fences are directly related to the effectiveness and the service life. The influence of wind load shall be considered during the design, while some anti-theft measures can be adopted to prevent damage caused by persons or animals. The specific calculation*

method is outlined in the relevant regulations for traffic sign structure design. While the physical structure of traffic signs mainly experiences stress on the upwind side, this side is in a netting structure whose reduction factor varies according to the grid porosity and the size of the hedgerow covering area.

8.1.2 The design of fencing may follow these guidelines:

1 Collect the topographic data for the highway roadside and the area within the right-of-way of highways, and the information about the locations of maintenance centers, interchanges, bridges and culverts, tunnels, service facilities, and the locations of the urban areas and villages along the route.

2 Determine a reasonable, effective, aesthetic and economical design scheme according to the design designations shown in Chapter 2 of the *Guidelines*.

8.2 Provision principles

8.2.1 Except for the highway sections conforming to one of the following conditions, fences must be continuously provided on both sides of motorways and access-controlled Class-1 highways. Fencing may be deployed on other highways as needed, such as:

1 Highway sections with natural barriers on the roadside, such as a canal, pond or lake.

2 Fill sections with drops, such as retaining walls or stone pitched walls higher than 1.5 m.

3 Bridges and tunnels, excluding road sections at abutments or tunnel portals where connection with roadway fences is needed.

4 Cut sections where the heights exceed 20 m and slope gradients are steeper than 70°.

8.2.2 Fencing shall form an enclosure at the conical slope of abutments or end walls where fences meet a bridge, tunnel or underpasses for vehicles or pedestrians. For sections with a high frequency of pedestrian passage, high strength structures may be applied for the enclosure facilities.

8.2.3 Fencing may directly cross a culvert with a span of less than 2 m, but it shall be enclosed around the culvert to prevent persons or animals from entering.

8.2.4 The centerline of fencing may be positioned at 20-50 cm from the highway reserve boundary within the boundary.

8.2.5 In order to meet the needs for maintenance management of highway, bridges and passageways, accessible doors may be provided at suitable locations along fencing for motorways and access-controlled Class-1 highways.

8.2.6 For motorways and access-controlled Class-1 highways where pedestrians and animals are incapable of inadvertently entering into the median area, fencing may be placed along the outer side of the road only. If pedestrians and animals may inadvertently enter into the median area at the inner side of a roadway, fencing shall be placed along the inner side of the road at specific locations as needed. When bridges, passage, or underpasses for vehicles or pedestrians are encountered along sections of separate formations, the provision for fencing shall comply with Clause 8.2.2 of the *Guidelines*.

8.3 Form selection

8.3.1 Fencing may take the form of welding grid, barbed wire grid, woven grid, steel plate grid, fenc wall, green fence, or a combination of barbed wire grid and green fence. A comprehensive comparison analysis of the performance, budgeting, aesthetic effects, and coordination with the highway landscape, construction conditions and maintenance shall be made based on the requirements for functionality of the enclosure.

Background:
The form of fencing shall be selected based on the separation functional requirement sand a comprehensive comparison analysis of the performance, cost, aesthetic effects, and the coordination with the highway landscape, construction conditions and maintenance needs.

1 *Cost Comparison: ranked by cost per unit from high to low, i. e. steel plate grid, electric welding grid, electric welding coil grid, weaving grid, and barbed wire grid.*

2 *Comparison of maintenance in the later stage: damage to the surface of and partial damage to the steel plate grid, electric welding grid, barbed wire grid are easy to repair and its maintenance cost is low. Partial damage to the weaving grid will affect the grid as a whole. The damage is difficult to repair, and its maintenance cost is high.*

3 *Comparison of the performance of terrain adaptability: steel plate grid and electric welding grid have a poor climbing performance and are generally used for flat lands. If the steel plate grid and electric welding wire gird are to be applied in bumpy road sections, they shall be designed*

as a staircase, or the mesh shall be designed in parallelogram to climb the slope, which is difficult to construct. The performance of the electric welding coil grid and weaving grid have a better climbing performance. The flexibility of weaving grid and the corrugated structure of electric welding coil grid are adaptable to the rolling terrain, but special mechanical equipment is required during the construction. Barbed steel wire has a strong adaptability to various forms of terrain, and its climbing performance is excellent. It is convenient for construction without special equipment in heavily rolling terrain.

4   *For an appearance comparison, steel plate grids, electric welding grids, and weaving networks provide a good structural appearance and are preferred forms of fencing the interchanges, service areas, scenic tourist areas, and the roadsides of towns. Barbed wire grids can be placed in the sparsely populated area that is far from urban areas.*

5   *In recent years, cases of stolen fencing have been frequent, and prevention is difficult even though highway operation and management agencies have increased monitoring. Given the need for maintenance and management of fencing, agencies should replace the fences with separation walls, thus reducing the risk of being stolen. With the best separation, sturdiness and durability, and a high cost, fencing can be used in one of the following circumstances after verification: 1) road sections where highway maintenance is difficult because the highways are far away from the urban area and thus welded wire grid and barbed wire grid fencing are often damaged or stolen; 2) road sections where the highway landscape and highway culture are important and thus fencing can be used as the carrier of highway landscape design according to the needs of highway construction and management; 3) road sections with concentrated human activities on the outer side of the highway, road sections where dangerous chemicals such as flammable and explosive chemicals are stored or produced on the outside of the highway, and road sections with hazards.*

8.3.2   Electric welding grid, weaving grid, and steel plate grid may be used for the fencing in the following road sections:

1   Road Sections near densely populated urban areas;

2   Road sections along scenic spots, tourist areas, and attractive sites;

3   Interchange roadsides, service areas, and parking areas, and buildings for management and maintenance.

8.3.3   The following sections may choose barbed wire grid. If needed, barbed wire grid may be combined with green fence.

1 Sparsely populated sections;

2 Highway reserve land;

3 Road sections that are enclosed for crossing ditches;

4 For road sections frequented by small animals, barbed wire grid with variable holes may be used. The wire spacing on the upper part of the grid can be larger than that of the lower part.

8.3.4 The following road sections may be suitable for fence wall:

1 Road sections where the welded grids and barbed wires are prone to be vandelized;

2 Road sections where the separation walls are included in the landscape design;

3 Road sections with greater safety hazards on the outside of the highway.

8.3.5 According to local conditions, green fences may be used if its function can be guaranteed.

8.4 Structure requirements

8.4.1 The mesh, post, strut, post, gate post and connecting fencing pieces made of metal material shall be in compliance with the provisions of the current standard entitled *Fencing* (GB/T 26941). Hedgerows, which can be shrubs or small arbors, shall be able to prevent pedestrians and animals from entering. The steel components of the fencing shall be fabricated with anti-corrosive technology such as hot-dip galvanizing, zinc-aluminum alloy coating, plastic dipping, or double coating, and the processed steel components shall meet anti corrosive requirements specified in the current standard entitled *Fencing* (GB/T 26941).

Background:
The strength and rigidity of the fencing shall be guaranteed under the wind load. The gate does not provide any crash protection and its structure shall be designed according to the wind conditions for the area where it is placed. Detailed requirements for different forms of fencing have several components. The welded grid can be classified into the sheet grid and the roll grid. The metal wire used in the sheet grid and the horizontal wire used in the roll grid shall be the low carbon steel wire whose mechanical properties shall conform to the requirements specified in the current standard entitled Low-Carbon Steel Wires for the General Propose (YB/T 5294). The vertical wire used in

the roll grid shall be high-strength steel with a strength of at least 650 MPa. The barbed steel grid is classified into the general grid and the reinforced grid. The strand and the barbed wire adopted in the general grid shall be low-carbon steel wires whose mechanical properties shall comply with the requirements specified in current standard Low-Carbon Steel Wires for the General Propose (YB/T 5294). The strand and barbed wire in the reinforced grid shall be high-strength low-alloy steel wires whose tensile strength should not be lower than 700 MPa. Additionally, the breaking force of the whole strand of the barbed wire should not be lower than 4,230 N. The steel wire of the woven grid and the tension steel wire shall be low-carbon steel wire whose mechanical properties conform to the requirements specified in the current standard Low-Carbon Steel Wires for the General Propose (YB/T 5294). The low-carbon steel plate shall be employed in the steel plate grid, whose chemical and mechanical properties shall conform to the requirements in the current Hot Rolled Steel Sheets and Strips of the Carbon Structural Steel and the Low-Alloy Structural Steel (GB 912) and Cold Rolled Steel Sheets and Strips of the Carbon Structural Steel (GB/T 11253). The fencing can adopt the reinforced concrete structure and mansonry structure, which should be in accordance with the specifications of the current Code for the design of Concrete Structures (GB 50010) and Code for the Design of Mansonry Structures (GB 50003), respectively. Bushes and small trees can be placed to create hedgerows and shall be able to prevent pedestrians and animals from entering the highway.

The steel components of the isolation fence shall be processed with anti-corrosive technology such as hot-dip galvanizing, zinc-aluminum alloy coating, plastic dipping and double coating, etc., and the processed steel components shall meet the anti-corrosive requirements specified in the current Separation Fencing (GB/T 26941).

8.4.2 With various forms and materials for the fencing, the size of the fence mesh may be designed based on the size of the expected animal along the highway. The size commonly used for the welded grid and the woven grid includes 100 mm × 50 mm and 150 mm × 75 mm, etc. The mesh shall be larger than 50 mm × 50 mm. The following factors shall be considered when choosing the size:

1 It should not be easy for people and small animals to climb over the fencing and enter the motorways.

2 In the section where there are many small animals, the barbed steel grid with adjustable holes can be adopted.

3 The strength of the structure and the grid.

4 The harmony with the landscape along the highway.

5 The cost-effectiveness and performance.

Background:
The mesh size shall be determined by comprehensive consideration of the potential for people to climb over the fence, the coordination of the whole structure, and the strength (tightness) of the grid. On condition that the mesh isolation and the strength and rigidity of the gate can be guaranteed, grids with adjustable holes should be adopted to reduce the engineering cost and improve the price-performance ratio of the gate.

8.4.3 Where the fencing cannot be continuously installed because of the terrain limitations, the fencing may be naturally disconnected at certain points, and the disconnecting points may serve as the ends of the fencing.

Background:
If the fencing cannot be continuously installed at some places (such as steep hills, lakes, rivers and deep ditches, etc.) because of the varying terrain on both sides of the highway, the ends of the gate shall be properly designed.

8.4.4 In the road sections where the terrain undulates, roll grids may be installed along the grade, or the sheet grid may be used for the rebuilt terrain as the stepped grade. See Figure 8.4.4.

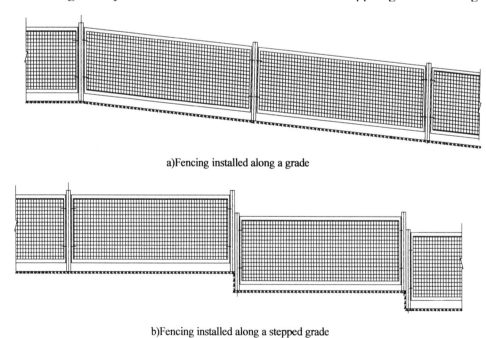

a)Fencing installed along a grade

b)Fencing installed along a stepped grade

Figure 8.4.4 Example of fencing on sections with undulating terrain

Background:
The woven grid, the roll welded grid, and the barbed steel grid are highly adaptable to undulating

terrains. The steel plate grid, the welded grid (sheet), and the woven grid (roll) are not adaptable to varying terrain and shall built into the stepped grade to be installed on the undulating terrain, or shall be specially made into parallelogram shape to be installed along the grade. Where the terrain undulates significantly, to the design can flatten out the terrain to make the gate as even as possible to avoid sudden change in certain sections.

In areas where the terrain undulates significantly, it is necessary to avoid the use of the steel plate mesh and the welded mesh, both of which have poor performance in climbing.

8.4.5 A corner shall be designed at the point where the direction of the fencing changes.

Background:
In order to ensure the effectiveness of the fencing, the ends shall be enclosed at the beginning and end of the gate. On a road section where the gate needs to be disconnected, a corner shall be designed at the point where the direction of the fencing changes. The design of the gate shall ensure the structural stability, the easeof construction, and the uniformity of the post and the fencing.

9 Netting

9.1 General

9.1.1 The design of netting shall meet the following requirements:

1 Netting should be capable of preventing objects and rocks from falling into the right-of-way.

2 Netting includes netting for falling objects and rockfall netting. Netting for falling objects should be 1.8 m to 2.1 m above the bridge deck unless there are special considerations, and rockfall netting shall be installed based on the area that requires rockfall prevention and the terrain of roadside slopes.

3 Where calculating the structure of the netting, relevant information for traffic signs may be considered. The rockfall netting shall be capable of with standing the impact force of falling rocks from the slope.

Background:

3 *The structure of the netting is directly related to its effectiveness and service life. The impact of the wind load shall be considered as a major influence during the design, while some structural features such as anti-theft measures can be adopted to prevent damage caused by people and livestock. For specific structure calculation methods, relevant regulations for the design of traffic sign structures can be consulted. Physical structures of traffic signs mainly sustain the stress on the upwind side. The upwind side of the netting is a reticular structure, and the void ratio is applicable to the reduction coefficient. In addition, netting is usually attached by wild akala plants, which are too difficult to remove and the ventilation of the barriers will be reduced. Therefore, different void ratio values shall be employed where calculating the wind load based on local conditions. Moreover, the impacts of the rockfall shall be taken into consideration apart from the wind load.*

9.1.2 The design of netting shall be implemented according to the following sequence:

1 Collect data on the geology, terrain, bridges and passageways, etc. along the highway roadside and the highway boundary.

2 Determine a reasonable, effective, aesthetic and economical scheme whose design designation is shown in the Chapter 2.

9.2 Netting for falling objects

9.2.1 Netting for falling objects shall be installed in accordance with the following principles:

1 Netting for falling objects shall be installed on both sides of vehicle or pedestrian structures crossing over railways, drinking water protected areas, motorways, or access-controlled Class-1 highways.

2 Netting for falling objects shall be provided for highways passing over a navigable river or another highway with high traffic volume.

3 If netting for falling objects is required on a bridge of separate structure, the netting shall be installed at the inner sides of the bridge.

4 Netting may not be placed on the road section with sound barriers.

5 Netting for falling objects shall be anti-corrosive and have earthing for lightning protection. The earthing for lightning protection shall have a resistance less than 10 Ω.

6 The extent of installation of netting for falling objects is the width of the protected areas of railways and highways, etc. (where an overpass structure and a highway intersect with a skewed layout, the width shall be the oblique width) and the areas with an extension of 10-20 m on both sides. The extent of installation of netting for falling objects on the highways passing over railways shall also comply with relevant provisions of the railway authorities.

9.2.2 Netting for falling objects can be classified as the steel plate net, the woven net, the welded net and the solid plate, etc. in terms of the type of the nets. In selecting the netting types, the factors of the strength, aesthetics, and harmony with the surroundings of the road and ease of construction and maintenance, etc. must be taken into account.

9.2.3 The structures of the netting for falling objects shall meet the following requirements:

1 Netting may adopt the same type of metal net as the fencing. The mesh size of netting for falling objects should not be larger than 50 mm × 100 mm, and the mesh size of the netting for falling objects installed on the highway crossing over the railways should not be larger than 20 mm × 20 mm.

2 The netting for falling objects installed on the overpass bridge over the railway electrification sections shall be installed with the warning sign stating 'Danger! High Voltage!'

3 The height of netting for falling objects installed on overpass bridges over high-speed railways shall not be less than 2.5 m above the bridge deck, and the height for overpass bridges over conventional railways shall be not less than 2.0 m above the bridge deck.

9.3 Rockfall netting

9.3.1 Rockfall netting shall be installed according to the following principles:

1 For motorways and Class-1 highways, where there is a possibility of rockfall within the boundary, if there are highway traffic safety concerns according to rockfall safety assessments, hazardous rocks with potential of rockfall shall be treated, or rockfall netting shall be installed.

2 For sections of Class-2 or lower highways, where rockfall is possible and with traffic safety concerns, rockfall netting may be provided as required.

3 Rockfall netting shall be adequately provided upon sufficient consideration of factors pertaining to terrain conditions, geological features, distribution of hazardous rocks, trajectory of rockfalls and their interactive relationship with highway construction, etc. Rockfall netting should be provided on a terrace with gentle slopes, or wide and gently sloping grounds at the toe of slopes adjacent to a highway.

Background:
Rockfall netting of the motorway and the Class I highway shall be able to prevent damage from rockfall and ensure safety on highways. For other sections where rockfall danger exists, a comprehensive consideration shall be made including factors such as safety, economy, and aesthetics, etc. to determine the feasibility of rockfall netting, warning signs or other devices to ensure highway safety.

9.3.2 The structural design of the rockfall netting shall include:

1 The type of rockfall netting selected shall be based on the kinetic energy of the falling rocks.

2 The height of the rockfall netting shall be determined based on the bouncing height of the falling rocks.

3 The installation of the rockfall netting shall be determined according to the length and direction of the rockfall netting.

4 Proper components such as steel posts, flexible anchors, bases and connectors, etc. shall be selected, and the steel post spacing shall be calculated.

5 The vertical orientation of the base and the system shall be installed based on analyses, and anti-tip screws shall be utilized if necessary.

6 An anchor pulling system shall be designed.

7 The type and specifications of supporting devices such as support cables, decompression rings, steel wire rope nets, seam ropes and grills shall be selected and determined.

Background:
The calculations for rockfall include three parts: the calculation of jumping, bouncing and impact. However, the rockfall motion is very complex and influenced by numerous factors such as the terrain and topography of the slope and the strength and volume of the rock, and there is no acknowledged appropriate calculation method for the rockfall motion. The results gained by current calculation methods are approximate values with great deviation. At present, the design of the rockfall netting mainly relies on experience, or to ensure that the rockfall of a certain volume, speed and height can be passively intercepted and will not impact road safety.

9.3.3 The form selection of the rockfall netting shall conform to the following rules:

1 The steel wire rope nets and ring nets may be used for rockfall netting and a steel wire grill may be attached where small falling rock need to be intercepted. See Figure 9.3.3-1.

2 The type and installation method shall be decided after considering several factors including the protection energy, structural form, the aesthetics, the harmony with the surroundings of the highway, and the ease of construction and maintenance, etc., as is shown in Figure 9.3.3-2.

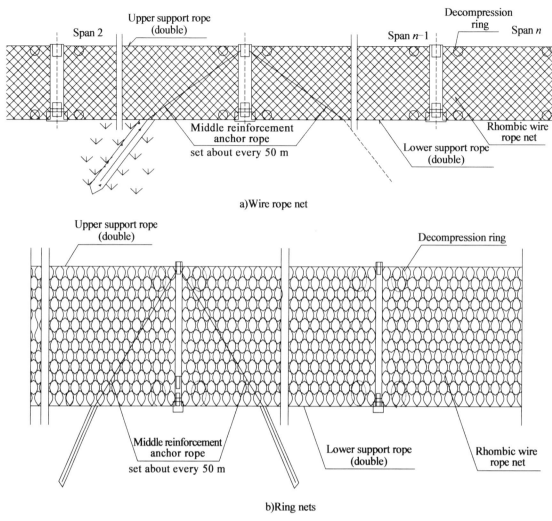

Figure 9.3.3-1 Example of rockfall netting

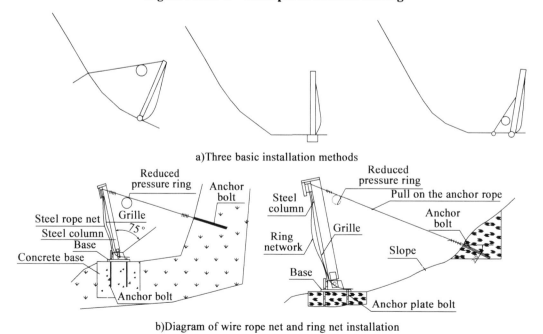

Figure 9.3.3-2 Examples of commonly used installation forms for passive rockfall netting

Background:

1 *The subgrade protection features that take active protective measures to prevent the damage of rockfall, including the active protection net, belong to the range of subgrade protection techniques, and shall be implemented in accordance with the specifications of the current Code for the Design of the Highway Subgrade (JTG D30). Passive rockfall netting can be divided into the steel wire rope net and the ring net in terms of the mesh sheet. The ring net is rarely used because of its limited capacity, and the steel wire rope net is adopted as the main net type in almost all of the passive rockfall netting. Actual examples are presented in Figure 9-1.*

a) Steel wire rope nets　　　　　　　　　　b) Ring nets

Figure 9-1　The installation example of the netting for falling objects

2 *The installation method of the rockfall netting is determined according to its protection energy, structural form, feature composition, the harmony with the surroundings of the highway and the ease of construction and maintenance.*

9.3.4　The structure of the rockfall netting shall meet the following requirements:

1　The mesh size of the rockfall netting should be selected based on the frequency and specification of the rockfall it prevents.

2　The rockfall netting shall be easily spreadable, highly impact resistant and highly industrialized.

3　All steel components shall be processed with anti-corrosion technology in accordance with the current *Technical Specifications for the Anti-Corrosion of the Steel Structures in Highway Traffic Engineering* (GB/T 18226).

Background:

1 *The structural requirements of the rockfall netting depend on the actual situation. According to the current Flexible Safety Net for Protection of Slope Along the Line, the specifications of the*

mesh includes rectangular, right-angled, and angled diamond mesh with side length of 2 m × 2 m, 4 m × 4 m, 4 m × 2 m, 5 m × 6 m, 5 m × 5 m, 5 m × 4 m and 5 m × 3 m and mesh with the sizes of the mesh holes of 300 mm, 250 mm, 150 mm, 120 mm and 100 mm. The selection of the specifications of the barrier depends on the size of the falling rocks. The impact resistance capability is not determined by the strength of the steel rope and the decompression ring. A layer of steel wire grid (ring net) should be added for intercepting small falling rocks.

2 *The structure of the rockfall netting depends on the protection capacity. The rockfall netting usually employs the slope flexible passive protection system, which primarily consists of steel wire rope or circuit netting (with an added layer of steel lattice for the interception of small gravels), connection system (bolt, pulling rope, pedestal and prop rope), decompression rings and steel posts. The capacity of passive protection barrier is limited. Data suggest that protection capacity of the three commonly used types of barriers, namely the RX-025, the RX-050 and the RX-075 are 250 kJ, 500 kJ, 750 kJ respectively. The protection capacity should be higher, theoretically, and the RX-075 is one of the most commonly used types with strong protection capacity. The principles of the system determine that an oversize protection capability is either inappropriate or not economical.*

The types, net patterns, structural configurations and protection functions of the commonly used rockfall netting are shown in Table 9-1.

Table 9-1 Commonly used rockfall netting

Model numbers	Net types	Structure configurations	Protective functions
RX-025	DO/08/250	Steel post + prop rope + pull anchor system + suture rope + depression ring	Intercepting the rockfall with an impact energy below 250 kJ
RX-050	DO/08/200	Same as RX-025	Intercepting the rockfall with an impact energy below 500 kJ
RX-075	DO/08/150	Same as RX-025	Intercepting the rockfall with an impact energy below 750 kJ
RXI-025	R5/3/300	Steel post + prop rope + pull anchor system + suture rope	Same as RX-025
RXI-050	R7/3/300	Same as RXI-025	Same as RX-050
RXI-075	R7/3/300	Same as RX-025	Same as RX-075
RXI-100	R9/3/300	Same as RX-025	Intercepting the rockfall with an impact energy below 1,000 kJ
RXI-150	R12/3/300	Same as RX-025	Intercepting the rockfall with an impact energy below 1,500 kJ
RXI-200	R19/3/300	Same as RX-025	Intercepting the rockfall with an impact energy below 2,000 kJ

continued

Model numbers	Net types	Structure configurations	Protective functions
AX-015	DO/08/250	Same as RX-025	Intercepting the rockfall with an impact energy below 150 kJ
AX-030	DO/08/200	Same as RX-025	Intercepting the rockfall with an impact energy below 300 kJ
AXI-015	R5/3/300	Same as RXI-025	Same as AX-015
AXI-030	R7/3/300	Same as RX-025	Same as AX-030
CX-030	DO/08/200	Same as RX-025	Same as AX-030
CX-050	DO/08/150	Same as RX-025	Same as AX-050
CXI-030	R7/3/300	Same as RXI-025	Same as AX-030
CXI-050	R7/3/300	Same as RX-025	Same as AX-050

Note: 1. The numbers next to the model types indicate the impact energy the barrier is capable of absorbing. For instance, 050 indicates a maximum of 500 kJ energy can be absorbed by the system, and '150' stands for a maximum of 1,500 kJ energy can be absorbed by the system.

2. This table is taken from *the Slope Flexible Safety and Protection Netting along the Railway*. One point that needs clarifying is that the flexibility of the passive protection system is limited, and the system may suffer from penetrating destruction where other parts remain undestroyed as a result of the bullet effect where falling rocks drop at a speed over 25 m/s with the kinetic energy below the protection level of the system. Therefore, active protection system or rockfall netting are needed if the speed of the falling rocks is high.

10 Anti-glare Devices

10.1 General

10.1.1 The anti-glare devices consist of glare screens, anti-glare nets and plantings.

10.1.2 The design of anti-glare devices shall meet the following regulations:

1 Anti-glare devices shall be designed according to the principle of partial shielding with the shielding angle for tangents to be not less than 8°, and the shielding angle for horizontal curves and vertical curves to be 8°-15°.

2 The provision of anti-glare devices shall not affect stopping sight distance.

3 The material used for anti-glare devices shall not be retroreflective.

4 Relevant information for traffic signs can be found in the structural calculation for anti-glare devices.

Background:
1 *Anti-glare devices are needed to not only effectively block the glare from the headlights of oncoming vehicles, but also to meet requirements for sufficient transverse sight distance, provide good view to beveled front direction, and provide less psychological effects on drivers. If the complete shielding is adopted, the vision will be narrowed conversely, the patrol vehicle for road management may not have intervisibility of the opposite direction, and drivers may suffer additional perception challenges. Meanwhile, traffic conditions for the opposite direction is an important reference for vehicles either at daytime or nighttime, and one of the key points is that the driver can estimate the longitudinal distance between two-way vehicles based on the light from the oncoming vehicle headlights, where the driver can adjust their driving status*

accordingly. From the testing results of oversea countries when two opposing vehicles are very close (less than 50 m), the light will not affect their sight distance. However, when the distance reaches a certain length, the glare will have great influence on the sight distance. Anti-glare devices do not need large shielding angles to obtain good shielding effect. Therefore, it is not necessary for anti-glare devices to shield all light from oncoming vehicles. The adopted partial shielding theory allows partial amounts of oncoming light to pass through anti-glare devices, and the amount of through light should not make drivers feel uncomfortable.

2 *On curves with small radii and a narrow median, the sight distance of the outer traveled way is possibly affected by anti-glare devices. Therefore, before the implementation of anti-glare devices, analysis of stopping sight distance is necessary to ensure that anti-glare devices would not reduce the stopping sight distance. The influence of anti-glare devices on the stopping sight distance increases with the decrease in width of central dividing strips and radius of curve. Therefore, sufficient attention is required regarding the possible sight distance issue caused by setting anti-glare devices on curves.*

If the anti-glare devices on curves affect the sight distance, the height of anti-glare devices may be reduced. The reduced height anti-glare devices may block most glare from the oncoming vehicle headlights, and drivers can see the top of the last vehicle in the traveled way. Generally, the height is about 1.2 m. In addition, another alternative method is to place anti-glare devices closer to the inside of curves. However, such method does not work well on curves with relatively small radii, and the landscape may not benefit this situation either. As a result, the method is usually used on curves with a relatively large radius.

If the aforementioned methods cannot achieve good anti-glare effects and landscape effects, anti-glare devices should not be used on the median. If the anti-glare devices are needed, the central dividing strip may be widened to get a sufficient lateral clearance from the edge of traveled way to the anti-glare devices, thereby ensuring adequate stopping distance. The Tomei expressway in Japan used the method of widening the central dividing strip, and remarkable results have been achieved, which makes the Tomei expressway beautiful and comfortable with continuous greenery. This is one of differences between the Tomei expressway and the Meishin expressway.

4 *Mechanical calculations for wind-load resistance of the anti-glare devices can be omitted on the premise that they meet all the structural requirements. Yet the mechanical calculation shall be conducted for the glare screen, the connecting pieces and its foundation in areas that are frequently stricken by typhoon, coastal areas with strong wind or areas with fallen trees and damaged road facilities. The specific calculation method can refer to the methods stated in the traffic sign section.*

10.1.3 The design of anti-glare devices may follow the requirements below:

1 Collect data on the width of the median along the highway, the structural form of the barriers, various kinds of construction techniques, and the distribution of nearby road network and the horizontal and vertical curves of the highway.

2 Determine the location and scheme for the installation of the anti-glare facilities. See Chapter 2 for the *Guidelines*.

10.2 Calculation of the shield angle

10.2.1 The shielding angle β_0 for straight sections is shown in Figure 10.2.1, and shall be calculated by Equation (10.2.1),

$$\beta_0 = \tan^{-1}\left(\frac{b}{L}\right) \qquad (10.2.1)$$

Where:
  b—The width of the anti-glare panels (m);
  L—The longitudinal spacing of the anti-glare panels (m).

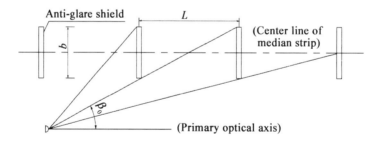

Figure 10.2.1 Calculation of shielding angle

10.2.2 The shield angle β of the horizontal curves shall calculated by Equation (10.2.2)

$$\beta = \cos^{-1}\left(\frac{R - B_3}{R}\cos\beta_0\right) \qquad (10.2.2)$$

Where:
  R—Radius of horizontal curve (m);
  B_3—Lateral distance between the driver and the anti-glare facility (m).

10.2.3 The shield angle of anti-glare net shall be determined by the width of the mesh and the thickness of glare screen.

10.3　Provision principles

10.3.1　For motorways and Class-1 highways, if the width of the central dividing strip is less than 9 m and one of the following conditions is met, anti-glare devices should be installed:

1. Sections with high traffic volume at night and the percentage of large trucks and buses is more than or equal to 15% of the traffic volume.

2. Circular curves with super-elevation.

3. Sections of concave vertical curve with radius equal or close to the minimum radius as specified in the prevailing *Technical Standards of Highway Engineering* (JTG B01).

4. Sections on separate roadways, and the height difference between the traveled ways of the two directions is less than or equal to 2 m.

5. Highway sections severely affected by glare from neighboring or intersecting highways and railways.

6. Highway sections near the twin-arch tunnel portals.

Background:
1. *When two opposing vehicles meet on the highway, the extent of drivers affected by glare is closely related to the lateral distance between the two vehicles. The research of the Influence on Sight Distance by Headlights of Two Meeting Vehicles conducted by Transport and Road Research Laboratory (TRRL) in Britain indicates: The larger of lateral distance ($S = 15m$), the smaller of the longitudinal distance, and the larger of the sight distance, especially when the two vehicles are very close to each other, the sight distance would apparently increase. If the lateral distance $S = 40$ m, the sight distance is almost independent from the longitudinal distance.*

The anti-glare experiments conducted by Research Institute of Highway Ministry of Transport also show that if the lateral distance between the two meeting vehicles exceeds 14 m, the light from the other vehicle would not make the driver experience glare. This result is consistent with the British research.

Domestic and foreign researchers generally agree that: the ideal anti-glare design eliminates glare caused by headlights of oncoming vehicles by providing enough lateral distance. For 6-lane motorways of other countries, apart from meeting the traffic demand at daytime, there are very few, if any, vehicles on the inside lane (the lane closest to the median) at night, and there are few vehicles in the middle lane. As a result, when two vehicles from opposite directions meet, the lateral distance is sufficient and the glare effect caused by the opposite vehicle headlights is eliminated. Vehicle driving regulations for motorways in Britain stipulate that vehicles are prohibited from using the right-side lane (In Britain, vehicles drive on the left, and overtake by the right) except either for overtaking another or if the right-side is occupied. As a result, the lateral distance is sufficient between the opposite traffic flow and there is no significant glare effect. In this case, the anti-glare devices may not be used.

Regulation on the Implementation of the Road Traffic Safety Law of the People's Republic of China enforced on May 1, 2004 stipulates that: If there are two or more lanes in one direction, the left lane is the fast lane and the right lane is designated for slow vehicles. If the width of the central dividing strip is 7 m, and the width of two marginal strips is $2 \times 0.75 = 1.5$ m, the median width is 8.5 m. If two vehicles in opposing direction are both driving in the fast lanes and meet, the lateral distance between them is 12.25 m ($S = 8.5 + 2 \times 3.75/2 = 12.25$ m). Therefore, if the width of central dividing strip exceeds 9 m, the glare effect can be effectively reduced, or the influence of glare to the driver may be negligible. Therefore, the Specification stipulates that there is no need for anti-glare devices when the width of central dividing strip is greater than or equal to 9 m.

2-7 *The setting of anti-glare devices depends on a lot of factors. High traffic volume at night or high proportion of large vehicles are main factors for setting anti-glare devices. For the convenience of design, the proportion of large vehicles is quantified herein for the requirements of setting barriers. A principle is specified for highway sections with serious glare effects from adjacent highways and railways. For other sections such as horizontal curves, vertical curves, weaving areas, and double-arc tunnel portal areas, etc., whether the anti-glare devices are needed or not may be determined according to the extent of glare affecting drivers. If the cross-section of highway subgrade is separated, and two directions of traveled ways are not on the same horizontal plane, the theoretical calculation and practical experiences both show that the glare effect on the driver is serious if the elevation difference between the two directions is less than or equal to 2 m, and then the anti-glare devices are needed. If the elevation difference exceeds 2 m, the glare effect is weak, and in this case, the roadside barriers are usually placed along the higher roadway to also block some glare. As a result, the anti-glare devices are not needed.*

During the design of anti-glare devices, the location and form of anti-glare devices need to be selected according to relevant provisions in the Guidelines, combining the specific highway traffic and on the basis of necessary cost-benefit analyses.

10.3.2 For at-grade intersections of Class-1 highways without access-control, the height of anti-glare devices may be reduced gradually from the nominal value to zero over a length of 100 m (80 km/h design speed) or 60 m (60 km/h design speed) from each end of the median openings. Otherwise anti-glare devices should not be installed. Anti-glare devices should not be provided on sections passing through villages and towns.

Background:

Drivers are usually caught unprepared where pedestrians either climb the anti-glare devices or jump over on road sections without any enclosure treatment. Trees planted at a certain interval may appear human-like standing beside the roadway especially at night with the headlight of the vehicle illuminating them. Therefore, drivers would be less likely to recklessly speed up even in the sections with good road conditions and would steer vehicles away from the median subconsciously. Statistical data suggest that the crash rate increases on the road sections without any enclosure treatment after the placement of the anti-glare devices, especially fatal crashes, which is related to the failure to respond to emergencies due to poor lateral visibility. Therefore, prudent consideration must be taken prior to the placement and the selection of the type of anti-glare devices on the road sections without enclosure. If anti-glare devices are needed, the forms and heights of the devices shall be carefully considered to prevent pedestrians and livestock from crossing and to guarantee a decent lateral visibility. The anti-glare devices shall be discontinuous, or the height of the devices shall be gradually reduced at median openings or intersections of the Class-1 highway without access-control, so as to prevent from late response in incidents due to the continuous devices. According to the requirements for stopping sight distance, the length of the opening of anti-glare devices shall be 100 m in order to allow the vehicle traveling close to the median to make a complete stop from the time drivers spot a passerby, where the design speed is no less than 80 km/h. If the design speed is 60 km/h, the opening of the anti-glare devices shall be approximately 60 m. As a result, anti-glare devices are not recommended to be installed within a certain range of the openings of the intersection and the median openings of Class-1 highways. The broken distance on at-grade intersections can be reduced due to factors such as the tendency to decelerate at median openings, at-grade intersections or outer side lane.

10.3.3 On sections with continuous lighting devices along a highway route, anti-glare devices may not be needed.

Background:

For highway sections with continuous lighting, vehicles usually drive with their low beam headlights on, so the glare effect is weak when two vehicles meet. Obviously, anti-glare devices may not be needed in this case.

10.3.4 If anti-glare devices are provided continuously, the following provisions shall be satisfied:

1 Short gaps without anti-glare devices between two highway sections with anti-glare devices shall be avoided.

2 Each structural section of anti-glare facility shall be independent, and the length of each structural section should not be over 12 m.

3 Transition sections shall be adopted when there is a change in structure form, height or position. The length of transition sections should be 50 m.

Background:
1 *Continuity has to be considered when setting anti-glare devices. Short gaps without anti-glare devices between two highway sections have to be avoided. This is due to a high potential glare risk to unprepared drivers, thus resulting in a traffic crash. In addition, the visual perception and landscape are less than desirable.*

2 *The anti-glare devices are needed to be manufactured and installed in an independent structural section with a certain length. The length of section is usually less than 12 m depending on the material and craft conditions. It is inevitable that the anti-glare devices be damaged by vehicles since they are exposed. To reduce the severity of damage and to facilitate maintenance or replacement, anti-glare devices need to be separated from each other at regular intervals. It is not only good for processing, transportation and installation, but also necessary from the point of view of preventing temperature stress impacts. The length of each independent section of anti-glare devices may be coordinated with the spacing of barriers. The length may be 4 m, 6 m, 8 m, 12 m or longer.*

3 *In principle, the height of anti-glare devices placed along a highway needs to be the same. If different anti-glare structures are connected, the height needs to be transitioned smoothly to avoid sudden changes. The heights of anti-glare devices on sag vertical curves need to be calculated based on the radii of vertical curves and the longitudinal grades, and the heights need to be transitioned gradually in certain lengths of sections (transition section) to accommodate the visual features. The length of the transition section is related to visual features, structure size, rangeability and vehicle speed (the class of highway). The length should be greater than 50 m in general. However, in the design, an appropriate length of transition section needs to be determined according to specific conditions. In addition, the width change of anti-glare panels is generally slight, so the length of the transitions may be shorter.*

10.4 Form selection

10.4.1 The form of the anti-glare devices shall be determined after careful consideration of factors such as the performance of various anti-glare devices, horizontal and vertical alignments and climatic conditions of the highway, sense of security and feeling of constriction by the driver, landscape requirements, coordination with surroundings, construction conditions, economic efficiency, as well as maintenance and repair.

Background:
Anti-glare devices can adopt a number of non-planting forms on the highway, including latticed or grid-patterned anti-glare mesh, fan-shaped slotted glare screen and the plate type recommended in this Guidelines. As for manufacturing materials, metal and synthetic materials can be utilized for anti-glare devices. After decades of development and device testing and phasing-out, glare screens and anti-glare mesh are the most commonly used anti-glare devices worldwide.

Through robust data analysis and investigation, the Research Institute of Highway Ministry of Transport conducted a comprehensive comparison study on the performance of glare screens and mesh from the following eight criteria, in order to meet the technology demand in the 'Seventh Five-Year Plan' National Science and Technology Key Programme.

1 *Effective reduction of the headlight glare from the on-coming traffic;*

2 *Few psychological impacts on the drivers (driving quality impact, monotonous sense);*

3 *Economic efficiency;*

4 *Good landscape (aesthetic appearance);*

5 *Simple construction and convenient maintenance;*

6 *Low wind resistance, less snow coverage;*

7 *Effective prevention man-made sabotage and vehicle damages;*

8 *Good visibility.*

According to the research (shown in Table 10-1): anti-glare panels are an economical, aesthetically pleasing form with low wind resistance, less snow coverage, and few psychological impacts on drivers and its performance will be better where the anti-glare panel with appropriate width is matched with concrete barriers. Thus, the anti-glare panel is determined as the best structural form of the device. Therefore, the anti-glare panel and tree planting are mainly recommended in this Guideline as the basic form of anti-glare device used in China.

Table 10-1 Comprehensive comparison of different anti-glare facilities

Features	Tree planting (shrub)		Glare screen	Anti-glare mesh
	Intensive	Separate		
Aesthetics	Good		Good	Fairly poor
Psychological impact on drivers	Small	Great	Small	Less
Wind resistance	High		Small	High
Snow cover	Severe		Good	Severe
Natural landscape coordination	Good		Good	Not good
Effect of anti-glare	Better		Good	Fairly poor
Economic efficiency	Poor	Good	Good	Fairly poor
Construction difficulty	Fairly difficult		Easy	Difficult
Maintenance level	Large		Small	Small
Lateral visibility	Poor	Better	Good	Good
Prevention on pedestrian crossing	Better	Poor	Better	Good
Landscape effect	Good		Good	Poor

10.4.2 On motorways and Class-1 highways, anti-glare panels and tree plantings should be adopted alternately to prevent glare effects. After technical and economic justification, other anti-glare forms may also be used. The anti-glare mesh may be used on the median and the shield may be used on the road with heavy-snow coverage.

Background:

For two forms of devices including anti-glare panels and tree plantings (shrubs), the anti-glare panels shall be used as the main form where the median is narrow, and tree planting shall be adopted on highways with relatively wide medians, large terrain change, and natural landscape requiring protection and suitable climate for tree growing. A combination of anti-glare panels and tree plantings is an ideal method due to economic efficiency, landscape, maintenance and the monotonicity. The combination of the cable barrier and the glare screen will lead to poor highway landscape where the cable barrier is applied. Besides, the cable barrier is a flexible structure that cannot effectively protect the anti-glare panels. Although the side impact of vehicles may not damage the cable barrier, the anti-glare panels may be damaged or deformed, providing difficulties in repair. A combination of tree planting with cable barriers will not only prevent glare effects, but also make up for the disadvantages of the cable barrier's undesirable directive function as well as provide a satisfying highway landscape. Tree planting is the best option on road sections with cable barriers. It shall be emphasized that none of these provisions are absolute. The selection of the form shall depend on specific situations after careful analysis based on the eight aspects listed in Clause 10.4.1.

10.4.3 Anti-glare planting should not be used if the distance between median barriers is smaller than the plants crown diameter, or trees affect the communication channels under the median, or the shrubs are to be located in the cold, arid and semi-arid areas or the roadbed filling materials is made from poor water-stability material.

Background:
The type of the trees planted shall be determined by the width of the median. Artificial anti-glare devices shall be adopted if the trees are to occupy the clear zone.

10.5 Structural requirement

10.5.1 The width and spacing of anti-glare panels shall meet the requirements, and the materials shall meet the current requirements stipulated in *Anti-glare board* (GB/T 24718); the space between anti-glare planting shall be determined by the calculation of the effective crown diameter.

10.5.2 The thickness, height and length of anti-glare mesh shall be 2-3 mm, 50-110 cm and 200-400 cm respectively, but the mesh size shall be determined through calculations.

Background:
The design elements of anti-glare panels include: light-shading angle, anti-glare height, plate width, and spacing between plates. Among these, the shading angle and the anti-glare height are the most important. The anti-glare panel partially blocks the glare of the oncoming traffic because of its width. That is to say, after the anti-glare panel of a certain width is installed on the median at a certain spacing, the car headlight will be blocked by two neighboring plates, where the horizontal light (light-shielding angle) with the main optical axis of the headlight casts on the anti-glare panels. So the shielding angle is an important parameter in the design. The distance between anti-glare panels ranges from 50 cm to 100 cm so that they can match the interval of the barriers, and this arrangement is also easy to process and manufacture. In addition, the width of the plate calculated according to the spacing shall be well matched with the width of the top of the barrier.

10.5.3 The height of the anti-glare device may be calculated according to the Equation 10.5.2.

1 H stands for the height of anti-glare facilities in straight sections:
$$H = h_1 + (h_2 - h_1)B_1/(B_1 + B_2) \qquad (10.5.3)$$

Where:

h_1—The height of the car headlight (m), as is shown in Table 10.5.3;

h_2—The height of driver view line (m), as is shown in Table 10.5.3;

B_1, B_2—The distance (m) between vehicles and centerline of anti-glare devices on roadway. $B = B_1 + B_2$, as is shown in Figure 10.5.3.

Table 10.5.3 The height of the driver view and the height of the headlight

Type	View height h_1 (m)	Headlights height h_2 (m)
Large vehicle	2.0	1.0
Small vehicle	1.30	0.8

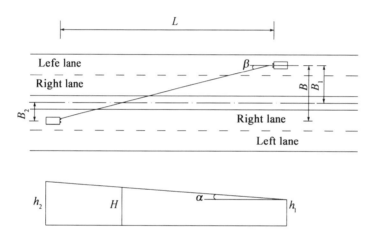

Figure 10.5.3 Minimum height calculation scheme of anti-glare devices

2 On vertical curve section, the height of the anti-glare device shall be calculated based on the size of the longitudinal grade before and after the vertical curve to determine whether the height meets the light-shading requirements where the vertical curve radius is smaller than the general minimum radius stipulated in the current *Technical Standards for Highway Engineering* (JTG B01).

3 The height of anti-glare devices should not be more than 2 m.

Background:

The height of the anti-glare device is directly related to the height of the driver view line and the height of the vehicle headlights. In the highway alignment design, the standard height of driver view line in China is 1.20 m. However, in the actual condition, the driver view line varies greatly due to factors such as the structure of the vehicle and the characteristics of the driver in actual conditions. According to surveys, the recommended height of the driver view line in China is 1.30 m for small vehicles, 2.20 m for buses and 2.00 m for trucks. The recommended headlight height is 0.8 m for small vehicles, and 1.0 m for large vehicles.

On the crest vertical curve, the driver can see headlight glare from the opposing traffic from a relatively low angle, and the glare will be sheltered by the anti-glare devices as the two vehicles approach and the view line moves upward. Therefore, in the crest vertical curve, the lower edge of the anti-glare devices shall be close to or in contact with the highway surface or dense bushes planted in the median in order to eliminate the effect of such glare. The range of device placement shall be at least 120 m away from the top of the crest vertical curve, since the minimum longitudinal distance of two vehicles where drivers do not suffer glare is about 120 m, as is the illumination distance of long-shot headlights.

In the sag vertical curve, the driver can see the glare from the headlight of the opposing vehicle from a higher angle. Therefore, the height of anti-glare devices should be proportionately increased according to the radius of the section and the size of the longitudinal grade around the curve. In general, the corresponding height of the anti-glare device in each typical section of the sag vertical curve can be obtained after calculation or computer drawing, and the average value shall be installed as the height for the whole sag curve. Planting trees that can reach a certain height is an ideal form of anti-glare device for sag curves, as it provides a pleasant landscape for the driver.

In order to coordinate the height of the anti-glare device with the cross-section of the highway, and to prevent the device from falling on the roadway after a crash, and to avoid the impacts while driving, the height of the anti-glare devices should not exceed 2 m in general.

10.5.4 Anti-glare devices should be installed independently. Where they need to be coordinated with barriers due to specfic constraints, the structural design shall meet the requirements as follows.

1 Where fixed on the top of concrete barriers, anti-glare devices may be installed by independent structural segments.

2 Where fitted with corrugated beam barriers, anti-glare devices may be installed on the barriers with connecting pieces or be embedded with supporting posts in the median.

3 The combination of anti-glare device and barrier shall not affect the function of the barrier, such as containment, attenuation and redirection.

10.5.5 The single piece length of anti-glare mesh should not be more than 2.5 m on road sections of horizontal or vertical curves.

Background:

From the placement principles of anti-glare devices and the median barrier, the most basic factors to be considered are similar. In general, the anti-glare devices are usually placed on the highway section where median barrier is also required. As a result, the anti-glare devices and the median barriers are often installed together as a whole. Many advantages can be obtained from this combination. First, the investment into the anti-glare devices will be greatly decreased, since the barrier can function as the supporting structure and thus the investment and cost can be reduced. Second, the barrier can protect the anti-glare device, which is not crash-proof, and this design lowers the risk of damage from a vehicular impact. The maintenance costs can be reduced as a result. Practice shows that anti-glare devices and barriers can complement each other to improve the landscape on highways.

There are two ways to design the structure of the glare screen and the barrier in median if the two are to be installed together:

1. *A combination of anti-glare panels and the concrete barrier, which depends on the pre-embedded pieces (generally anchor bolts) on the top of the concrete barrier.*

2. *A combination of anti-glare panel and corrugated beam barrier. Steel beam (such as channel steel) can be installed on the independent barrier post, and the anti-glare panel fixed on the channel steel or on the combined barrier post.*

10.5.6 When using trees as anti-glare devices, the species shall be determined according to local climate. The selected species shall thrive with well-developed roots, dense foliage, few fallen leaves, low maintenance workload, and successful application experience.

Background:

The Guidelines do not impose excessive requirements on trees serving as anti-glace devices, since tree species vary greatly in different locations that have different climate features and require different height of the anti-glare devices. These guidelines recommend selection of species that thrive with well-developed roots, dense foliage, few fallen leaves, low maintenance workload, all based on successful application experience. The height of the trees and the distance between bushes shall be determined flexibly based on the height and the effective diameter of the tree crown.

11 Escape Ramps

11.1 General

11.1.1 An escape ramp consists of approach lane, arrestor bed and emergency service lane.

11.1.2 Escape ramps shall be provided with highway safety devices, such as traffic signs, road markings, delineators, etc.

11.1.3 Escape ramps on motorways should be equipped with lighting, surveillance and other management facilities. Escape ramps on other classes of highways may be equipped with lighting, surveillance and other management facilities as needed. Indicative signs with emergency call numbers shall be provided at suitable locations of an emergency ramp on all classes of highways.

11.1.4 Escape ramps shall be equipped with a robust drainage system, in order to prevent from icing and pollution of the arrester beds.

11.2 Provisions of the escape ramps

11.2.1 On continuous downgrades where sustained braking of trucks over a long period of time entails a high risk of braking failure, the needs for escape ramps and their specific locations on a highway section shall be determined according to considerations of traffic composition, traffic characteristics, traffic crashes and road geometric alignments, such as grades, and length of grades, horizontal curves, etc. in conjunction with roadside conditions. The installation and the specific location of the escape ramp shall be made in compliance with the provisions as follows.

>   1 On road sections with long and steep down grades, the placement of the escape ramp shall be considered based on the findings and suggestions of road safety audit, where the average

longitudinal grade and the length of the grade satisfy the requirements stated in Table 11.2.1 and the percentage of the trucks in the traffic composition reaches 20%-30%.

Table 11.2.1 **Average longitudinal grade and grade length for consideration of escape ramps on continuous long and steep down grades**

Average grade (%)	2.5	3.0	3.5	4.0	4.5	5.0	5.5	6.0
Grade length (km)	20.0	14.8	9.3	6.8	5.4	4.4	3.8	3.3
Relative height difference (m)	500	450	330	270	240	220	210	200

2　On operating road sections with long down grades, the black spot with frequent brake failure shall be regarded as a suitable location for escape ramp. The specific location of the escape ramp shall be determined based on the analysis of the crash characteristics of trucks on a long and steep downgrade, the testing data of the brake drum temperature, the location of the road alignment, the bridge and the tunnel, the roadside terrain as well as the visibility requirements.

Background:

The escape ramp was originated in the United States, and the first escape ramp to rescue the runaway vehicle in California 1956. The number of escape ramps in U. S. has increased rapidly. Statistics in 1990 showed that 170 escape ramps was provided in 27 states of the United States. The Grade Severity Rating System-GSRS developed by the Federal Highway Administration (FHWA) has been the most widely used tool for analyzing the necessity for escape ramps in long and steep downhill grades. GSRS uses the predefined temperature limit (260 degrees) of brake drum to establish the maximum safety speed on downhill grades, which is defined as the speed at the bottom of the ramp where the emergency braking happens, and the temperature of the brake drum will not exceed the predefined temperature limit. The system model is acknowledged by the World Road Association as the main technical method of predicting temperature rising of the brake drum on a long downhill grade.

In some other documents and design manuals, United States government also introduces guidelines for the placement of escape ramps such as: A POLICY ON GEOMETRIC DESIGN OF HIGHWAYS AND STREETS by American Association of State Highway and Transportation Officials (AASHTO) in 2001, the dissertations published by American Society of Civil Engineers (ASCE), the Highway Design Guidelines from Arizona and Highway Design Manual from North Carolina.

In addition to the United States, many foreign countries also have conducted extensive researches on escape ramps, such as Highway Planning and Design Guide from Queensland Australia, Geometric Design Manual from South Africa, both of which stipulate how to install escape ramps according to the actual situation of the country.

Compared with foreign countries, China started late in the provisions and research of escape ramps. In 1998, the first escape ramp was completed on Badaling Motorway in Beijing, which reduce the damage and loss caused by crashes. In recent years, the number of escape ramps has risen dramatically, but related specifications or guidelines have not yet been published. There is no uniform standards for the provisions of escape ramps. Technical Standards for Highway Engineering (JTG B01—2014) stipulates that escape ramps shall be provided based on RSA on long and steep downhill grades. There is no detailed provision requirements for escape ramps in the Design Specification for Highway Alignment (JTG D20—2006). At the present stage, the installation of escape ramp mainly depends on the crash rate for the operating highways, and the subjective judgments of the designers for the new built highways.

Based on the summarization of domestic and foreign research results and experiences in the establishment of escape ramps, the Guidelines proposes an installation method of escape ramps. For the operating highways with long downhill grades, the escape ramps shall be installed on sections where trucks are more likely to suffer from brake failures based on past crash record. For new built highways, factors such as vehicle configurations, grade, length of grade, horizontal curve, and traffic characteristics shall be taken into consideration and escape ramps shall be installed on sections where trucks suffer a greater risk of braking failure after long-time continuous braking. In general, where the proportion of natural traffic of large and medium-duty trucks in the traffic composition accounts for more than 50%, it is regarded as a relatively high proportion. Given the small probability of crashes, it is recommended that escape ramps shall be provided where the traffic volume of large and medium-sized trucks accounts for more than 30%, and even lower proportion of traffic composition.

Where determining the location of the escape ramp, the temperature rise model of the brake hub can be used to predict the position where the truck may suffer from the brake failure. In recent years, some research institutes and universities in China have established a temperature rise model of the brake hub based on the actual conditions of trucks in China, or have revised the models recommended by the World Road Association to predict the possible locations of brake failure of freight cars after calibration, which provides a theoretical basis for the location selection of the escape ramp.

11.2.2 Escape ramps should be located on right hand side of highway sections with satisfactory sight distance on continuous downgrades, in advance of horizontal curves on the mainline where vehicles cannot make safely negotiate, or in advance of populated areas. Escape ramps should be placed along the tangential direction of small radius horizontal curves. If they are provided on tangents or large radius curves, the intersecting angle between the escape ramp and the mainline should be less than 5°.

11.2.3 The positioning and form of escape ramps should be determined in consideration of the topography and highway alignment. They should be sited away from bridges, and shall be sited away from tunnels.

11.3 Geometric design of escape ramps

11.3.1 The decision sight distance preceding of the entrance of escape ramps should be not less than that the value specified in Table 11.3.1. When conditions are constrained, the decision sight distance shall be greater than 1.25 times of the stopping sight distance of the mainline.

Table 11.3.1 Decision sight distance for entrance of escape ramps

Entrance design speed to arrester bed (km/h)	120	100	80	60
Decision sight distance (m)	350-460	290-380	230-300	170-240

11.3.2 The length of the approach road should be not less than 70 m. The width of the approach entrance should be 3.8-5.5 m. The width of its end shall be the same as that of the arrestor bed. The end and the arrestor bed shall be smoothly connected. The approach shall be ended at the rear of the triangular area, as shown in Figure 11.3.2.

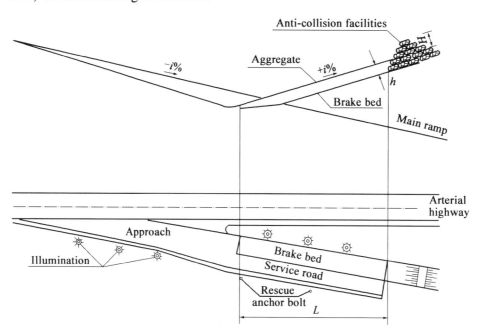

Figure 11.3.2 Structure diagram of escape ramps

11.3.3 The horizontal and vertical alignment of the escape ramp shall be in tangent.

11.3.4 The longitudinal grade of the escape ramp shall avoid any possibilities of longitudinal overturning and sliding and shall be controlled below 15%.

11.3.5 The width of arrester bed for escape ramps should be 4-6 m. The arrestor bed shall be of equal width or gradually widened, instead of gradually narrowed.

11.3.6 The emergency service lane should be on the same plane with and be close to arrestor bed. The width of the emergency service lane should be 5.5 m allowing the access of tow trucks and maintenance vehicles.

11.3.7 The length of the arrestor bed shall be determined based on the speed of the runaway vehicles, the longitudinal grade and the material of the arrestor bed. The calculation for the length of the escape ramp can be seen in Equation (11.3.7), and the reference value is shown in Table 11.3.7.

$$L = \frac{v^2}{254 \times (R + G)} \quad (11.3.7)$$

Where:
   L—The length of the arrestor bed in the escape ramp (m);
   v—The speed of vehicles driving into the arrester bed of the escape ramp (km/h);
   R—The coefficient of rolling resistance;
   G—The grade (percentage) divided by 100.

Table 11.3.7 The recommended value for the design entrance speed of arrestor bed of escape ramp in different grades

Highway class	Entrance speed (km/h)
Motorway, Class-1 highway	100-120
Class-2 highway	80-100
Class-3 and Class-4 highway	60-80

Background:
The speed of the runaway vehicle entering the arrester bed is a key parameter to calculate the length of the escape ramp. US believes that although it is very rare for runaway vehicles to exceed 130 km/h though data observation, it is still possible to reach that speed. Therefore, the A POLICY ON GEOMETRIC DESIGN OF HIGHWAYS AND STREETS stipulates that the minimum entering speed of escape ramps shall be 130 km/h, but the recommended speed is 140 km/h. In South Africa's GEOMETRIC DESIGN GUIDE, the entering speed of escape ramps is same with that in the US. The British standard (MANUAL FOR ROADS AND BRIDGES) points that the speed shall be determined by the designer based on the actual situation, but the entering speed shall be no less than 60 mph (96.5 km/h).

Based on the research on the speed range of the runaway vehicles (80-120 km/h) and economic

efficiency, the recommended speed of entering the arrester bed is shown in the Table 11.3.8.

In addition to the positive value, the G-value of the arrester bed of the escape ramp can also be a negative value, 0° or a value close to 0° applying to uphill, downhill and level escape ramp respectively.

The uphill arrester bed decelerates the vehicle through the gravity gradient resistance and the aggregate rolling resistance; while the level and downhill arrester bed decelerate the vehicle through the aggregated rolling resistance only.

Compared with the uphill arrester bed, the level and downhill arrester bed fail to decelerate the speed and dissipate the energy thus the length of arrester bed shall be increased accordingly. The advantage of the uphill arrester bed is that the escape ramp is easy to locate and that the filling workload can greatly be reduced because the longitudinal grade of arrester bed conforms to the mainline. While the downhill arrester bed may bring difficulty to wreckers which need to pull the vehicles upward.

The escape ramp with level arrester bed is basically on the same place with the mainline, vehicles suffering from brake failure can decelerate to a safe speed and drive out of the escape ramp by itself or can pull over and wait for rescue. For level arrester beds, the aggregates inside the arrester bed may fly to the nearby roadside and thus may impose safety hazards on the vehicles on the main line.

11.3.8 Where the length of the escape ramp fails to meet the requirements, the arrestor nets or energy dissipation facilities may be installed in the proper position in the middle or latter part of the arrestor bed, and these facilities should be burglarproof. See Equation (11.3.8) for the working principle of arrestor nets, and Figure 11.3.8 for the overall structure of arrestor net escape ramp.

$$E_{energy} = W_{net} + W_{friction} + E_{potential} \quad (11.3.8)$$

Where:

E_{energy}—The kinetic energy of runaway vehicles entering the escape ramp;

W_{net}—Work of arrester net;

$W_{friction}$—Work of ground friction;

$E_{potential}$—Potential energy of vehicle on the adverse grade of escape ramp.

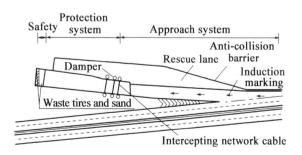

Figure 11.3.8 Schematic diagram of arrester net escape ramp

Background:

The installation of energy dissipation facilities at the end of the escape ramp that meets the length requirements provides higher safety insurance for runaway vehicles. It is not recommended to use energy dissipation facilities or arrester nets as a means to compensate for the length of the escape ramp. The length of the escape ramp shall try to meet the required length. If the escape ramp cannot reach the length required due to terrain restrictions, the length can be compensated by installing deceleration and energy dissipation facilities at the end of the ramp or installing arrester nets or arrester mesh in the middle or later part of the ramp. The above mentioned measures shall be adopted through verification before application.

Motorways in Yunnan MengXin and Sichuan Yalu introduced an arrester net for use in traditional gravel bed escape ramps. Arrester net is a damper energy dissipation and deceleration system that can meet the protection requirements for different runaway vehicles with different speed and mass on the long downhill grade and shorten the length of the escape ramp through adjusting the damping force of the dampers at both sides of the roadways, the spacing and the amount of the dampers.

The height of the arrester net shall be generally 1.3-1.5 m, and the length for vehicle interception shall not be smaller than the width of the arrester bed. The arrester net should be erected in an upright position on the arrester bed of the escape ramp supported by brackets. The bracket shall be made of steel components such as the rectangular section and the H-section, while the steel wire rope used for the arrester net shall be fiber core steel wire with the nominal tensile strength greater than 1,770 MPa. The nominal diameter of the steel rope shall be greater than 20 mm, and the spacing between multi steel ropes shall be no more than 15 cm. The ends of the arrester net at the front of the arrester bed shall be connected to the damper through the steel wire rope of the main arrester wire. The two ends of the arrester net at the end of the arrester bed shall be effectively anchored on the concrete base which can be with the main cable through the damper. The concrete base can be integrated with the concrete barrier of the arrester bed.

11.4 Pavement materials and technical requirements of arrester beds and escape ramps

11.4.1 An impact attenuating device or facility such as crashworthy barrels or waste tires, etc. shall be added at the end of the arrester bed of the escape ramp.

11.4.2 The material of the arrester bed should be pebble or gravel with relatively higher coefficient of rolling resistance, better property of embedment and the material should not be prone to hardening and washaway by rain. The particle size of the material should be 2-4 cm. See Table 11.4.2 for coefficients of rolling resistance of different materials.

Table 11.4.2 The rolling resistance coefficient R value of different materials

Surface material	R	Surface material	R
Carbonate cement concrete	0.01	Loose crushed aggregate	0.05
Asphalt concrete	0.012	Loose gravel	0.1
Compacted gravel	0.015	Sand	0.15
Loose sandy earth	0.037	Pea gravel	0.25

11.4.3 The aggregate thickness of the arrester bed in the escape ramp shall be 1.1 m, and the minimal thickness shall be not less than 1 m.

11.4.4 The aggregate thickness of the arrester bed shall be gradually increased from 7.5 cm at the entrance of the arrester bed to the complete thickness within 30-60 m, as shown in Figure 11.4.4.

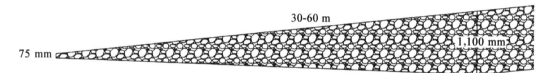

Figure 11.4.4 Gradual transition of the aggregate of the arrester bed

11.4.5 For the recovery service lane, cement concrete pavement should be adopted. The design of roadbed and pavement shall meet the corresponding regulations of the Class-3 and Class-4 highways specified in the *Specifications for Design of Highway Subgrades* (JTG D30) and *Specifications for Design of Highway Cement Concrete Pavement* (JTG D40).

11.5 Supporting facilities for safety and rescue

11.5.1 Safety devices installed on the escape ramps shall conform to the following provisions:

1 Information signs about grade length should be installed at the top of long and steep downgrades, and information signs should be installed repeatedly at appropriate locations in advance of the escape ramp.

2 Advance signs of 2 km, 1 km and 500 m should be installed in advance of the escape ramp. The sign of the escape ramp shall be installed at the entrance of the approach of the escape ramp.

3 Regulatory signs of 'No Parking' and informatory signs of 'exclusive for runaway vehicles' should be installed at the entrance of the approach.

4 Pavement lettering marking 'exclusive for service lane' shall be installed at the paved surface of the service lane.

5 Concrete barriers should be installed on both sides of the uphill arrester bed.

6 Delineators with red reflectors shall be installed on both sides of the arrester bed, better to with 12 m spacing. Delineators need not be installed on the right side of the service lane.

Background:
Aggregates inside the arrester bed may fly to the nearby roadside and thus may impose a safety hazard to running vehicles nearby as runaway vehicles enter the arrester bed. As a result, concrete barriers should be installed on the side of the arrester bed which is close to the adjacent roadway to contain the flying aggregates.

11.5.2 Warning or regulatory signs as well as traffic separation devices shall be installed at the entrance of the service lane. Service lane and the arrester bed shall be separated by post delineators or crashworthy barrels to prevent runaway vehicles from using the service lane as the escape ramp.

Background:
The emergency lane on the right side of the arrester bed is designed for the rescue of the crashed vehicle and cleaning up of loads. In consideration of the convenience for rescue, the service lane and the arrester bed are usually separated by post delineators or crashworthy barrels. If a barrier is adopted as separation, an easily openable movable door shall be installed to facilitate load handling and transport by rescue vehicles.

11.5.3 The service lane shall be equipped with a ground anchor to prevent movement of the rescue tow truck, and the tensile strength should be not less than 200 kN.

11.5.4 Installation of terminal energy dissipation facilities shall be in accordance with the following provisions:

1 Impact attenuator facilities such as aggregate pile, sand barrel, waste tire, and arrester nets shall be added at the end of the arrester bed. The size of aggregate piles shall be in accordance with the requirements of Figure 11.5.4. The size and quantity of the impact attenuator shall be designed according to the model and the speed of the vehicle as well as the structural form of the escape ramp after verification.

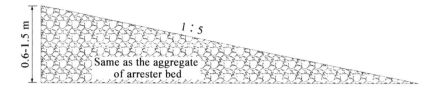

Figure 11.5.4　Aggregate pile

2　The fill material of the energy dissipation facilities shall be the same as that of the arrester bed.

11.6　Antifouling and drainage systems

11.6.1　Cross-slopes, transverse drainage pipes and the longitudinal drainage ditches shall be provided on the surface of arrester bed base.

11.6.2　Geotextile or stones shall be paved between the base and the aggregate of the arrester bed.

12 Other Highway Safety Devices

12.1 Wind fences

12.1.1 The design of highway wind fences shall comply with the following provisions:

1 The design of wind fences shall effectively reduce the adverse effects of crosswinds on live traffic.

2 For highway sections where traffic is affected by strong crosswinds, overall consideration shall be given to wind fences in coordination with traffic signs, pavment markings (including colored anti-skid markings) and other devices.

3 If wind fences are installed on a bridge, their aerodynamic stability and loading on the bridge structure shall be verified.

4 When wind fences are not located within right-of-way, the agricultural and industrial land should not be occupied to install these fences.

5 The structure loading calculation of wind fences can be referred to in Section 3.5.

Background:
Wind fences in the Guidelines are essentially different from the subgrade sandstorm protection devices installed in the windy and sandy highway sections in subgrade engineering. The windproof devices for the subgrade engineering are structures used to protect the subgrade from wind erosion. The wind fences in the Guidelines are highway safety devices and their functions are to reduce the wind speed and in turn reduce the impacts of crosswinds on the stability and safety of vehicles driving on the traveled way under strong winds. However, researches and practices both proved that wind fences cannot eliminate the impacts of strong crosswinds on road safety, and various

other measures such as speed limit, highwind advisory, and anti-sliding pavement are also needed to reduce the impacts. Therefore, wind fences are typically not the only measure provided.

The wind fences shall be kept a certain distance off the edge of shoulders. Permissions from related parties are needed when wind fences are located outside the highway right-of-way, and they should not occupy agricultural and industrial land.

12.1.2 The data of the wind force, wind speed and wind direction along the highway shall be collected before designing of the wind fences. Wind speed and direction observation shall be conducted on road sections with probability of strong crosswind during the construction, and an effective and reasonable design scheme shall be determined based on the results of the observation.

Background:

The design of wind fences shall depend solely on the data provided by the meteorological department because the data usually covers a large area and therefore are not particularly accurate on a specific section and the data provided are measured at 10 m above the pavement surface while the speed requirement of wind fences is the one measured below 5 m above the pavement surface, (except the wind fence on bridge section). In addition, highway construction will change the original landform, and the filled subgrade will have influences on the wind speed distribution near the ground, which may lead to the inconsistency between the actual situation and the data collected. Therefore, observation shall be conducted during the later stage of subgrade construction to collect data on the real and actual wind speed and wind direction, so as to ensure an effective and reasonable design of the wind fences.

12.1.3 When the angle between crosswinds and the longitudinal axis of highway is greater than 30° and one of the following criteria is met, wind fences may be provided along the roadside on the upwind side:

1 Sections with design speed greater than or equal to 80 km/h, and the perennial wind force is greater than Level 7.

2 Sections with design speed less than 80 km/h, and the perennial wind force is greater than Level 8.

3 Sections at tunnel portals, mountain passes and on large bridges with instantaneous wind speed greater than values specified in Table 12.1.3.

Table 12.1.3 **Wind speed for safe driving**

Highway design speed (km/h)	100	80	60	40	20
Wind speed (m/s)	15	17	19	20	20

Background:

Wind fences are not mandatory safety devices. Speed limit and other measures can also improve the safety level of sections with strong wind. Moreover, there are not many cases of using wind fences for domestic highway projects, so the terminology used in the Guidelines is 'may', indicating that it is not mandatory to provide wind fences and it is just an alternative safety device for designers to choose.

According to the relevant research carried out in the Road Traffic Safety Technology Action Plan, the impacts of strong crosswinds on road safety mainly include vehicle sideslip and rollover. Since the critical wind speed of vehicle sideslip on the inside of horizontal curve is the lowest, this shall be used as the limit state under the conditions of strong crosswinds. The analysis of critical wind speeds for safe driving was carried out for four different types of vehicles under the limit state of sideslip, and the wind speeds for safe driving with sideslip were obtained, as shown in Table 12-1.

Table 12-1 Wind speed for safety driving with sideslip (m/s)

Vehicle type/Road pavement condition		Vehicle speed (km/h)				
		100	80	60	40	20
Small vehicles	dry	36.5	38	39	39	39
	wet	30.5	32.5	34	34	34
Minibus, light passenger vehicles	dry	19.5	21.3	22.5	23	23
	wet	15.5	17.5	19	20	20
Medium passenger vehicles	dry	25	27	28	28.3	28.5
	wet	19.5	22	23.5	24.3	24.3
Container vehicles, Buses	dry	26	28	29.5	30	30
	wet	17.0	20	22	23.5	23.5

The wind speed in Table 12-1 refers to the maximum speed within the height of 5 m above the road surface.

The classification of vehicles in Table 12-1 is based on the aerodynamic shapes of vehicles. It can be seen that the minibus and light passenger vehicles (including multi-purpose vehicles) are most susceptible to strong wind impacts due to their higher aerodynamic drag coefficient and lower self-weight. When designing wind fences, these two types of vehicles shall be the primary consideration. The safe wind speed shown in the table is the maximum instantaneous wind speed, meaning that when instantaneous wind speed reaches the value in the table, the vehicle traveling on the horizontal curve will sideslip under the joint effects of centrifugal force and wind force.

However, if the setting conditions are all based on the instantaneous wind speed, wind fences will need to be considered for many road sections. Besides, in perennial strong wind areas, the distribution of wind speed is relatively uniform, and drivers will control their driving speed by themselves. Therefore, the cost-benefit ratio of setting wind fences based on the instantaneous wind speed is not high. The Guidelines refers to the concept of wind force for common highway sections. Wind force is a result of average wind speed. Using wind force as the basis to determine whether to install wind fences is more economical and rational. However, in some special sections with uneven wind speed distribution, such as tunnel portals or mountain passes, drivers cannot expect in advance that they will face strong winds and they often enter the strong wind area suddenly from the weak wind area. At this time, the lack of preparation and high speed of vehicle create more crash-prone situations. Therefore, for these special sections, it is required to use the maximum instantaneous wind speed as the control indicator of setting condition. In meteorological definition, the instantaneous wind speed generally refers to the average wind speed within 3 s. For high-speed railways passenger lines in China, the risk level for safe operation or speed limit of high-speed trains are determined by the maximum instantaneous wind speed of two-year return level. The study conducted by the railway authority considered that the maximum instantaneous wind speed of two-year return level provided an intuitive indicator with the safety level and risk grade. Based on this, designers may refer to the 3 s average wind speed of two-year return level within the height of 5 m above road surface and take it as the instantaneous wind speed.

According to relevant research in Japan and China, when the angle between the wind direction and the axis of the road is less than 30°, the effect of wind fence is no longer obvious. Therefore, wind fence may be considered only when that angle is greater than 30°.

12.1.4 The porosity of the wind fences should not be higher than 30%. While the rate can be increased on bridge, the porosity should be no higher than 60%.

Background:

The porosity of the wind fence is related to the efficiency of it. The researches in the US, Japan and China show that the investment benefit ratio is higher if the porosity ranges from 20% to 30%. The wind tunnel test in our country proves that the porosity is the fundamental parameter of wind fences efficiency. The efficiency of wind fence with small porosity (e.g. 10%-20%) is as high as 75%-90% (i.e. where the wind speed is reduced to 10%-25%), but if low-ventilation-rate wind fence is used on the bridge, it will bring very large aerodynamic drag load to the bridge structure system, leading to decrease in dynamic stability. Wind tunnel test has proved that the wind fences with porosity between 40%-60% can not only block the wind, but also avoid the increase of aerodynamic drag and decrease of stability. Therefore, it is recommended to control the porosity below 30% in non-bridge sections and increase the porosity to 60% in bridge sections. To guarantee the safety of bridge structure, the aerodynamic drag of the bridge shall be analyzed where wind fences are installed on the bridge.

Research in China suggests that the design in which porosity of the lower half part of the wind fences are 30% and the upper half part is 0% can achieve better efficiency. Designers can employ the above-mentioned method according to the actual situation after detailed analysis and justification.

12.1.5 Wind fences should be installed on the edge of the unpaved shoulder. The height of the top of the wind fences should be no less than 3 m on a two-lane highway, and should be no less than one fifth of the width of the subgrade on a four-lane highway. The height of the wind fences shall be specifically analyzed where the wind fence is a certain distance away from the road shoulder or there are more than 4 lanes on the highway.

Background:

The porosity and height of wind fences are the key indicators for the effectiveness of the wind fences. Research shows that in the area above the wind fence, the effect fades away significantly. Wind tunnel test shows that where the wind fences height is 3 m, the wind speed at the height of 5 m is about 30 percent higher than that at the height of 3 m. The Clause 54 of the Road Safety Law of the People's Republic of China stipulates that 'the height of heavy or medium trucks and loads on semi-trailers must be no more than 4 m from the road surface, the height of the container trucks must be no more than 4.2 m; passenger cars must not carry cargo except for the luggage rack outside of the car and the built-in luggage. The luggage rack height of a passenger car shall not exceed 0.5 m from the roof of the vehicle and shall not exceed 4 m from the road surface'. Thus, the height of vehicles on the highway is generally not higher than 4.2 m. Considering that at wind fences of 3 m have a significant impact on the reduction of wind speed even at the height of 4.2 meters, it is recommended that the height of wind fences shall be no less than 3 m balancing economic efficiency and safety.

Wind tunnel experiment demonstrates that on the downwind side of wind fences, the wind speed reduction effect of the wind fence decreases as the horizontal distance increases. Within the range of twice the height of the wind fence behind the fence, the wind speed decreases, and the wind speed reduces more greatly near the ground. Where the distance is larger than twice the height of the wind fence, the wind speed increases gradually. In order to ensure the protective effect of the wind fences can cover the whole highway, the height of the wind fences shall be increased as the width of subgrade increases. According to the result of the wind tunnel test, the height of the wind fences shall be no less than 1/5 of the width of the subgrade. Considering that the speed of the vehicles is relatively lower and the width is relatively smaller on the two-lane highway, a minimum height of 3 meters can basically ensure the protection effect on the entire roadway, and therefore only the four-lane highway is regulated in the Guidelines.

Installing the wind fence on the edge of the road shoulder is the most economical installation method and the height of the fence is also easy to determine. Where the wind fences are located far away from the shoulder, the subgrade itself has a great influence on the characteristics of the wind and the recommended height of the Guidelines cannot be adopted under this circumstance. Likewise, if the subgrade is too wide, the speed change on the downwind side of the fence is more complex. Therefore, if there are structures with wind-blocking effect such as subgrade between the wind fence and the roadway or if the highway is too wide, the height of the wind fence shall be determined using technical methods such as simulation analysis.

12.1.6 Wind fence structures are designed by the limit state method, and the importance coefficient of the structure is tabulated in Table 3.5.1-2.

Background:
The finite element method and the limit state method can be used in the design of wind fence structure, and the latter is the same as the method used in traffic sign structure design.

The wind-resistant standard of wind fences in Japanese motorway is 60 m/s which occur every 100 years. This standard is too high for most areas in China. The designed speed of the traffic sign structures in China is calculated in flat and open areas at 10 m from the ground and is the average maximum wind speed within 10 minutes, which shall not be slower than 22 m/s and shall occur every 50 years. In the Guidelines, the design standard for traffic sign structure is used for reference.

12.1.7 The horizontal bar arrangement shall be adopted where a grid bar structure is designed. If the wind fence is to be installed on the roadside barrier, the roadside barrier shall be concrete barrier and where designing the structure, the influences on wind load of the wind fences and the driving safety shall be taken into consideration. If the wind fences are installed on bridges, the bridge structure performance shall be checked.

Background:
There are a lot of wind fence manufacturers with a variety of products. Wind fences can be divided into grid bar structure, perforated plate, flexible network structure in terms of structural form; the materials used for wind fences include wood, metal and composite materials. Wind fences which can adjust porosity and height are also available. The Guidelines do not specify the structure and material of the wind fences, which can be chosen according to actual conditions, on the premise of meeting the requirements of porosity, height and strength.

According to the results of domestic and foreign wind tunnel tests, where adopting the grid structure, the horizontal grid layout has better effect, and therefore is recommended for grid structure wind fences. Given to the limited width of the road shoulder, the wind fence needs to be installed on the barriers on many occasions. Since wind fence is a wind-resistant structure that is relatively high and bears a great wind load, therefore a relatively large wind load is passed on to the barrier and the effect of the wind load shall be considered where designing the barrier. Besides, the possibility of wind fences being damaged and collapsing on the road due to deformation and the damage of the barriers and the possibility of secondary crashes shall be considered if the wind fences are to be installed on the barriers. Therefore, it is recommended to choose concrete barrier with smaller deformation if the wind fences are to be installed on the roadside barriers. If the wind fences are to be installed on bridges, the aerodynamic drag of the bridges as well as the wind load passing to the bridge structures by the wind fences shall be calculated and checked to prevent the wind load from damaging the bridge structures.

12.2 Snow fences

12.2.1 The design of highway snow fences shall comply with the following requirements:

1 Snow fences shall be designed to effectively reduce the adverse impacts of snow drift on live traffic. Concurrently, subgrade protection shall also be taken into account.

2 Snow fences shall be installed on the upwind side of a highway. Multiple rows of snow fence may be provided for highway sections in open areas with extra-heavy snow fall and very strong winds.

3 If snow fences are located outside the highway right-of-way (ROW), they should not occupy agricultural and industrial land.

4 The structure design and analysis of snow fences may refer to Section 3.5 of the *Guidelines*.

***Background*:**
Snow fences specified by the Guidelines are used primarily to protect vehicles by reducing snow on the road. In the meantime, the subgrade could be protected as well on the premise of reducing the covering snow. According to relevant research in the United States, crashes caused by the low-visibility formed by drifting snow has been reduced by 70% where the snow fences are constructed. Providing snow fences is an effective highway safety strategy in areas with heavy snowdrifting.

A certain separation distance shall be kept between the snow fence and the subgrade of the highway. As a result, snow fence is installed outside the highway ROW and under that circumstance, the occupation of the agricultural or industrial land should be avoided.

12.2.2 Data of snowfall, wind force, wind speed and wind direction along the highway shall be collected in advance. After determining the capacity and the protection range, snow fences shall be designed based on terrains along the highway.

12.2.3 Permanent snow fences can be installed on sections with a large amount of snow accumulation, a long duration and little change in wind direction. While in sections with variations in wind direction, strong wind and heavy snow, portable snow fences may be used.

Background:
Snow fences are generally placed along highways where snowdrift is relatively heavy based on both domestic and overseas experiences. However, reliable quantitative results on provisions of snow fences are lacking at present. Most of the available design settings are based on field observation and experience.

Snow fences may be divided into two basic forms, i.e. permanent and portable in general. Permanent snow fences is not be movable, while portable snow fences may be moved at any time according to snow, wind direction and wind forces. The Guidelines adopts the relevant provisions for permanent and portable snow fences in the prevailing Specifications for Design of Highway Subgrades (JTG D30).

12.2.4 The porosity of snow fences shall be determined according to the amount of snowdrift and the conditions of the snow storage site behind the snow fences. The porosity should be in the range of 40%-70%.

Background:
The porosity of snow fences is the most important index affecting the snow trapping efficiency. The Snow Fence Guide (SHRP-W/FR-91-106) of US indicates that the most suitable porosity is 40%-50%, and the most commonly employed rate in the United States is 50%. Related researches in China finds that with the increase of porosity, the maximum snow trapping efficiency increases as well and reaches the maximum value where the porosity is at 66%, after which the maximum snow trapping efficiency starts to drop dramatically (Figure 12-1). It can be seen that results gained from domestic researches are similar to those obtained in foreign countries such as the US. The Guidelines adopts domestic results and recommended the upper limit of the porosity at 70%. However, the higher the porosity, the longer the snow dunes in downwind side fence will be, and the larger the larger the snow storage sites will be required. As a result, 50%

porosity is the most common application in China. However, in the case of sufficient snow storage capacity is available, a higher porosity of 66% can be employed to achieve better snow trapping efficiency.

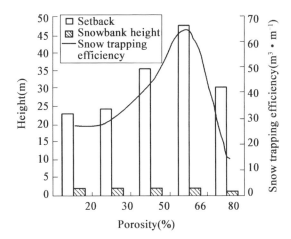

Figure 12-1　The relationship among the snow trapping efficiency, the length of snowbanks in the downwind side and porosity in 2 m high snow fences

12.2.5　The snow fence height shall be determined according to the snow transport in the heavy-snow area, the porosity of the snow fences and the terrains, and should not be lower than 3.0 m. Where the snow fence height is greater than 6 m, double or multiple rows of snow fences shall be considered.

Background:

The snow fence height is related to snow storage capacity of the snow fences. In general, the larger the snow storage capacity, the greater the snow fence height will be.

The Snow Fence Guide (SHRP-W/FR-91-106) of the United States proposes a method to determine the snow fence height based on the snow storage capacity, which is measured in tonnes/ meter. The basic principle is using 10% of the annual snowfall as the water-equivalent winter precipitation, and the relocated precipitation is 70% of it. The specific calculation method is the descriptive geometry method: the curve in Figure 12-2 is the relocated precipitation which is 70% reduction of the 10% of the annual snowfall; the X-axis represents the fetch, and the Y-axis is the snow transport (tonnes/m). The curve shall be selected according to the relocated precipitation for calculation, and the X-axis shall be defined according to the fetch and the corresponding Y-axis is the snow storage capacity. The Y-axis in Figure 12-3 is the snow storage capacity and the horizontal axis is the height of snow fences. According to the calculated snow storage capacity, the snow fence height can be determined by the curve (The porosity of the snow fences is usually in the range of 40%-50% in America).

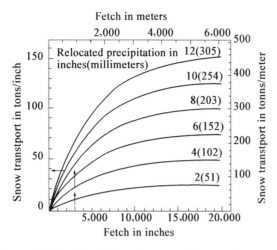
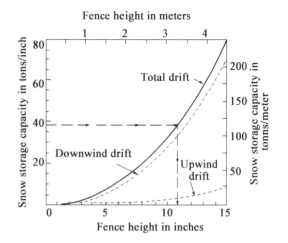

Figure 12-2 Variation of seasonal snow transport with fetch and relocated precipitation

Figure 12-3 Snow Storage capacity in relation to fence height

In China, an empirical equation, as in Equation (12-1), is proposed defining the relationship among the height of snow fences the snow trapping efficiency and the porosity. This equation can also be used to estimate the height of snow fence. But because there are many factors affecting the snow trapping efficiency of snow fences, such as the location of the highway (upwind or downwind), the cross-section form of the subgrade (embankment, cutting or half cutting), these methods can only be used as references. It is better to perform numerical simulation analysis in the design of snow fences in order to achieve better effects.

$$Q = 1,081 \times \frac{H}{100 - d} \tag{12-1}$$

Where:

Q—Snow trapping efficiency of snow fences (m^3/m);

H—The snow fence height (m);

d—Porosity, in percent.

The snow fence height has great influences on snow trapping efficiency. In general, the greater the height is, the higher the efficiency will be. However, because snow particles in snowdrifts mainly concentrate within a 2 m range above the ground, the improvement of snow trapping efficiency slows down as the snow fence height increases. The Snow Fence Guide (SHRP-W/FR-91-106) requires the minimum snow fence height shall be no less than 2.4 m, while the Specifications for Design of Highway Subgrades (JTG D30—2015) of China recommends the snow fences height shall be no less than 3 m. Most snow fences are higher than 3 m during practices in China, and therefore the Guidelines adheres to the requirements in the Specifications for Design of Highway Subgrades (JTG D30—2015). Research shows that as the snow fences height reaches 6 m, the increase in the snow fence height will not improve the snow trapping efficiency. Therefore, if there is the possibility of applying over 6 m height snow fence due to high demands of snow trapping efficiency, the fence height shall be kept within 6 m, and snow fences in double rows or multiple rows shall be deployed instead of a single row.

12.2.6 A gap between the bottom of the fence and the ground shall be retained, which should be 5-10 cm higher than the depth of maximum local precipitation.

Background:

A gap between the snow fences and the ground shall be retained to prevent premature failure of the snow fence as it is buried by snow. As the air flows through the gap, a compression acceleration effect will be produced, which will affect snow cover besides snow fences. The larger the gap is, the smaller the snow storage near the snow fences will be, and the longer the setback will be. Therefore the bottom gap of the fences shall be determined according to the local conditions. Generally, the gap is 5-10 cm higher than the maximum snow depth in the local area. In the US Snow Fence Guide (SHRP-W/FR-91-106), it is recommended that the gap at the bottom of snow fences shall be in the range of 10%-15% of the snow fence height. If it is difficult to determine the maximum snow water equivalent in the area, this regulation can be referred to as guidance.

12.2.7 The length of the snow fences shall cover the entire snow-prone section, and the snow fence shall be extended to a distance no less than 20 times of snow fence height at both ends.

Background:

Because of the detour flow effects of the wind, the drifts at the ends of the snow fences is much stronger and longer. Especially where the intersection angle between the wind direction and the orientation of the snow fences are relatively small, the length of the snow at the ends of the snow fence may be 2 times as long as that at the middle part of the fences. If the snow fences are not long enough, the snow cover will extend to the roadways. Therefore, the length of the snow fence could be increased at the ends of the fence. Typical three types of arrangement of z-shaped snow fence, flying-geese shaped or herringbone shaped snow fence could be adopted.

The US Snow Fence Guide (SHRP-W/FR-91-106) stipulates that both sides of the protected area to intercept winds that vary up to 30° on either end of the prevailing wind directions (Figure 12-4), which is 20 times the snow fence height according to the trigonometric function relation.

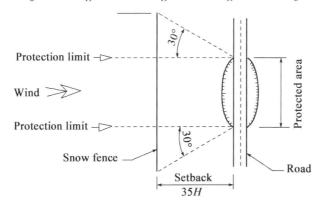

Figure 12-4 Schematic diagram of extension length of snow fence

12.2.8 The application method and placement of snow fences shall be in accordance with the following provisions:

1. The snow fence shall be placed on the upwind side and be perpendicular to the wind direction. The intersection angle between the snow fence and the wind direction should be no less than 75°, even with topographic restriction. The broken-line type snow fence or multiple rows of fences in flying-geese pattern shall be adopted.

2. The distance between adjacent snow fences should be no less than 25 times the snow fence height if multiple-row of snow fences are installed.

3. The distance between snow fences and highway shoulder should be at least 35 times the snow fence height. It should be no less than 25 times the snow fence height where there topographic constraints.

4. If the highway is to be located on hill slopes, the adaptability of snow fences shall be evaluated, and the placement of snow fences shall depend on the fetch value.

Background:
Snow trapping efficiency is best where the snow fence is perpendicular to the prevailing wind direction. Domestic practice and research show that where the intersection angle between wind direction and snow fence is reduced to 40°, the snow fence efficiency becomes insignificant. The U. S. Snow Fence Design Guide (SHRP-W/FR-91-106) requires that snow fences shall be perpendicular to the prevailing wind direction with a deviation less than 25°. The Guidelines learn the rules from the U. S. Snow Fence Design Guide (SHRP-W/FR-91-106), and the principle in the Guidelines is that the snow fence shall be kept as perpendicular as possible to the prevailing wind direction in order to achieve better snow trapping efficiency. Where the intersection angle is small, the flying geese installation method below can be adopted, as is shown in Figure 12-5.

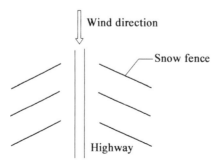

Figure 12-5 Snow fence layout when the wind direction and highway orientation are the same or with a small intercepting angle

A long snow dune will appear at the downwind side of the snow fences because of the snow trapping effect of snow fences (Figure 12-6). In order to prevent the snow dune from extending onto the road, it is necessary to keep a certain distance between the snow fence and the road shoulder edge. Domestic studies show that the setback distance usually reaches 20-25 times the height of a snow fence. U. S. Snow Fence Design Guide (SHRP-W/FR-91-106) requires the setback distance shall be at least 35 times the snow fence height. In consideration of the protection of the highway subgrade by snow fences and the need for a certain distance to ensure safety, the regulations of the Guidelines are consistent with that of the U. S. Snow Fence Design Guide (SHRP-W/FR-91-106), but the setback distance can be 25 times the snow fence height.

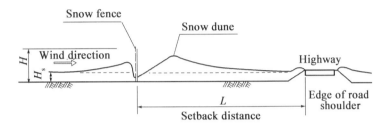

Figure 12-6 Snowbank schematic diagram in the downwind side

Where installation of multiple rows of snow fences is needed, the spacing between adjacent snow fences shall be 25 times the snow fence height in order to avoid the snow fences behind being affected by the snow dunes at downwind side of the snow fences, as is shown in Figure 12-7.

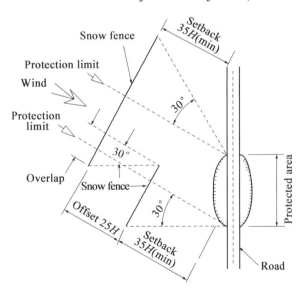

Figure 12-7 Schematic diagram of multi-row snow fence

Studies show that where snow fences are constructed on upwind slopes to prevent highway snowdrift hazards, the snow trapping efficiency will be small and the wind-resistant distance will get shorter (short snow dune), the steeper the slope the shorter the dune, with reduced effectiveness.

Similarly, where snow fences are constructed on the downwind slope to prevent highway snowdrifts, the snow trapping efficiency will be large and the wind-resistant distance will be longer (snow dune is short), the steeper the slope the longer the dune with reduced effectiveness. Therefore, if the snow fences are to be constructed on steep slopes, the effect and applicability of snow fence shall firstly be analyzed, and the appropriate placement locations shall be determined in accordance with the setback distance. Generally speaking, snow fences on downwind slope has a better performance than those on upwind slope. Topographic conditions permitting, the snow fence on downwind can be placed at the top of slope.

12.2.9 The snow fence structure is designed by limit state method, and coefficient for importance of structure is shown in Table 3.5.1-2.

Background:

Similar to wind fence, snow fence is also a wind load structure. Therefore, its structural design method is the same as that of the wind fence, and the requirements for structural calculation in the Guidelines are consistent with that of the wind fence.

12.2.10 Where a grid structure is adopted, horizontal bar layout is preferred. The position and snow fence height shall be determined according to their characteristics if wind directive structures or other non-grid structures are adopted.

Background:

For snow fences with grid structure, studies show that the snow trapping efficiency with horizontal structure is 8.4% larger than that of longitudinal structure. The main reason is that change of wind speed in vertical direction near ground is greater than the change in horizontal direction, and vortexes are generated in front of and behind the snow fence, which leads to a decrease in wind speed in the vertical direction, while snow fences with longitudinal grid structure decreases wind speed mainly in the horizontal direction. Therefore, snow fences with horizontal grid are preferred for adoption.

Although grid structure is more economical and the most commonly adopted structure, a great variety of new types of snow fences are now available. Some new snow fences are specially designed and developed, such as snow fences with wind directive function. The snow trapping principles and aerodynamic characteristics of these new snow fences are very different from those of ordinary ones. The heights and positions of new snow fences shall be determined in accordance with the structural features and aerodynamic characteristics, for example, some specially designed snow fences in Japan need to be placed close to road shoulder.

12.3 Snow poles

12.3.1 The design of highway snow poles shall comply with the following requirements:

1 Highway snow poles should be installed on the highway earth shoulder, and their location must not intrude the highway clearance profile.

2 The spacing between snow poles may be based on the spacing of delineators.

Background:
The snow poles are used to help drivers to recognize road geometric alignments when traveled ways are covered with snow. The location of snow poles may not be too far from the traveled way. It is better to be on earth shoulders if conditions allow. There are no uniform stipulations for the color of snow poles across the world. However, red, orange, and red and white are the most common colors(Figure 12-8). The colors of snow poles are needed to not only contrast with the white color of snow, but also contrast with the environmental background of the highway. Designers may select easily recognizable colors based on the environmental conditions of specific highway sections.

a)   b)   c)

Figure 12-8 Snow poles in oversea countries

12.3.2 Snow poles may be provided on highway sections with snow-covered traveled way due to heavy snowfall, or snowfall of long duration.

Background:
Snow poles are highway safety devices which may be used for snow-covered highway sections. Their need is based on the comprehensively consideration of the severity of snow accumulation and snow removal maintenance operation. Snow poles are not required as safety devices for highway sections where snow can be removed and maintained in a timely manner. Therefore, the Guidelines uses the word "may", and designers shall make decisions according to prevailing circumstances.

12.3.3 The height of snow poles above the road surface should range from 1.5-2.4 m.

Background:

The effectiveness of snow poles is greatly influenced by the surroundings, and therefore the specification and size of snow poles should not be unified. The recommended diameter and height of snow poles in the Guidelines fall within the range adopted by foreign countries. In principle, the higher the poles, the better the recognition effect will be. However, short poles can also have a good performance on sections with an open roadside. Snow poles can be designed specifically according to the surrounding situations. In general, the height of snow poles shall be 1.2 m higher than the maximum historical snow cover depth.

12.3.4 Reflective sheeting shall be attached to snow poles on sections with heavy nighttime traffic. The reflective sheeting should be yellow in color and wrap in a full circle around the pole, and may be placed with certain spacing between two sheeting. The longitudinal length and interval of reflective sheeting should each be 20 cm.

Background:

The attachment of reflective sheeting on the snow poles can promote the recognition of the poles during nighttime and snowfall conditions. The length of and the spacing between reflective sheeting are determined based on the requirements of the guard post at the entrance of the road. Experience suggests that the length and the placement spacing of 20cm can be easily identified by drivers. The yellow color of the reflective sheeting forms a clear contrast with the snow background, and white reflective sheeting shall be avoided.

12.4 Height restriction gantries

12.4.1 The design of height restriction gantries shall adhere to the following provisions:

1 Height restriction gantries may be installed if the vertical clearance of a bridge or tunnel structure is less than 4.5 meters. Height restriction gantries should be installed if the vertical clearance of a bridge or tunnel structure is less than 2.5 meters.

2 Anti-crash or height restriction warning devices can be installed if restriction of vehicle height is required according to the regulations of traffic operation and management.

3 Height restriction gantries shall be installed in coordination with height restriction warning signs. The vertical clearance of the barrier shall not be smaller than the height restriction indicated on the sign. Vehicle height monitoring and warning system can also be installed

if required.

4 Object marking of the height restriction barrier shall be in yellow and black colors, and reflective film should be adopted as object markings.

5 Height restriction barriers must not affect the operation of emergency vehicles such as fire engines and ambulances.

6 The vertical clearance of the height restriction barrier can be designed as adjustable in accordance with actual needs.

7 When an over-height vehicle collides with the height restriction gantry, the components and detached parts of the gantry shall not endanger the safety of personnel inside or outside of the vehicle.

***Background*:**

Height restriction gantries are to protect bridges and tunnel structures from being hit by over-height vehicles. The Clause 54 of the Regulation on the Implementation of the Road Traffic Safety Law of the People's Republic of China stipulates: A motor vehicle shall be loaded in conformity with the verified loading capacity, and overload is strictly prohibited. the dimensions of loaded trucks shall comply with the following provisions:

1 The height of heavy, medium trucks, and semi-trailers must not exceed 4 meters from the ground, and the height of container vehicles must not exceed 4.2 meters;

2 Height of other cargo motor vehicles must not exceed 2.5 meters from the ground…

As the legal height of vehicles will not exceed 4.2 meters, height restriction gantries need not be installed for bridges and tunnels with a vertical clearance of 4.5 meters or more. When the vertical clearance of bridge or other structures is between 2.5 and 4.5 meters, there is a possibility that loaded trucks may hit the bridge or the structure. In this case, it is better to install upstream height restriction gantries. But if there are no over-height trucks on the highway passing underneath the bridge and the bridge is less likely to be hit, height restriction gantries need not be provided. Therefore, the requirement for such a condition in the specification is 'may'. In the design process, designers shall determine whether to provide the device according to the types of vehicles passing the bridge. When the vertical clearance of the bridge is less than 2.5 meters, it is possible that regular cargo motor vehicles hit the bridge structure. In this case, the provision of height restriction gantry shall be determined by whether there are over-height trucks on the highway that will cross underneath the bridge. Therefore, height restriction gantries 'should' be installed according to the Specification.

In order to ensure the safety of vehicles, the vertical clearance of height restriction gantries must be clearly conveyed to drivers and over-height warning signs are needed upstream of all height restriction gantries. The vertical clearance of height restriction gantries must not be less than the height limit value of over-height warning signs.

Height restriction gantries, when hit, may cause damage and harm to vehicles and occupants. Therefore, it is necessary to comprehensively consider the structural safety of bridges and tunnels and the safety of drivers where designing height restriction gantries. Based on overseas practices, a warning height restriction gantry installed upstream of a rigid gantry structure but with a flexible structure with the same height can be adopted.

12.4.2 Where height restriction gantries are installed ahead of a bridge or tunnel, another similar height restriction gantry and warning signs with the same height restriction should be installed at the entrance of intersections leading to the road section. The distance between the height restriction gantry and the bridge or tunnel structure shall be no less than the distance needed for the impact vehicle to stop. The distance shall be determined in accordance with regulations of stopping sight distance specified in the *Technical Standards for Highway Engineering* (JTG B01). Where a road crosses a motorway in the form of an underpass and there is a high proportion of trucks, article 12.4.1 can be referred to for the installation of height restriction gantries.

Background:
Height restriction gantries can be divided into two categories, namely, height restriction warning gantry and anti-crash height restriction gantry. Warning gantry uses flexible structures such as suspending horizontal bars that will not damage the impact vehicle, but will warn drivers. The vehicle can still pass through even if the height of the vehicle exceeds the restricted height. Anti-crash height restriction gantries, on the other hand, shall be strong enough to prevent vehicles from passing so as to protect the downstream highway structures. In order to prevent the damage to bridges and tunnels, and to avoid that overheight vehicles finding it impossible to pass through just ahead of the bridge, it is better to install height restriction gantries together with height restriction warning signs with the same restricted height at intersections leading to the highway section(Figure 12-9).

12.5 Speed humps

12.5.1 Speed humps may be provided for sections of Class-3 and Class-4 highways passing through towns and villages, or on local roads at the intersections where Class-3 and Class-4 highways intersect the arterial highways.

Figure 12-9 Foreign practices of height restriction warning gantry

12.5.2 The placement of speed humps shall meet the following provisions:

1 Speed humps should be placed in advance of the intersection of local road and arterial highway to control the vehicle speeds entering arterial highways.

2 In order to limit the vehicle speeds, speed humps may be placed on the sections in advance of villages and towns and the sections in advance of schools or intersections.

3 Speed humps shall cover the entire roadway and shall be placed together with corresponding speed hump signs, markings, and advisory speed signs or speed limit signs.

12.5.3 The structure of speed humps shall be designed in accordance with the following provisions:

1 The width of large speed humps should be 6,600 mm, and the central height should be 76 mm, as shown in Figure 12.5.3-1. The longitudinal edge of speed humps shall be gradually reduced to the height of highway shoulder, as is shown in Figure 12.5.3-2.

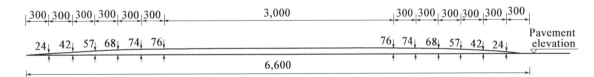

Figure 12.5.3-1 Cross-section diagram of speed humps (Unit: mm)

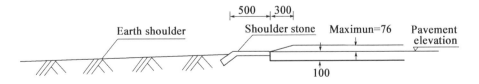

Figure 12.5.3-2 Vertical edge diagram of speed humps (Unit: mm)

2 Small speed humps can be prefabricated or cast in place. The width of prefabricated humps should range between 300-500 mm, and the central height should range between 30-50 mm. Cast-in-place humps can be casted on site with C20 concrete or concrete of higher classes. The width should range between 500-600 mm, and the central height should range between 50-60 mm.

Background:

Speed humps are installed on Class-3 and Class-4 highway sections before entering towns and villages, or on the local roads access to an arterial highway, to reduce the speed of vehicles and to improve the safety of pedestrians. As speed humps protrude above the pavement surface, incidents may happen when drivers fail to detect the presence of such an elevation difference in pavement surface, especially under weather conditions with low visibility, such as foggy days, dusk or nighttime or when the speed is too high. Therefore, speed humps shall be placed with supporting traffic signs and markings, including signs of advisory speed or speed limit, to warn drivers to slow down upstream of speed humps.

12.6 Convex mirrors

12.6.1 Convex mirrors may be provided on the outer side of small radius horizontal curves with limited meeting sight distance.

12.6.2 Convex mirrors should be installed in conjunction with visual guiding devices.

12.6.3 The diameter of the convex mirror shall be 600 mm, 800 mm or 1,000 mm in accordance with the design speed and the radii of horizontal curves.

12.7 Other devices

12.7.1 In addition to the various types of highway safety devices mentioned in this chapter, other necessary devices, such as lane separation devices, speed reduction pavement and rumble strips etc., may be provided as necessary.

Appendix A
A Sample of the Integrated Design of Safety Facilities at Tunnel Entrance and Exit

A.1 Marking placement sample of tunnel entrance and exit

A.1.1 Marking placement sample of tunnel entrance and exit (Figure A.1.1).

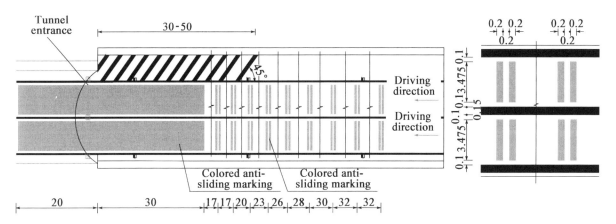

Figure A.1.1 Marking placement sample of tunnel entrance (Unit: m)

A.1.2 Marking placement sample of tunnel exit (Figure A.1.2).

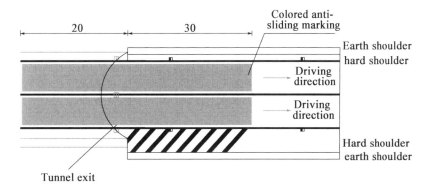

Figure A.1.2 Marking placement sample of tunnel exit (Unit: m)

A.2 Safety facility placement sample of tunnel entrance and exit

A.2.1 Safety facility placement sample of tunnel entrance and exit is shown in Figure A.2.1.

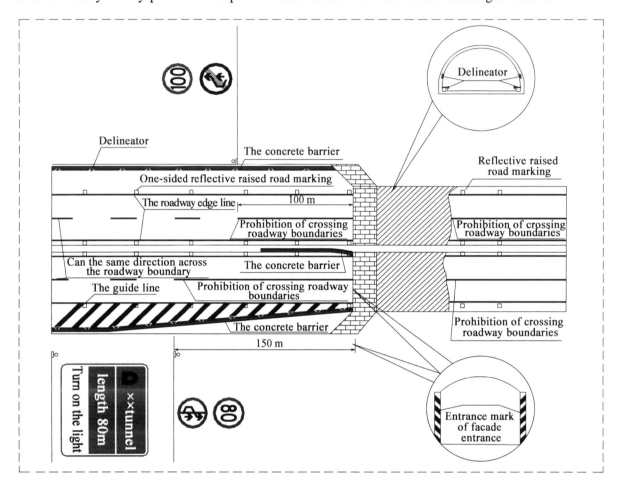

Figure A.2.1 Safety facility placement sample of tunnel entrance and exit

Appendix B
Calculation Methods for Clear Zone Width

B.0.1 Without considering the deployment of roadside protection facilities, clear zone width may be classified as suggested clear zone width and the effective recovery zone width.

B.0.2 Suggested clear zone width shall be determined based on the conditions of the highway horizontal alignment indicators, sub-grade filling and cutting and operating speeds in compliance with the provisions as follows:

1 Suggested clear zone width should be determined based on the conditions of sub-grade filling and cutting for tangent sections obtained in Figure B.0.2-1 and Figure B.0.2-2.

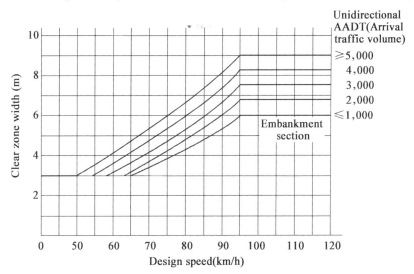

Figure B.0.2-1 Suggested clear zone width of tangent sections on embankments

2 Suggested clear zone width on curves should be modified based on the suggested clear zone width of tangent sections with the same sub-grade type and multiplied by the adjustment coefficient F_c, which can be obtained in Figure B.0.2-3.

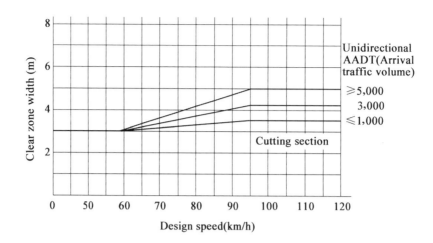

Figure B.0.2-2 Suggested clear zone width of tangent section in cutting

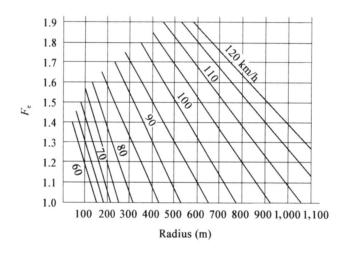

Figure B.0.2-3 Adjustment coefficient F_c for suggested clear zone width on curves

B.0.3 The effective recovery area width shall be the available width of a gentle, and unobstructed area extending outward from the outer edge of the traveled way, including paved shoulders, earth shoulders and utilizable foreslopes in compliance with the following provisions:

1 If the foreslope is flatter than 1 : 6, the effective width is the entire foreslope width.

2 If the foreslope is between 1 : 3.5 and 1 : 6, the effective width is 1/2 of the entire foreslope width.

3 If the foreslope is steeper than 1 : 3.5, the width of foreslope is not an effective width because an errant vehicle cannot be driven through such a slope.

4 If there are masonry ditches or drainage channels without cover plates along the roadside,

these do not form part of the effective width.

5   If there are non-removable street trees, flower planters, sign supports or other obstacles on the roadside, the width occupied by these obstacles does not form part of the effective width.

Appendix C
General Structural Design Sample of Cable Barrier, Corrugated Beam Barrier and Concrete Barrier and Variation Method

Some structural design samples provided in this appendix are derived from domestic researches, which have passed full-scale and real-vehicle crash test in accordance with the provisions of relevant standards and some are derived from foreign standard drawings, which have passed full-scale and real-vehicle crash tests for foreign barrier performance, and the protection degree is greater than or equal to the corresponding class of that in China. This appendix can be used as a reference for designers. It encourages all design units to independently develop or cooperate with barrier producing units, to develop barriers that are suitable for project characteristics and demands, and that can be put into application after safety performance evaluation.

C.1 General Structural Design Sample of Some Cable Barriers

C.1.1 General Structural Design Sample of Level 1 (C) Cable Barrier(Figure C.1.1).

C.1.2 General Structural Design Sample of Level 2 (B) Cable Barrier(Figure C.1.2).

C.1.3 General Structural Design Sample of Level 3 (A) Cable Barrier(Figure C.1.3).

Background:
This appendix provides two general structural design samples of third (a)-class cable barrier, among which sample a) is a general type widely adopted in China, while sample b) is a compact type from the "Research on Cable crash Prevention System of Highway Middle Zone" initiated by the Department of Transportation, Zhejiang Province in the year of 2013 and conducted by Zhejiang Provincial Highway Administration, Quzhou Municipal Highway Administration, Zhejiang Provincial Institute of Transportation Planning and Zhejiang Feihong Traffic Facilities Co. Ltd. The barrier have passed real-vehicle crash test with medium-size bus, and the maximum dynamic deformation value of the barrier is 2017 mm.

C.1.4 General Structural Design Sample of the Middle and End Section of Level 3 (A) Cable Barrier(Figure C.1.4).

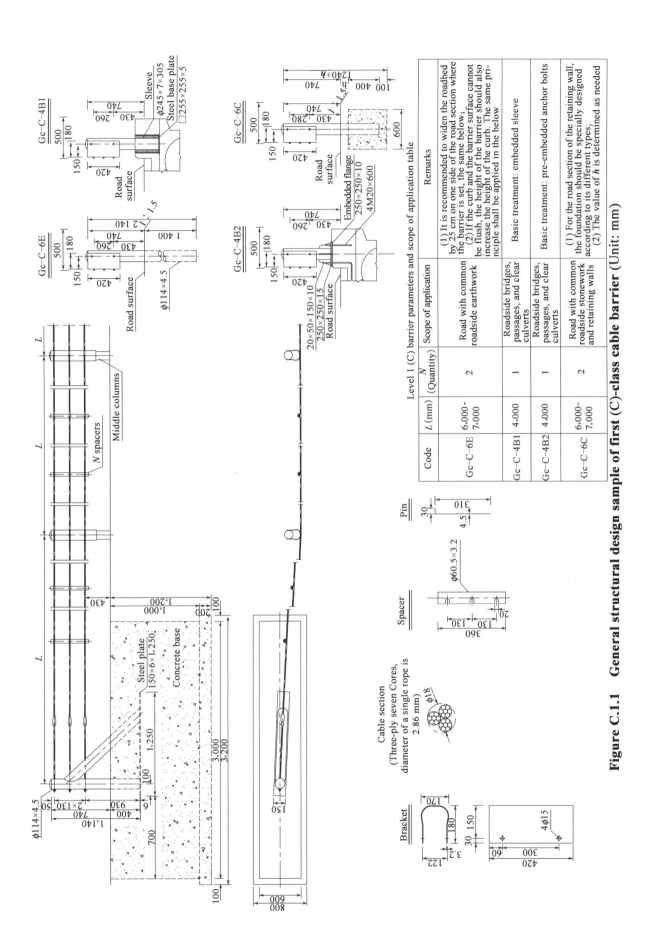

Figure C.1.1　General structural design sample of first (C)-class cable barrier (Unit: mm)

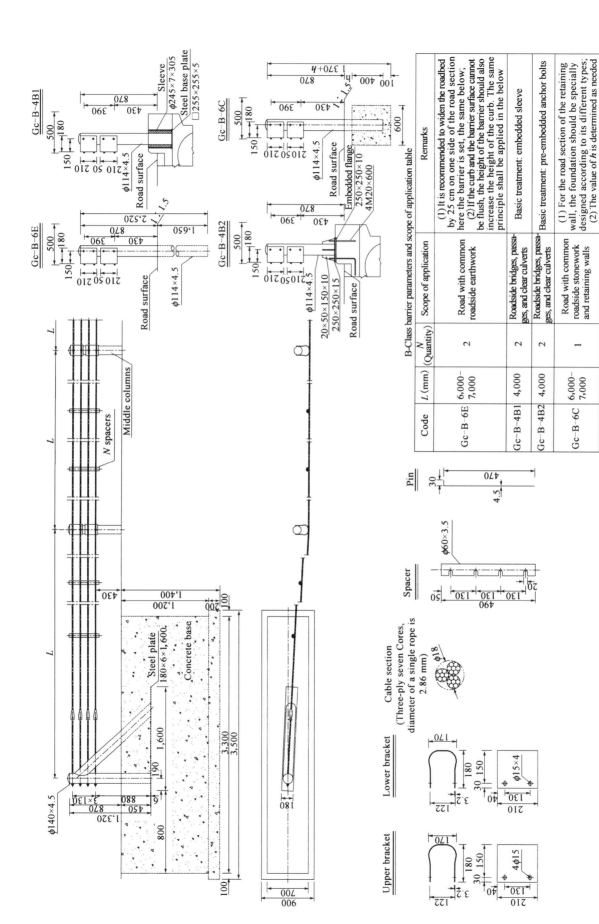

Figure C.1.2　General sructural design sample of second (B)-class cable barrier (Unit: mm)

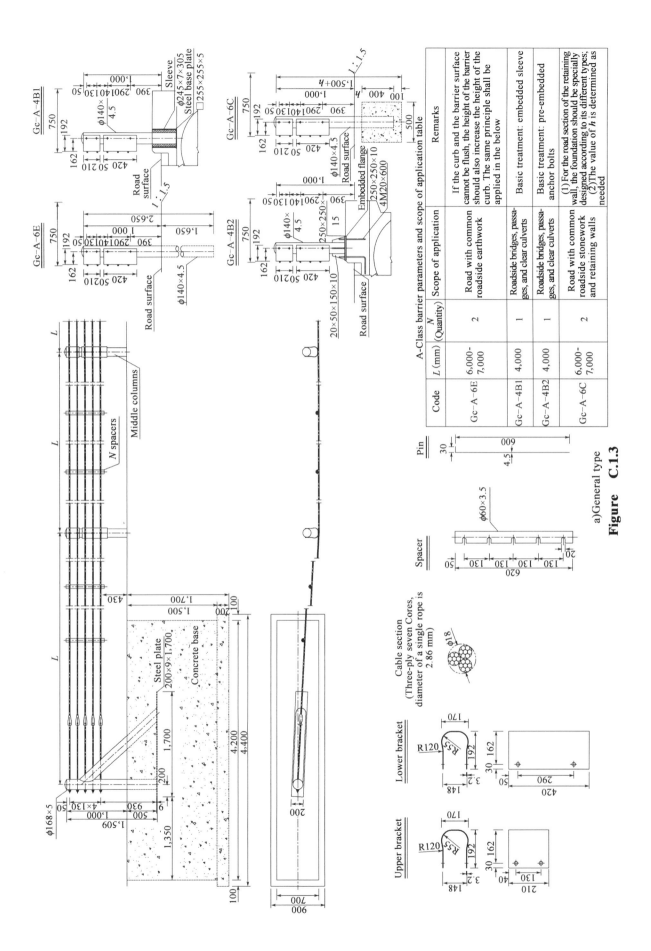

a) General type

Figure C.1.3

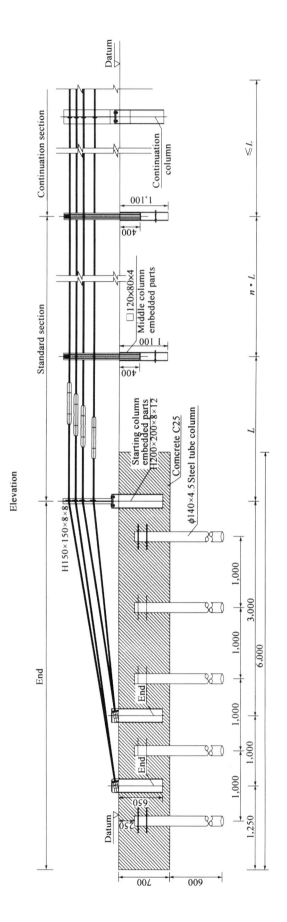

Figure C.1.3 General structural design sample of third (A)-class cable barrier (Unit: mm)

Note: L is the standard spacing of the vertical column, N is the number of standard spacing in the column.

b) Compact type

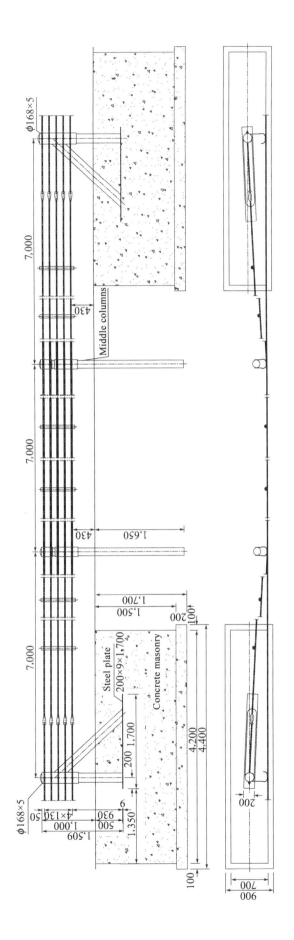

Figure C.1.4 General structural design sample of the middle and end section of third (A)-class cable barrier (Unit: mm)

227

Background:

This appendix provides two general structural design samples of third (a)-class cable barrier, among which sample a) is a general type widely adopted in China, while sample b) is a compact type from the 'Research on Cable crash Prevention System of Highway Middle Zone' initiated by the Department of Transportation, Zhejiang Province in the year of 2013 and conducted by Zhejiang Provincial Highway Administration, Quzhou Municipal Highway Administration, Zhejiang Provincial Institute of Transportation Planning and Zhejiang Feihong Traffic Facilities Co. Ltd. The barrier have passed real-vehicle crash test with medium-size bus, and the maximum dynamic deformation value of the barrier is 2017 mm.

C.2 General Structural Design Sample of corrugated beam barrier

C.2.1 General Structural Design Sample of Level 1 (C) corrugated beam barrier(Figure C.2.1).

C.2.2 General Structural Design Sample of Level 2 (B) corrugated beam barrier(Figure C.2.2).

C.2.3 General Structural Design Sample of Level 3 (A) corrugated beam barrier(Figure C.2.3).

C.2.4 General Structural Design Sample of Level 4 (SB) corrugated beam barrier(Figure C.2.4).

C.2.5 General Structural Design Sample of Level 5 (SA) corrugated beam barrier(Figure C.2.5).

C.2.6 General Structural Design Sample of Level 6 (SS) corrugated beam barrier(Figure C.2.6).

C.2.7 General Structural Design Sample of Level 7 (HB) corrugated beam barrier(Figure C.2.7).

C.2.8 General Structural Design Sample of Level 3 (Am) combined corrugated beam barrier(Figure C.2.8).

C.2.9 General Structural Design Sample of Level 4 (SBm) combined corrugated beam barrier(Figure C.2.9).

C.2.10 General Structural Design Sample of Level 5 (SAm) corrugated beam barrier(Figure C.2.10).

C.2.11 General Structural Design Sample of Level 6 (SSm) corrugated beam barrier(Figure C.2.11).

C.2.12 General Structural Design Sample of Level 7 (HBm) corrugated beam barrier(Figure C.2.12).

C.2.13 Structure Sample of Outstretch-type Ends of the Starting Section of Barrier(Figure C.2.13).

C.2.14 Structure Sample of the Ends of Separate-Type Meidan Barrier(Figure C.2.14).

C.2.15 Structure sample of triangle area barrier(Figure C.2.15).

C.2.16 Structure sample of barrier ends at tunnel entrance(Figure C.2.16).

C.2.17 Structure sample of concrete bridge barrier and corrugated beam barrier subgrade barrier at transition section(Figure C.2.17).

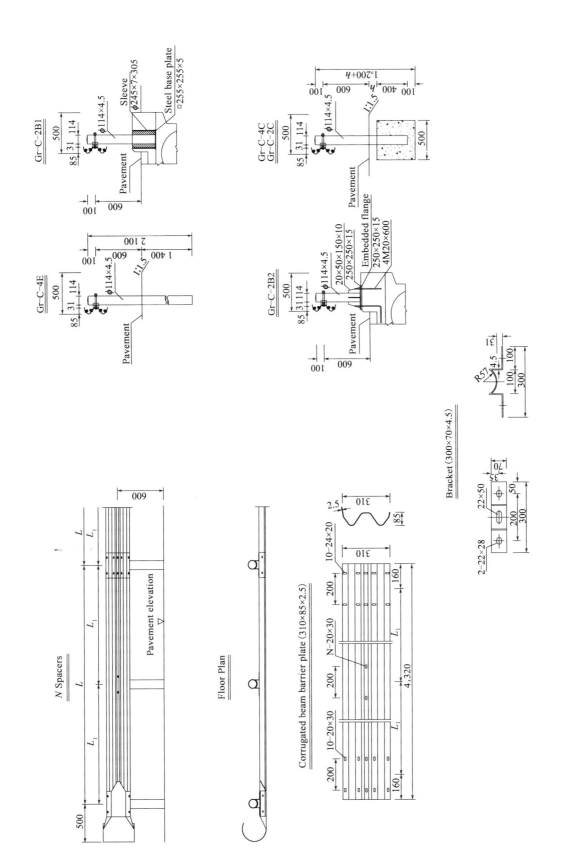

Figure C.2.1

Level 1(C) barrier Parameters and scope of application table

Code	L (mm)	L_1 (mm)	N	Scope of application	Note
Gr-C-4E	4,000	—	—	Roadside earth-work Normal section	(1)It is suggested for the road on side of this section of the barrier to by 25 cm, similarly hereinafter; (2)If the kerb stone and the barrier surface can not be flat, the height of the barrier should also increase the height of the kerb stone, similarly hereinafter
Gr-C-2E	2,000	1,000	2	Small radius section of roadside earth work	—
Gr-C-2B1	2,000	1,000	2	Roadside channel bridge, culver	Foudation treatment; reserved sleeves
Gr-C-2B2	2,000	1,000	2	Roadside channel, bridge, culvert	Foudation treatment; reserved sleeves
Gr-C-4C	4,000	—	—	Roadside sthone, normal section of retaining wall	(1)Retaining wall section, the foundation shall be specifically designed according to varied forms; (2)The value of h shall be determined as needed
Gr-C-2C	2,000	1,000	2	Roadside kerb stone work, small radius section of retaining wall	—

Barrier deformation and vehicle dynamic displacement index evaluation result of real-vehicle crash test

Test Item	Vehicle Model	Test Result
Maximum Lateral Dynamic Displacement Value:W, m	Minibus	0.23
	Medium Bus	0.25
	Medium Truck	0.56
Maximum Vehicle Dynamic Displacement Equivalent Value:VI_n, m	Medium Bus	0.19
	Medium Truck	0.91

Figure C.2.1 General structural design sample of Level 1(C) corrugated beam barrier

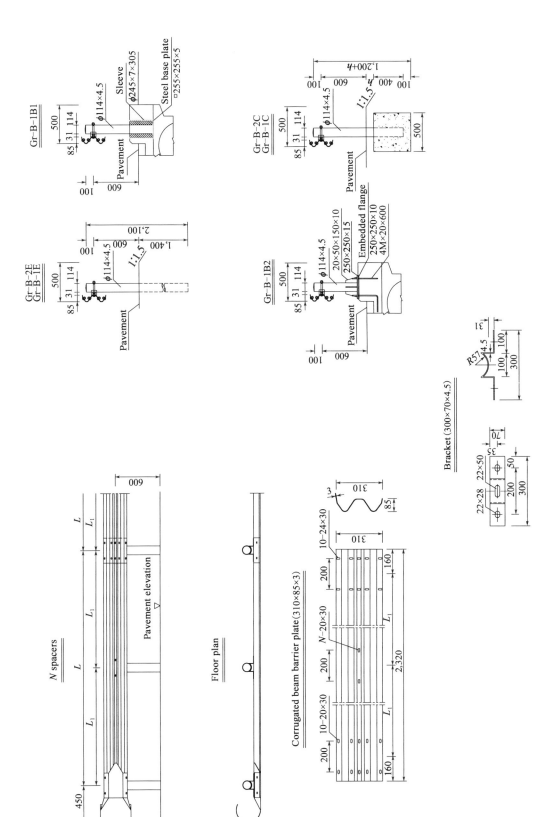

Figure C.2.2

B-Class barrier parameters and scope of applidcation table

Code	L (mm)	L_1 (mm)	N	Scope of application	Note
Gr-B-2E	2,000	—	—	Roadside earthwork Normal section	(1)It is suggested for the road on side of this section of the barrier to by 25 cm, similarly hereinafter; (2)If the kerb stone and the barrier surface can not be flat, the height of the barrier should also increase the height of the kerb stone, similarly hereinafter
Gr-B-1E	2,000	1,000	2	Small radius section of roadside earthwork	—
Gr-B-1B1	2,000	1,000	2	Roadside channel bridge, culver	Foudation treatment; reserved sleeves
Gr-B-1B2	2,000	1,000	2	Roadside channel, bridge, culvert	Foudation treatment; reserved sleeves
Gr-B-2C	2,000	—	—	Roadside sthone, normal section of retaining wall	(1)Retaining wall section, the foundation shall be specifically designed according to varied forms; (2)The value of h shall be determined as needed
Gr-B-1C	2,000	1,000	2	Roadside kerb stone work, small radius section of retaining wall	—

Barrier real-vehicle crash test deformation and vehicle dynamic displacement index evaluation result

Test Item	Vehicle Model	Test Result
Maximum Lateral Dynamic Displacement Value: W, m	Minibus	0.79
	Medium Bus	0.64
	Medium Truck	—
Maximum Vehicle Dynamic Displacement Equivalent Value: VI_n, m	Medium Bus	1.15
	Medium Truck	—

Figure C.2.2　General structural design sample of Level 2 (B) corrugated beam barrier（Unit:mm）

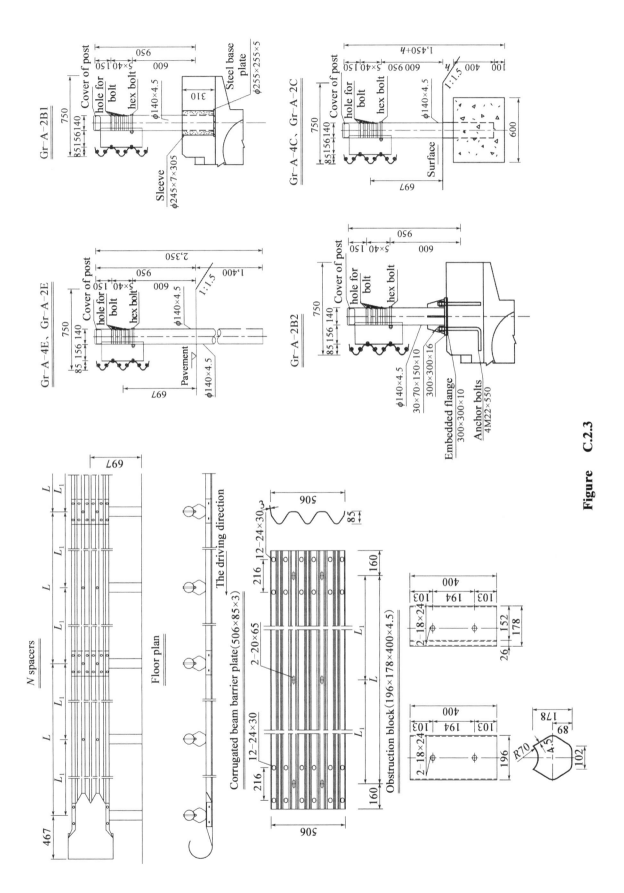

Figure C.2.3

A-Class barrier parameters and scope of application table

Code	L (mm)	L_1 (mm)	N (Quantity)	Scope of application	Remarks
Gr-A-4E	4,000	—	—	Road with common roadside earthwork	If the curb and the barrier surface cannot be flush, the height of the barrier should also increase the height of the curb. The same principle shall be applied in the below
Gr-A-2E	4,000	2,000	1	Small radius road section with roadside earthwork	—
Gr-A-2B1	4,000	2,000	1	Roadside bridges, passages, and clear culverts	Basic treatment: embedded sleeve
Gr-A-2B2	4,000	2,000	1	Roadside bridges, passages, and clear culverts	Basic treatment: pre-embedded anchor bolts
Gr-A-4C	4,000	—	—	Road with common roadside stonework and retaining walls	(1) For the road section of the retaining wall, the foundation should be specially designed according to its different types. The same principle shall be applied in the below; (2) The value of h is determined as needed. The same principle shall be applied in the below
Gr-A-2C	4,000	2,000	1	Small radius road section with common roadside stonework and retaining walls	—

Barrier real-vehicle crash test deformation and vehicle dynamic displacement index evaluation result

Test Item	Vehicle Model	Test Result
Maximum Lateral Dynamic Displacement Value: W, m	Minibus	1.10
	Medium Bus	1.15
	Medium Truck	1.35
Maximum Vehicle Dynamic Displacement Equivalent Value: VI_n, m	Medium Bus	1.55
	Medium Truck	2.73

Note: Where the barrier is located at downstream end, it can be installed in line with the barrier of the standard section, but its ends shall be reinforced in the way shown in C.2.13 in Appendix C.

a)

Figure C.2.3

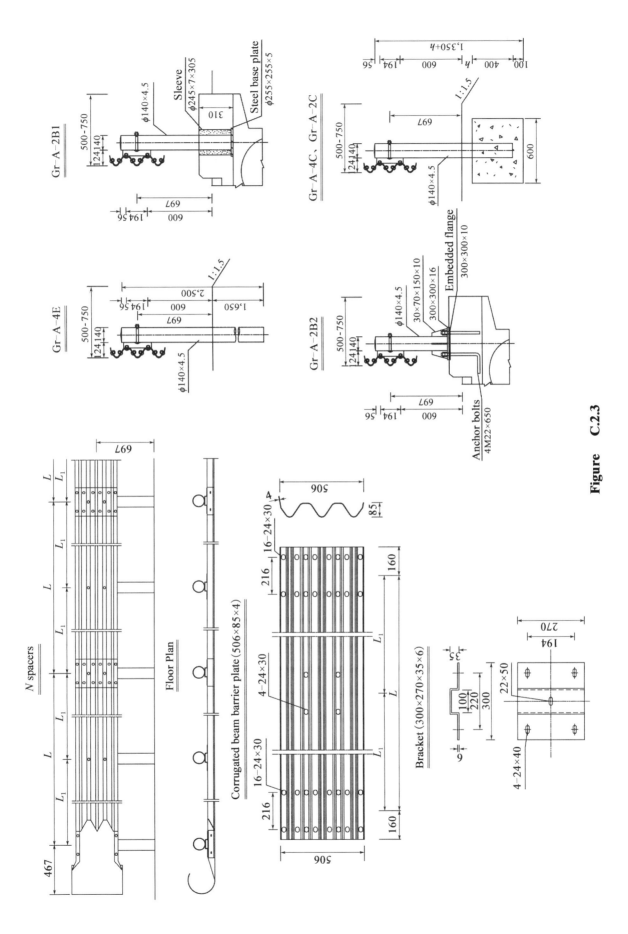

Figure C.2.3

A-Class barrier parameters and scope of application table

Code	L (mm)	L_1 (mm)	N (Quantity)	Scope of application	Remarks
Gr-A-4E	4,000	—	—	Road with common roadside earthwork	If the curb and the barrier surface cannot be flush, the height of the barrier should also increase the height of the curb. The same principle shall be applied in the below
Gr-A-2E	4,000	2,000	1	Small radius road section with roadside earthwork	—
Gr-A-2B1	4,000	2,000	1	Roadside bridges, passages, and clear culverts	Basic treatment: embedded sleeve
Gr-A-2B2	4,000	2,000	1	Roadside bridges, passages, and clear culverts	Basic treatment: pre-embedded anchor bolts
Gr-A-4C	4,000	—	—	Road with common roadside stonework and retaining walls	(1) For the road section of the retaining wall, the foundation should be specially designed according to its different types. The same principle shall be applied in the below; (2) The value of h is determined as needed. The same principle shall be applied in the below
Gr-A-2C	4,000	2,000	1	Small radius road section with common roadside stonework and retaining walls	—

Barrier real-vehicle crash test deformation and vehicle dynamic displacement index evaluation result

Test item	Vehicle model	Test result
Maximum lateral dynamic displacement value: W, m	Minibus	0.78
	Medium bus	1.33
	Medium truck	1.23
Maximum Vehicle dynamic displacement equivalent value: VI_n, m	Medium bus	1.53
	Medium truck	2.14

Note: This barrier can applied to soil shoulder with the width ranging from 50 cm to 75 cm, but the barrier shall be coincided with the left edge line of the soil shoulder or the left side elevation of the highway kerb.

b)

Figure C.2.3 General structural sample of Level 3 (A) corrugated beam barrier (Unit:mm)

Background:

This article provides two structure samples of Third (A)-class corrugated beam barrier barrier, among which sample a) is from the results of the 2014 annual scientific research project A-Class corrugated beam barrier Barrier Protection Performance Analysis and New Product Research and Development of Guangdong Provincial Department of Transportation, undertaken by Guangdong Highway and Transportation Society, Guangdong Nanyue Transportation Investment & Construction Co. Ltd, Beijing Zhongluan Traffic Technological Co. Ltd and Highway Research Institute of Ministry of Transportation, and the sample has been further optimized and adjusted.

Sample b) is based on the achievements of the Technical Research on Anti-crash Enhancement of Highway corrugated beam barrier Barrier from Ministry of Transportation in 2013, which was undertaken by Highway Research Institute of Ministry of Transportation and Fujian motorway Co Ltd., and the sample has been further optimized and adjusted. Both samples can be adopted according to the width of the soil shoulder, the deformation of the barrier, and the material stock, etc.

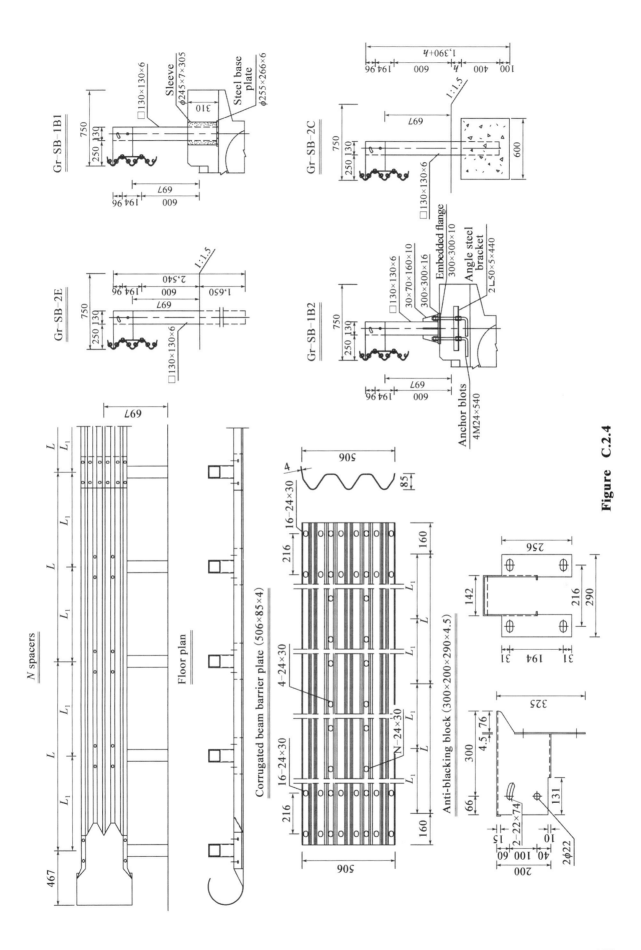

Figure C.2.4

SB-Class barrier parameters and scope of application table

Code	L (mm)	L_1 (mm)	N (Quantity)	Scope of application	Remarks
Gr-SB-2E	2,000	—	—	Road with roadside earthwork	If the curb and the barrier surface cannot be flush, the height of the barrier should also increase the height of the curb. The same principle shall be applied in the below
Gr-SB-1B1	2,000	1,000	8	Roadside bridges, passages, and clear culverts	Basic treatment: embedded sleeve
Gr-SB-1B2	2,000	1,000	8	Roadside bridges, passages, and clear culverts	Basic treatment: pre-embedded anchor bolts
Gr-SB-2C	2,000	—	—	Road with roadside stonework and retaining walls	(1) For the road section of the retaining wall, the foundation should be specially designed according to its different types. The same principle shall be applied in the below; (2) The value of h is determined as needed. The same principle shall be applied in the below

Barrier real-vehicle crash test deformation and vehicle dynamic displacement index evaluation result

Test item	Vehicle model	Test result
Maximum lateral dynamic displacement value: W, m	Minibus	0.85
	Medium bus	1.34
	Medium truck	—
Maximum vehicle dynamic displacement equivalent value: VI_n, m	Medium bus	2.27
	Medium truck	—

Figure C.2.4　General Structural Design Sample of Level 4 (SB) corrugated beam barrier (Unit:m)

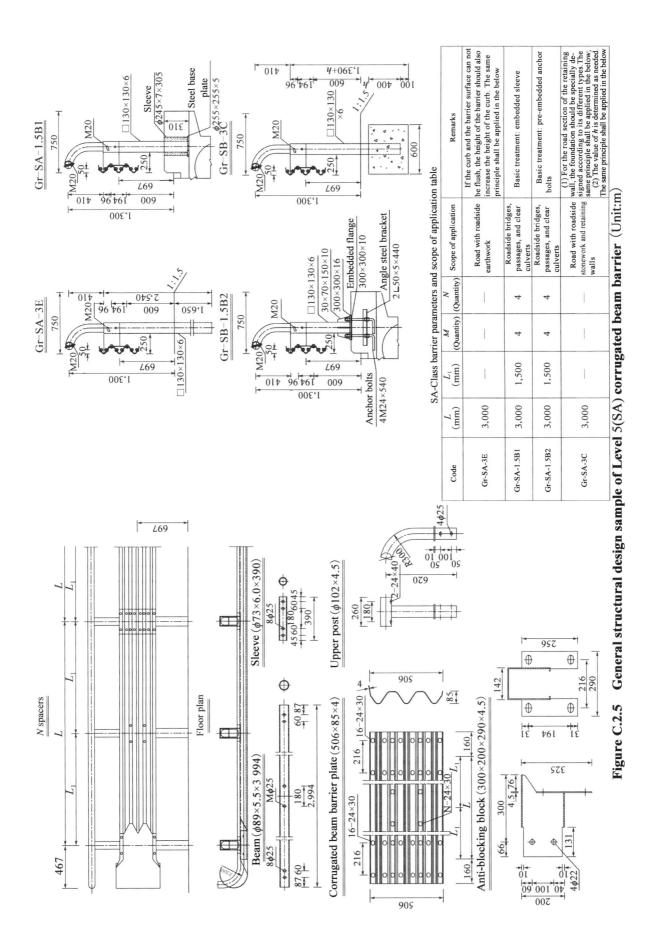

Figure C.2.5 General structural design sample of Level 5(SA) corrugated beam barrier (Unit:m)

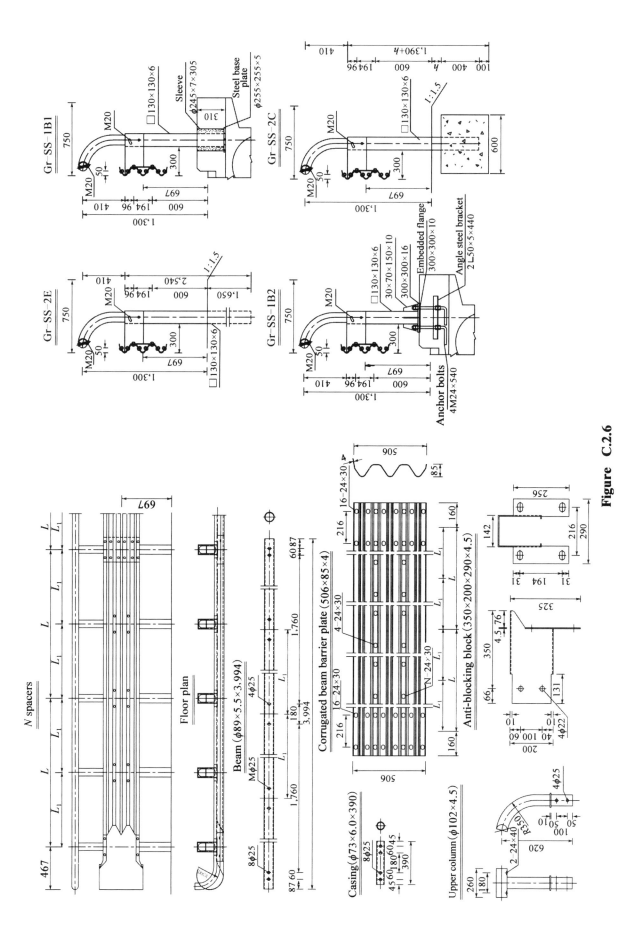

Figure C.2.6

SS-Class barrier parameters and scope of application table

Code	L (mm)	L_1 (mm)	M (Quantity)	N (Quantity)	Scope of application	Remarks
Gr-SS-2E	2,000	—	—	—	Rroad with roadside earthwork	If the curb and the barrier surface cannot be flush, the height of the barrier should also increase the height of the curb. The same principle shall be applied in the below
Gr-SS-1B1	2,000	1,000	8	8	Roadside bridges, passages, and clear culverts	Basic treatment: embedded sleeve
Gr-SS-1B2	2,000	1,000	8	8	Roadside bridges, passages, and clear culverts	Basic treatment: pre-embedded anchor bolts
Gr-SS-2C	2,000	—	—	—	Road with roadside stonework and retaining walls	(1) For the road section of the retaining wall, the foundation should be specially designed according to its different types. The same principle shall be applied in the below; (2) The value of h is determined as needed. The same principle shall be applied in the below

Barrier real-vehicle crash test deformation and vehicle dynamic displacement index evaluation result

Test item	Vehicle model	Test result
Maximum lateral dynamic displacement value: W, m	Minibus	0.74
	Medium Bus	1.76
	Medium Truck	1.61
Maximum vehicle dynamic displacement equivalent value: VI_n, m	Medium Bus	2.24
	Medium Truck	2.36

Figure C.2.6　General structural design sample of Level 6 (SS) corrugated beam barrier (Unit:m)

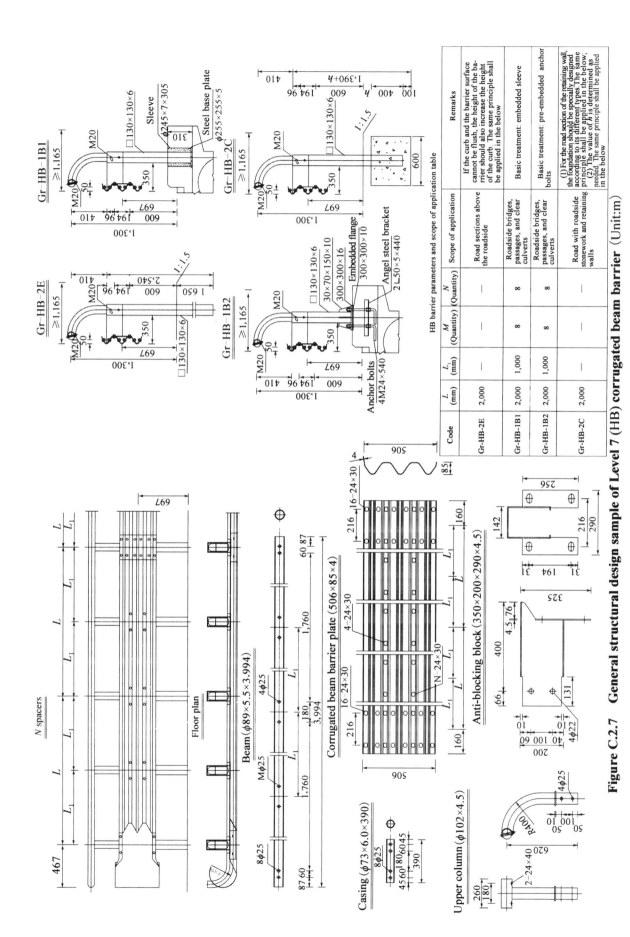

Figure C.2.7 General structural design sample of Level 7 (HB) corrugated beam barrier (Unit:m)

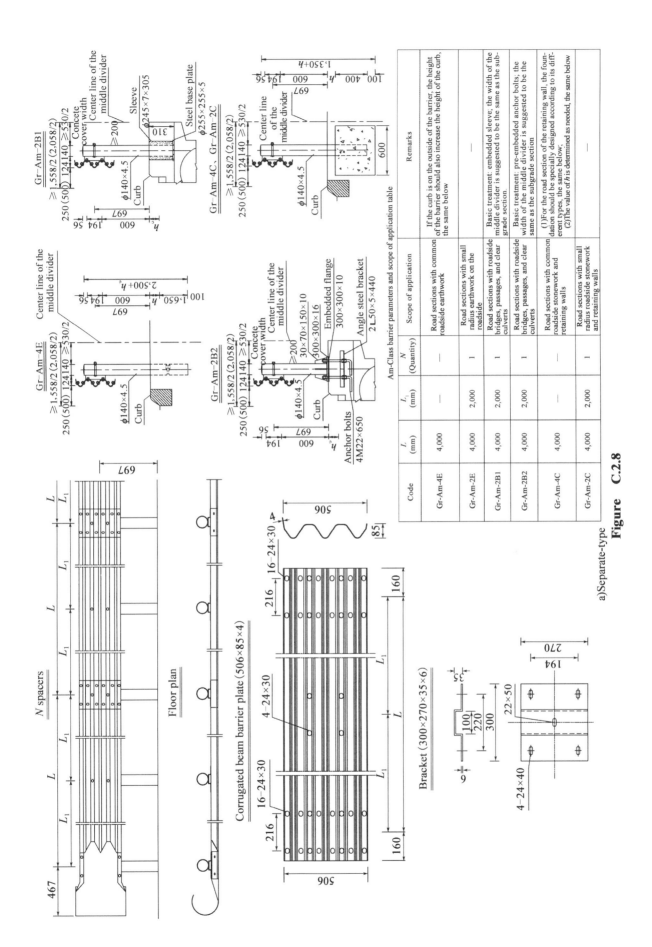

Figure C.2.8 a) Separate-type

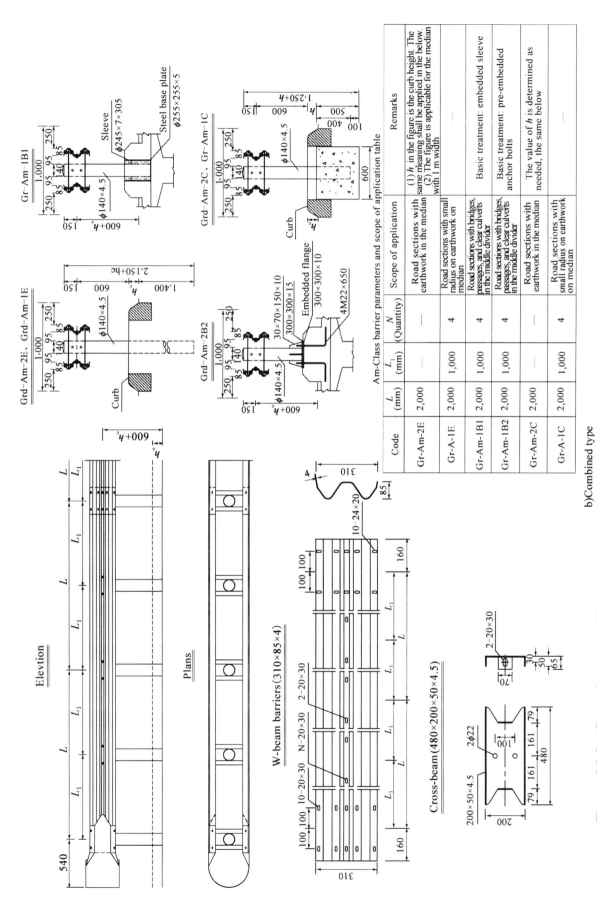

Figure C.2.8 General structural design sample of Level 3 (Am) combined type corrugated beam barrier (Unit:m)

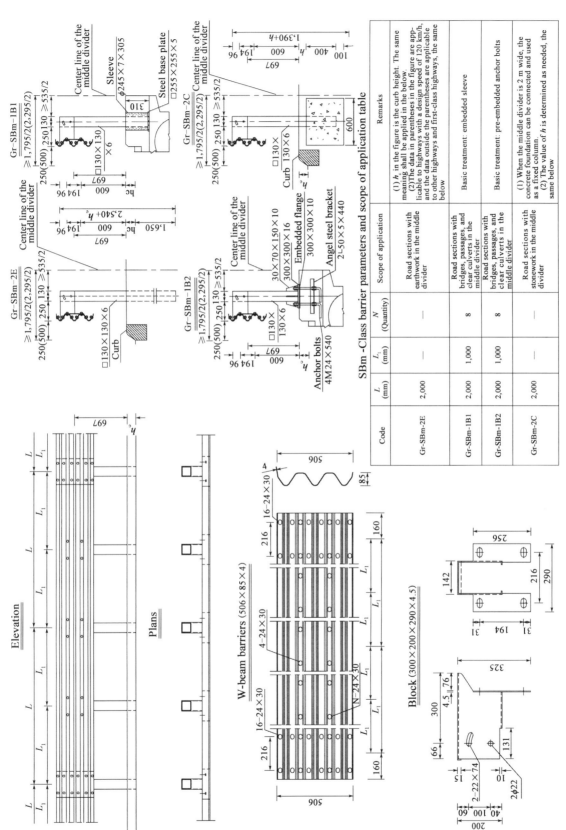

Figure C.2.9 General structural design sample of Level 4 (SBm) combined-type corrugated beam barrier(Unit: mm)

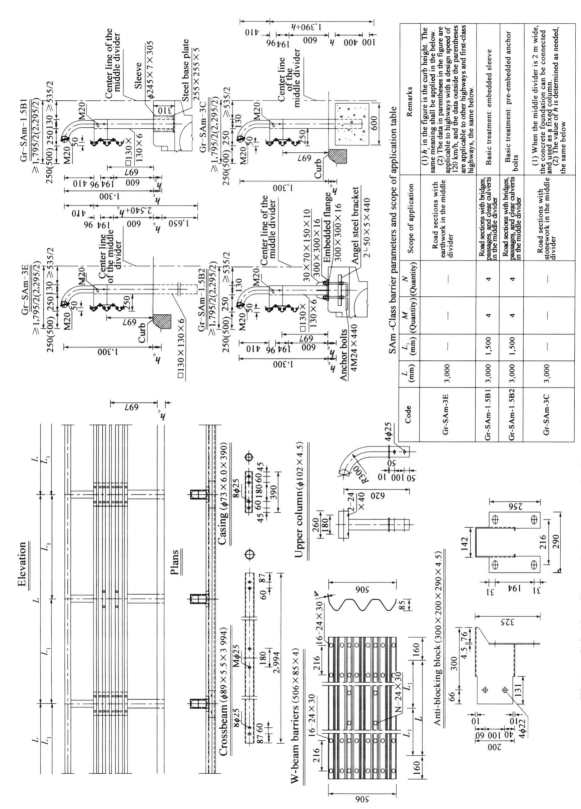

Figure C.2.10　General structural design sample of Level 5 (SAm) corrugated beam barrier (Unit:m)

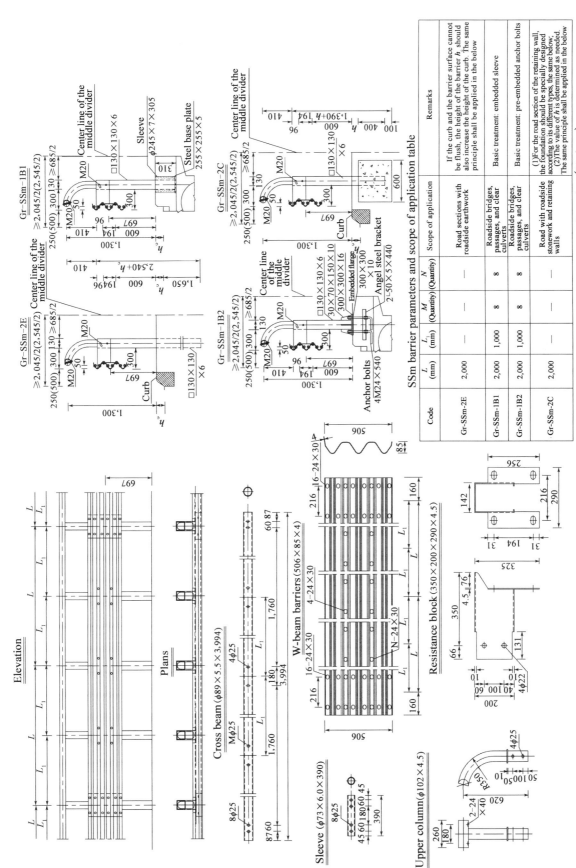

Figure C.2.11 General structural design sample of Level 6 (SSm) corrugated beam barrier (Unit:m)

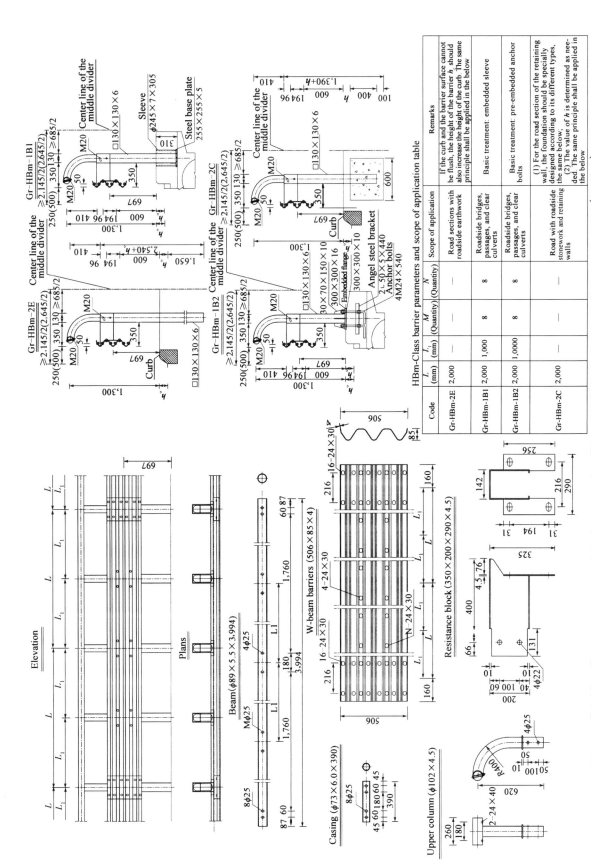

Figure C.2.12 General structural design sample of Level 7 (HBm) corrugated beam barrier (Unit:m)

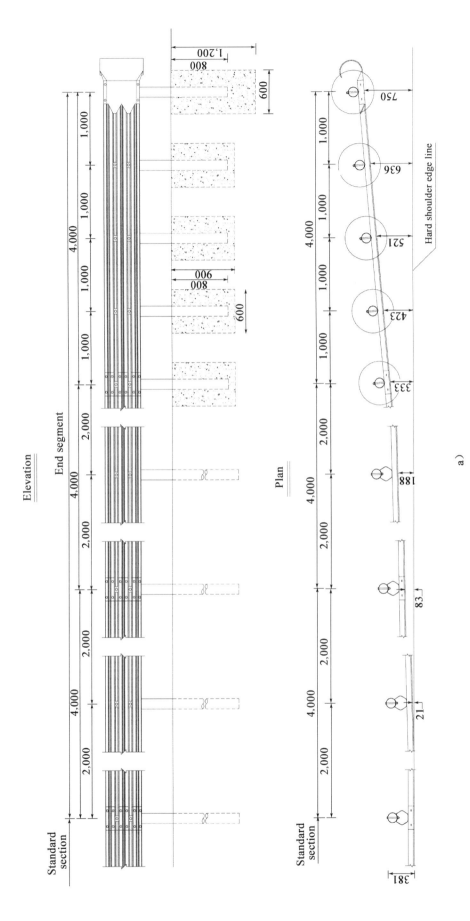

Figure C.2.13

Note: 1. In this pichture, an example of A class a wave beam barrier for the 750 mm section of the earth's shoulder is taken as an example to illustrate the method of handling the end of the barier.
2. This figure applies to the end processing method at the beginning of the barrier section of the filling section. At the end of the barrier located at the junction of the fill, the transition section of the barrier should extend to the cutting edge according to the abduction slope specified in the Table 6.2.2-2, and the length of the cut slope should not be less than 2-3 m.

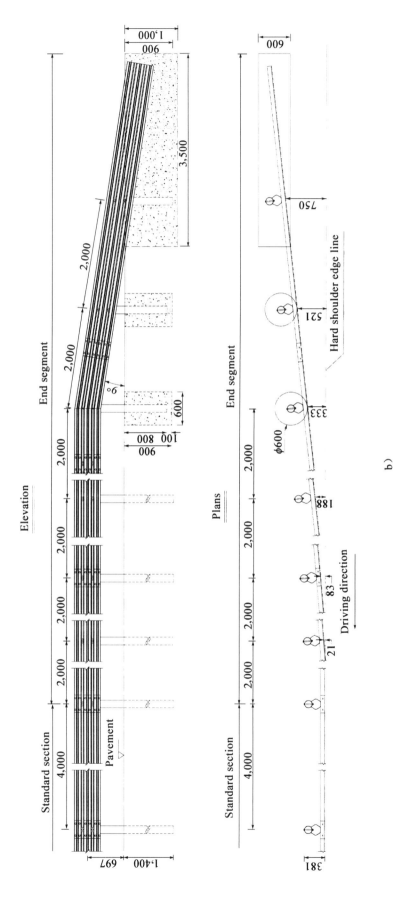

b)

Figure C.2.13

Note: 1. In this picture, an example of A class a wave beam barrier for the 750 mm section of earth's shoulder is taken as an example to illustrate the method of handling the end of barrier.
2. This figure applies to the end processing method at the beginning of the barrier section of the filling section.

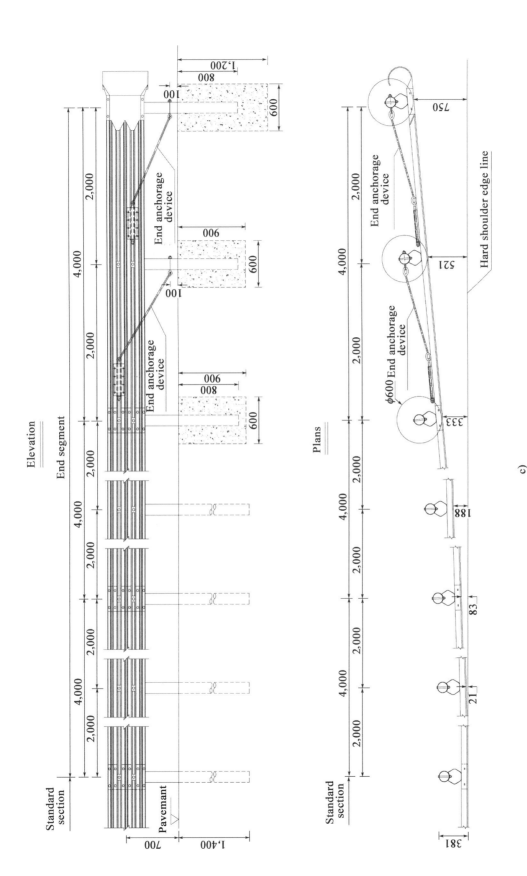

Note: 1. In this picture, an example of A class a wave beam barrier for the 750 mm section of earth's shoulder is taken as an example to illustrate the method of handling the end of barrier.
2. This figure applies to the end processing method at the beginning of the barrier section of the filling section.

Figure C.2.13　Structure sample of out stretch-type ends of the starting section of the barrier (Unit:mm)

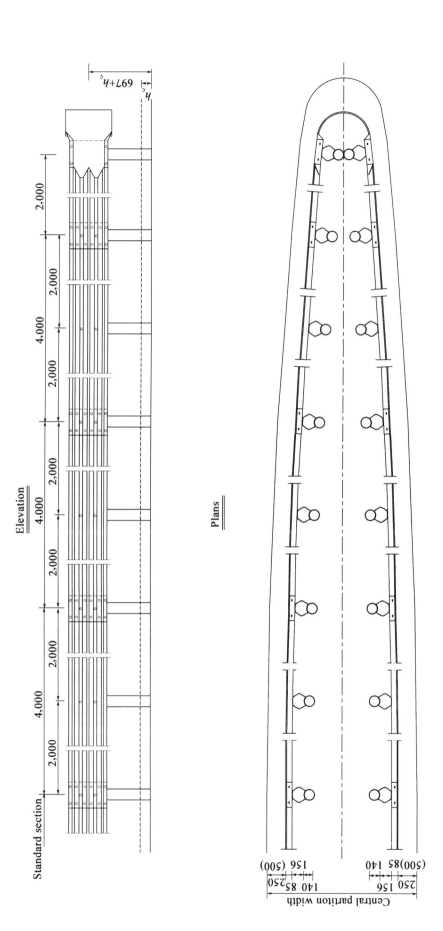

Figure C.2.14 Structure sample of the ends of separate-type median barrier (Unit:m)

Note: 1. This figure uses a Am-class separate barrier as an example to illustrate the method of handing the end of the middle divider barrier.
2. In this picture, h_c is the height of the road edge stone. The height of the barrier should be increased by h_c when the edge stone is protruded.
3. The end of the middle divider battier should be smoothly connected with the open barrier and become a whole.

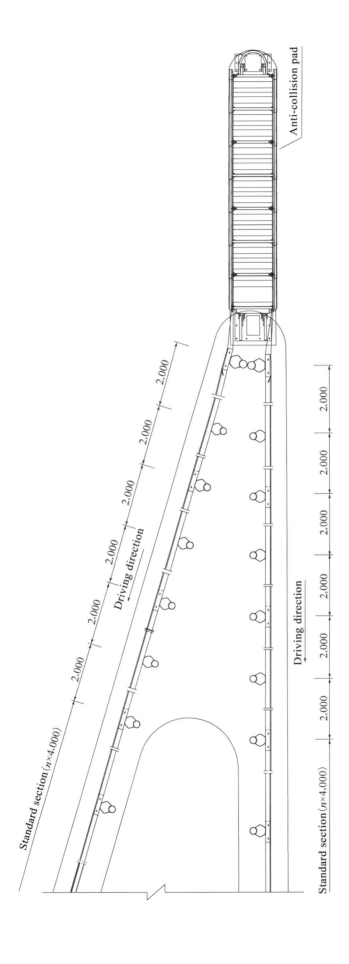

Figure C.2.15 Structure sample of triangle area barrier (Unit:m)

Note: This diagram is only applicable to the placement of A-class corrugated beam barrier barriers in triangle area.

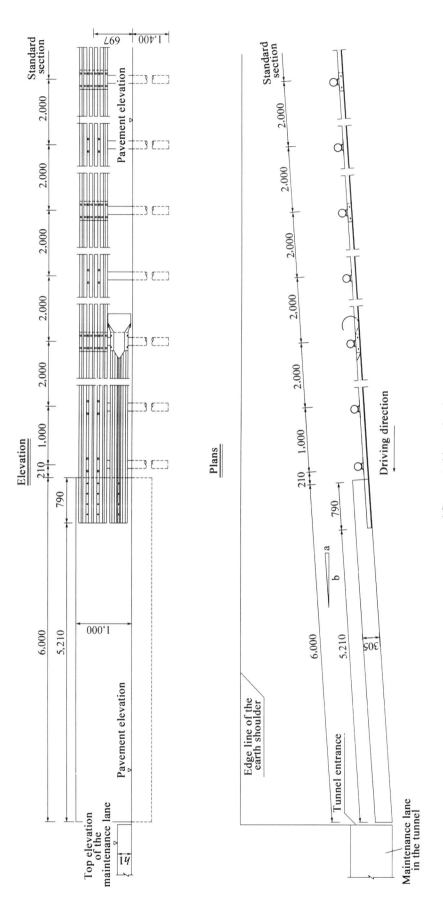

a) Corrugated beam barrier

Note: 1. This figure uses a Am-class separate barrier as an example to illustrate the method of handing the end of the middle divider barrier. For other grades of barriers, the specifications of the transition wing walls should be changed accordingly, and the basic treatment should be set according to the relevant provisions of this group.
2. The gradient rate (a:b) in the figure should not exceed the specified value in Table 6.2.2-2 of the *Guidelines*.
3. h_1 in the figure is the height of the Maintenance lane in the tunnel.
4. The width of the telescopic bracket at the end of the transition wing wall and the tunnel opening in the figure should comply with the relevant regulations.

Figue C.2.16

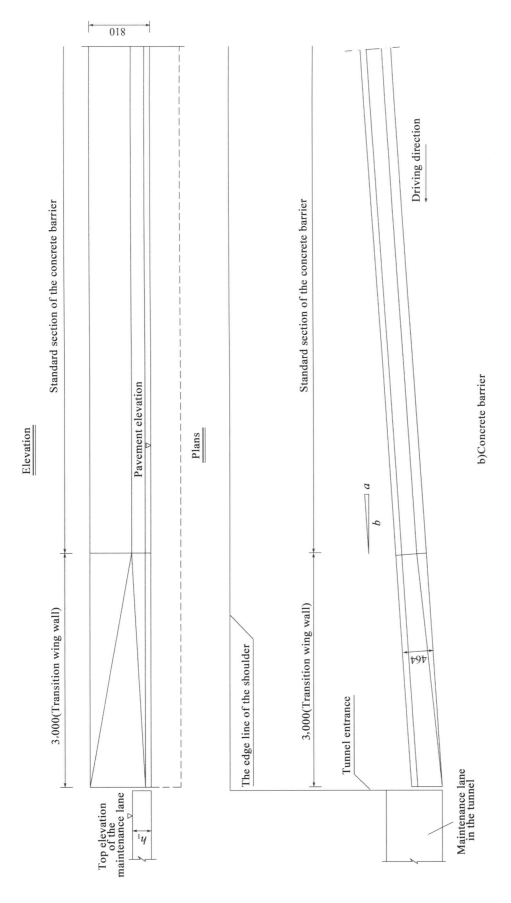

Figure C.2.16 Structure sample of barrier ends at tunnel entrance (Unit:mm)

Note: 1. This figure uses a Am-class separate barrier as an example to illustrate the method of handing the end of the middle divider barrier. For other grades of barriers, the specifications of the transition wing walls should be changed accordingly, and the basic treatment should be set according to the relevant provisions of this group.
2. The gradient rate (a:b) in the figure should not exceed the specified value in Table 6.2.2-2 of the *Guidelines*.
3. h_1 in the figure is the height of the Maintenance lane in the tunnel.
4. The width of the telescopic bracket at the end of the transition wing wall and the tunnel opening in the figure should comply with the relevant regulations.

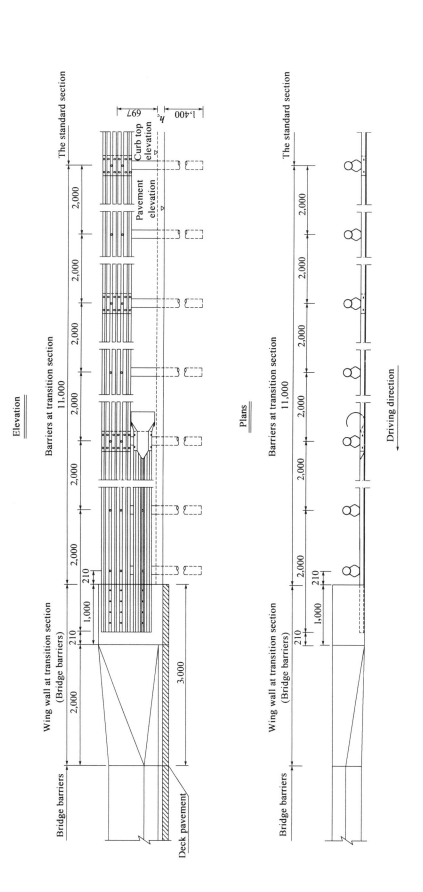

a) BT-1

Figure C.2.17

Note: 1. This diagram is applicable to the transition treatment of F-type concrete barrier on bridges and A-class corrugated beam barrier on the subgrade.
2. In the diagram, h_c stands for the height of the highway edge stone. The height of the barrier shall be increased by h_c where edge stone protrudes out of the barrier.

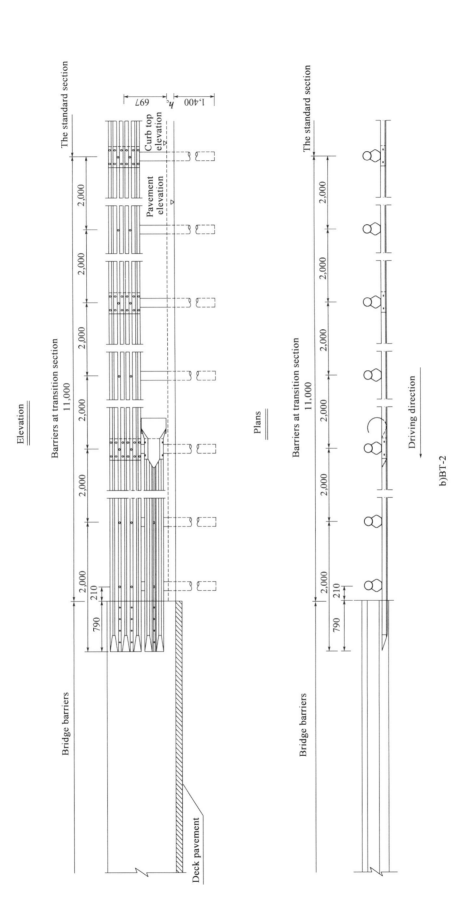

Note: 1. This diagram is applicable to the transition treatment of the single-slope concrete barrier on bridges and A-class corrugated beam barrier barrier on subgrade.
2. In the diagram, h_c is the height of the highway edge stone. The height of barrier shall be increased by h_c where edge stone protrudes out of the barrier.

Figure C.2.17 Structure sample of concrete bridge barrier and corrugated beam barrier subgrade barrier at transition section (Unit:mm)

C.3 General structure samples of some types of concrete Barrier

C.3.1 C3 General structure samples of A (C) class concrete barrier (Figure C.3.1).

C.3.2 C3 General structure samples of B (B) class concrete barrier (Figure C.3.2).

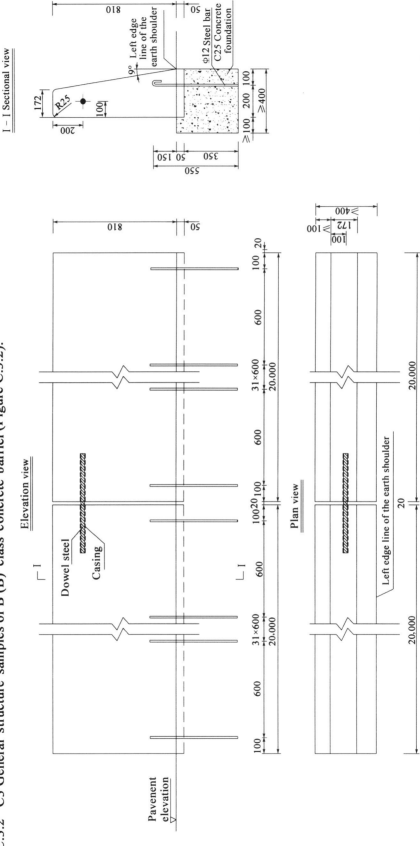

Figure C.3.1 General structure samples of A (C) class concrete barrier (reinforced concrete foundation) (Unit: mm)

Note: 1. This guardrail can be applied to road shoulder retaining wall sections greater than or equal to 400 mm.
2. The concrete foundation should be poured together with the road shoulder retaining wall. The φ12 steel bar can be pre-buried in the foundation, or when the concrete strength is not less than 80% of the standard strength, drill holes in the concrete foundation and use epoxy resin glue to implant,During the reinforcement layout and concrete pouring of the guardrail, the rebar planting process must meet the specification requirements.

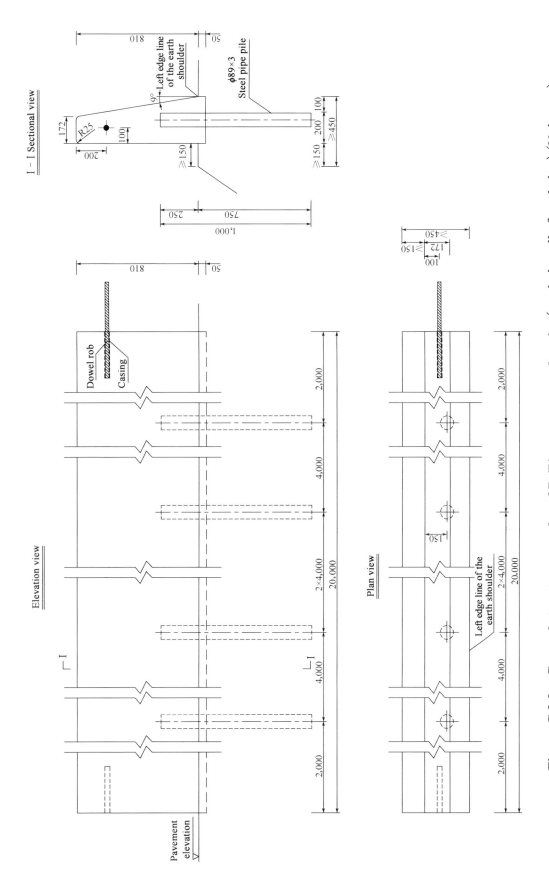

Figure C.3.2　General structure samples of B (B) cass concrete barrier (steel pipe pile foundation) (Unit: mm)

Note: 1. This barrier is applied for the roadway with 500 mm width verge.
2. Spacing of the steel poles of the concrete barriers are 4 m, which should be compacted into soil with accurate positions.

C.4 Variation method

Appendix C.1 and C.2 have determined the shape, size and material of crossbeams, cables, posts, obstruction blocks, and foundations required by cable barriers and corrugated beam barrier barriers to maintain its performance. Where these requirements cannot be satisfied for certain reasons, partial structure can be changed according to following methods through scientific analysis and reasonable justification of the on-site conditions, the types of vehicle to be protected and the structure of the barrier.

Background:

In many cases, the general structure examples provided in Appendix C.1 and C.2 cannot be completely adopted and need to be changed appropriately due to the influence of the factor such as the shoulder width, the grade of side slope, the matrix material and soil compactness. Appendix C.4 consults relevant regulations of Commentary of Standard Diagram of Vehicle fences (January 2008) in Japan for reference in solving practical problems.

C.4.1 Changes in shape and specifications can be made in accordance with the following provisions:

1 Where a change in the spacing between posts occurs due to the limitation of the field conditions, the distance between the embedded upright posts can be narrowed to the value stated in the Table C.4.1-1. The distance cannot be narrowed where installed installation concrete foundation.

Table C.4.1-1 The minimum separation distance between the cable barriers and the corrugated beam barrier barriers (Drive post)

Form	Position	Code	Minimum post spacing (m)
Cable barrier	Road side	Gc-C-6E, Gc-B-6E, Gc-A-6E	3.0
Corrugated beam barrier	Road side	Gr-C-4E, Gr-A-4E, Gr-SB-2E, Gr-SA-3E, Gr-SS-2E, Gr-HB-2E	1.0
	Median (Separate)	Gr-Bm-2E, Gr-SBm-2E, Gr-SAm-3E, Gr-SSm-2E, Gr-HBm-2E	
		Gr-Am-4E	2.0

2 Where the protruding amount of obstruction block needs to be changed due to the limitation of the field conditions, it shall be limited within the range of ±50% of the values shown in each specifications.

C.4.2 The varieties in supporting conditions can refer to following provisions:

1 The drive upright post

1) The post of the corrugated beam barrier and the middle post of the cable barrier

If the installed installation of the post cannot meet the supporting conditions required in general structure samples due to the site conditions, the backside soil weight of one post in the sample can be calculated and the sum of the weight of the soil and/or the weight of the concrete foundation can reach or exceed the backside soil weight of one post in the structure sample. The main calculation and evaluation process is as follows:

①The examination of the condition of installation and the condition of the foundation

Where the post is installed in the soil foundation, the strength of the post is determined by supporting conditions such as the width of the grade top of the soil foundation outside the post, the slope of the grade, the depth of the embedded post, and the foundation material. The above parameters are shown in the general structural example. Where the site conditions are different from the above parameters, the placement conditions and foundation conditions shall be checked, and the foundation with small bearing capacity shall be improved.

②Calculation of the back soil weight of post

According to the real-vehicle crash test, the vehicle crash load on the barrier will be borne by the counteraction of backside soil of the post. Therefore the supporting force of the post is closely related to the volume and density of the backside soil. The weight of the backside of a post can be calculated according to Figure C.4.2-1, and the supporting force of post can be evaluated accordingly. The weight of the backside soil of a post of a certain protection level in the general structural sample is shown in Table C.4.2-1.

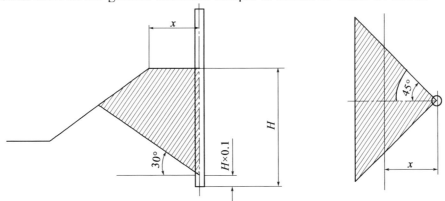

Figure C.4.2-1 The calculation range of the backside soil of one post of a certain protection level

Note: 1. The weight of the backside soil (T) = The volume of the backside soil(m^3) × The density of soil(t/m^3)
2. Where calculating the weight of the backside Soil of the median, the backside of the post can be regarded as a flat slope.

Table C.4.2-1 The backside soil weight of a post of a certain protection level

Code	The backside soil weight of a post(t)	Notes	
		post specifications (mm)	Standard burial depth (m)
Gc-A-6E	2.51	φ140 × 4.5	1.65
Gr-A-4E	2.34		1.65/1.40
Gc-B-6E Gr-B-2E	1.01	φ114 × 4.5	1.65/1.40
Gc-C-6E Gr-C-4E	0.82		1.40
Gr-HB-2E Gr-SS-2E	2.86	□130 × 130 × 6	1.65
Gr-SA-3E Gr-SB-2E	2.19		

③Evaluation of the weight of the backside soil of a post

The sufficiency of the supporting force of post shall be determined by comparing whether the weight of the backside soil of one post is greater or equal to that in Table C.4.2-1. If the calculated weight is smaller, the foundation shall be modified or the following schemes shall be adopted to ensure the weight of the necessary backside soil. If the distance of the grade top, grade slope, or burial depth is insufficient, the following schemes can be referred.

④The scheme based on independent concrete foundation

If the calculated weight is smaller, the insufficient quantity shall be determined first, then the shape and specifications of the concrete foundation shall be determined according to the top slope width of subgrade outside the post, slope of the side grade, the buried depth of the post, to supplement its weight.

⑤The scheme based on continuous concrete foundation

If the shape and specifications of the independent concrete foundation determined in ④ are not convenient for construction, or pipelines and other buried objects are in the soil foundation, and therefore the burial depth cannot be ensured, continuous concrete foundation can be taken into consideration.

⑥The scheme for shortening the spacing between posts

The scheme of shortening the spacing between posts can be adopted in accordance with the provisions of Table C.4.1-1 where an independent concrete foundation or a continuous foundation cannot be adopted due to the limitation of field conditions, the existence of buried objects or the shorter-than-required burial depth.

2) The end post of cable barriers

The shape and specifications of the concrete post foundation at the end of the cable barrier shall be determined on the presumption that can withstand the pretension force of the barrier and shall be determined, after calculating the overturning stability, sliding stability, and base stress. Where the shape and specifications cannot be guaranteed, the following calculation method can be employed to maintain the same or higher level of stability.

Design conditions: As is shown in Figure C.4.2-2 and Table C.4.2-2.

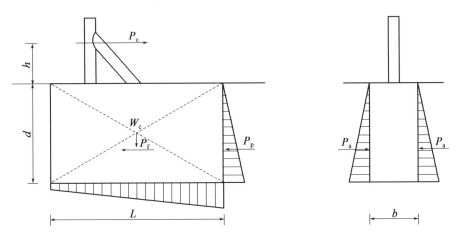

Figure C.4.2-2 Sample of concrete foundation of cable barrier end post

Table C.4.2-2 Design conditions for foundation of cable barrier end post

Protection level	Pre-tension (kN/each)	The number of cables	Load (kN)	Height of point of action (m)
C	9.8	3	30	0.60
B	12.5	4	50	0.65
A	22	5	110	0.70

①Shape and specifications of concrete foundation (height d × length L × width b); cable tension P_e (pre-tension × number of cables), height of point of action h.

②Torque of external force: $M_e = P_e \times (h + d)$

③The parameters related to foundation and concrete: the internal friction angle φ within the soil, the active earth pressure coefficient K_a, the passive earth pressure coefficient K_p, the friction coefficient of soil and concrete μ, the allowable stress of the soil $[\sigma]$, the soil density γ_s, the density of the concrete γ_c, the basic anti-sliding stability coefficient $s_f = 1.2$, the basic anti-overturning stability factor $s_o = 1.2$.

Stability calculation of foundation:

①Check of sliding stability of foundation:

Frictional resistance of the dead load:
$$P_w = \mu W_c = \mu \times d \times L \times b \times \gamma_c$$
Unilateral lateral active earth pressure:
$$P_a = K_a \times \gamma_s \times d^2 \times L/2$$
Frictional resistance of the unilateral lateral active earth pressure:
$$P_f = \mu \times P_a = \mu \times K_a \times \gamma_s \times d^2 \times L/2$$
Front passive earth pressure:
$$P_p = K_p \times \gamma_s \times b \times d^2/2$$
Resistance relative to sliding:
$$P_\gamma = P_w + 2P_f + P_p$$
Stability evaluation relative to sliding:
$$s_f \times P_e = 1.2 P_e < P_\gamma$$

②Check of the overturning stability of foundation

The distance from the foundation to the edge with the largest pressure side: $y = L/2$;
Resultant force eccentricity external forces:
$$e_0 = (M_e - M_p - 2M_f)/W_c$$

Where:
M_p—Moment caused by passive earth pressure in front, $M_p = P_p \times d/3$;
M_f—Moment caused by unilateral lateral active earth pressure, $M_f = P_f \times d/3$.
Anti-overturning stability factor:
$$K_0 = y/e_0 < s_o$$

③Foundation stress checking: $M = M_e - M_p - 2M_f$
$$\sigma = W_c/(L \times b) + 6M/(L^2 \times b)$$

Foundation stress checking results: $\sigma < [\sigma]$

2 Where installed in concrete foundation

The cable barrier and W beam barrier foundation installed on the concrete structures by the sleeve method shall be reinforced with front and rear reinforcing bars, the specifications of which are shown in Table C. 4. 2-3 and Table C. 4. 2-4 and Figure C. 4. 2-3. If the supporting conditions need to be changed due to site conditions and the structure of the constructions, etc. , the foundation fixing method can be determined according to the following method to achieve the same or higher supporting conditions.

Table C. 4.2-3　The shape of reinforcing bars of various protection level (Burial depth: 400 mm)

Code	Gr-SB-1B1 Gr-SA-1.5B1 Gr-SS-1B1 Gr-HB-1B1	Gc-A-4B1 Gr-A-2B1	Gc-C-4B1 Gc-B-4B1 Gr-C-2B1 Gr-B-1B1
a	$\phi130 \times 130 \times 6$	$\phi140 \times 4.5$	$\phi114 \times 4.5$
b	2	2	2
c	D22	D13	D13
d	1	1	1
e	D13	D13	D13
f	$\phi220$	$\phi220$	$\phi180$
g			

Table C. 4.2-4　The shape of reinforcing bar of various specifications (Burial depth: 300 mm)

Code	Gr-SB-1B1 Gr-SA-1.5B1 Gr-SS-1B1 Gr-HB-1B1	Gc-A-4B1 Gr-A-2B1	Gc-C-4B1 Gc-B-4B1 Gr-C-2B1 Gr-B-1B1
a	$\phi130 \times 130 \times 6$	$\phi140 \times 4.5$	$\phi114 \times 4.5$
b	2	2	2
c	D25	D22	D16
d	1	1	1
e	D25	D22	D16
f	$\phi220$	$\phi220$	$\phi220$
g			

1) Inspection of site conditions and structure of the constructions

Where installed installation up the barrier foundation on bridges, tunnels, clear culverts and retaining walls, the shape of the bridge deck base and the top of the retaining wall shall be affirmed, and its specification and concrete strength shall be determined in accordance with the condition of the base and the condition of the reinforcement and buried objects inside the retaining walls.

2) Evaluation on post strength

The maximum carrying capacity of the post root can be adopted as the design load to evaluate the post strength, which shall not be lower than the post strength in the general structural sample.

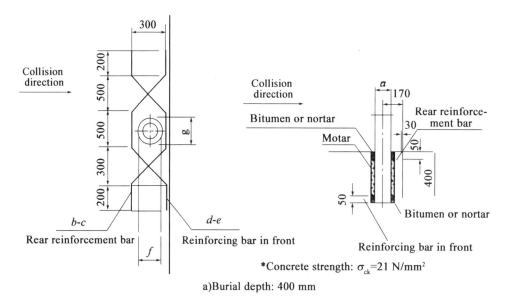

a) Burial depth: 400 mm

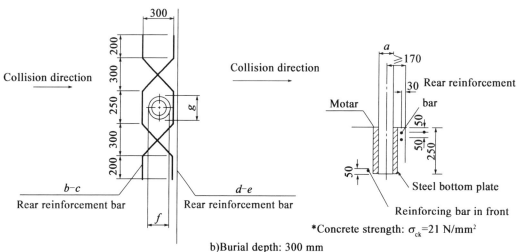

b) Burial depth: 300 mm

Figure C.4.2-3 Location of reinforcing bars for guardrails of different protection levels (Unit: mm)

Note: Where the barrier is located in the median, the reinforcing bars shall be installed symmetrically.

3) Adjustment scheme based on reinforcing bars

According to the assessment results of the post strength, special attention should be paid to the thickness of the concrete cover and the amount of steel bars etc, if the requirements can be reached by changing reinforcing bars.

4) Adjustment scheme based on anchor bolt connection mode

Where the allowable stress of the concrete used for foundation and the steel bar cannot meet the requirements of the post strength, the post can be fixed by anchor bolts. While calculating the post foot strength, the maximum load capacity of post root can be chosen as the design load to check the specifications of the flange, the stiffener and the anchor bolt.

Appendix D
Design Method of Testing Pieces of Bridge Railings

D.1 Basic structure

D.1.1 Typical structure of Bridge Railings is shown in Figure D.1.1. The distance between the bottom of the beam post and the pavement C_b, post retreated distance S, and the clear distance between beams C shall meet the following requirements:

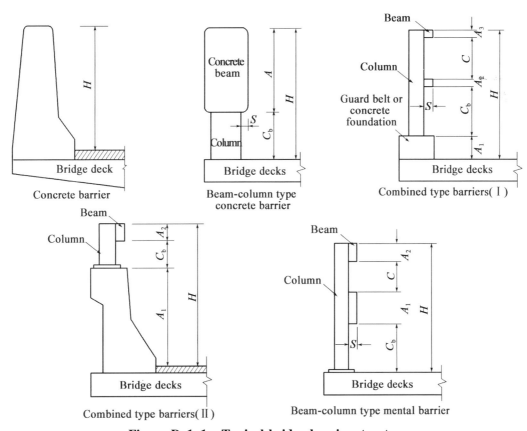

Figure D.1.1 Typical bridge barrier structure

1 Total contact height of the beam and the vehicle ΣA shall be no less than 25% of the total height of the barrier.

2 The clear distance C between beams corresponding to the retreated distance C of the post shall fall within or under the shaded area shown in Figure 6.3.5-2 a).

3 The ratio between the total height of the beams corresponding to the retreated distance S of the post and the height of the post ($\Sigma A/H$) should fall within or above the shaded area shown in Figure 6.3.5-2 b).

4 For the barrier functioning both as the barrier of the pedestrian path and the bicycle lane, the maximum vertical spacing between beams or posts shall also comply with the relevant provisions in Article 6.3.6 and 6.3.7.

D.1.2 The height of the bridge barrier shall be higher than or equal to the effective height of the anti-overturning loads of the vehicle. The relationship between the bridge barrier and the vehicle is shown in Figure D.1.2. The effective height of the anti-overturning load of the vehicle is as follows:

$$H_e = G - \frac{WBg}{2F_t} \tag{D.1.2-1}$$

Where:

G—The height (m) between the center of gravity of the standard vehicle after the loading test and the bridge deck may be obtained from regulations in Section 5.5 of the current *Standard for Safety Performance Evaluation of Highway Barriers* (JTG B05-01);

W—The weight (kg) of a standard vehicle after post-loading test corresponding to the required protection level can be obtained from regulations in Section 5.5 of the current *Standard for Safety Performance Evaluation of Highway Barriers* (JTG B05-01);

B—The distance (m) between the outermost elevation of the tire can be obtained from regulations in Section 5.5 of the current *Standard for Safety Performance Evaluation of Highway Barriers* (JTG B05-01);

g—Grvaity constant, $g = 9.8$ N/kg;

F_t—The lateral load (N) corresponding to the required protection level, that is, the vehicle crash load specified in Table 3.5.4.

The placement of the barrier components shall meet the following conditions:

$$\overline{R} \geq F_t \tag{D.1.2-2}$$
$$\overline{Y} \geq H_e \tag{D.1.2-3}$$

Where

$$\overline{R} \geq \Sigma R_t \tag{D.1.2-4}$$
$$\overline{Y} \geq \frac{\Sigma(R_i Y_i)}{\overline{R}} \tag{D.1.2-5}$$

Where:

R_i—Beam carrying capacity (N);

Y_i—The distance between beam i and the bridge deck (m).

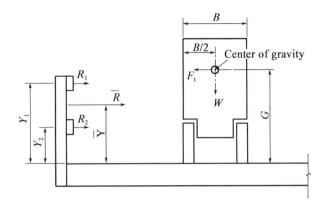

Figure D.1.2 Relationship between the bridge barrier and the vehicle

Background:

Equation (D.1.2-1) can be adopted to predict the effective height of the barrier and to avoid rollovers.

If the design load at H_e is among the components of the barrier, the load shall be proportionally distributed to the components to ensure that $\overline{Y} \geqslant H_e$.

Results obtained from the formula of the effective height of vehicle overturning load shall be checked according to test data and the experience of the existing barrier. For example, in the United States, the theoretical height requirement of TL-4 barrier based on this formula is 86 cm for concrete barriers. However, the widely used 81 cm-height barrier can also be accepted in practice, so for TL-4 level barriers the 81 cm height.

D.2 Design load

D.2.1　All loads shall be applied to the longitudinal beam components. The longitudinal load distribution to the post shall be consistent with the continuity of beam components. The lateral load distribution shall be consistent with the assumed failure mechanism of the barrier system.

D.2.2　The structural testing pieces of the new bridge barrier shall be designed in accordance with the limit state method. The load carried by the testing components is shown in Figure D.2.2, and the values are as follows:

　　1　Lateral crash load F_t and distribution length L_t: F_t is the crashal load, and the direction of the action is perpendicular to the barrier. The values and L_t are shown in Table 3.5.4.

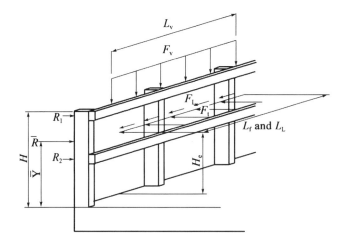

Figure D.2.2 Design load, vertical position and horizontal length distribution of metal barriers

Note: The figure takes beam barriers as an example to indicate the design load and its distribution.

2 Longitudinal crash load F_L and distribution length L_L: F_L is the crashal load, and the direction of the action is parallel with the barrier. The value is $F_t/3$ and the length of L_L is the same as L_t.

3 Vertical crash load F_v and distribution length L_v: F_v is the crashal load, the direction of the action is vertical downward. The value is the weight of the vehicle, while L_v is the length of the vehicle.

Background:

Figure D.2.2 shows the various design loads born by beam barriers only for illustration. Load and length distribution can be adopted for other barrier types.

D.2.3 Various load sub-factors, load combination value coefficients, etc. should be adopted in accordance with the prevailing *General Specifications for Design of Highway Bridges and Culverts* (JTG D60), in which horizontal and longitudinal loads should not be combined with vertical loads.

D.3 Design procedures of barrier testing components

D.3.1 For reinforced concrete and pre-stressed concrete barriers, the theory of yield line analysis and strength design can be adopted. The application methods of the yield line analysis where the crash happens at the standard section and the ends of the barrier are shown in Figure D.3.1-1 and Figure D.3.1-2.

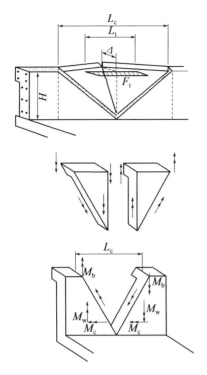

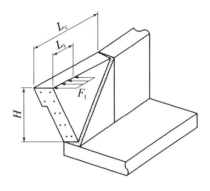

Figure D.3.1-1 The application methods of the yield line analysis if the crash occurs at the standard section of the barrier

Figure D.3.1-2 The application methods of the yield line analysis if the crash occurs at the ends of the barrier

The standard resistance R_w of the barrier to the horizontal load can be determined by the yield line method.

1 If crash occurs at the standard section of the barrier:

$$R_w = \left(\frac{2}{2L_c - L_t}\right)\left(8M_b + 8M_w + \frac{M_c L_c^2}{H}\right) \tag{D.3.1-1}$$

The critical length of yield line L_c shall be:

$$L_c = \frac{L_t}{2} + \sqrt{\left(\frac{L_t}{2}\right)^2 + \frac{8H(M_b + M_w)}{M_c}} \tag{D.3.1-2}$$

2 If crash occurs at the ends of the barrier or at expansion joints:

$$R_w = \left(\frac{2}{2L_c - L_t}\right)\left(M_b + M_w + \frac{M_c L_c^2}{H}\right) \tag{D.3.1-3}$$

$$L_c = \frac{L_t}{2} + \sqrt{\left(\frac{L_t}{2}\right)^2 + H\left(\frac{M_b + M_w}{M_c}\right)} \tag{D.3.1-4}$$

Where:

F_t—Lateral load acting on the top of concrete barrier (kN), as shown in Table 3.5.4;

H—Effective height of the barrier(m);

L_c—Critical length of yield line failure mode (m);

L_t—The longitudinal length of crash load distribution of crash(m), as is shown in Table 3.5.4;

R_w—The total lateral load carrying capacity (kN);

M_w—Bending bearing moment of the barrier on its vertical axis (kN·m);

M_b—Additional bending bearing moment (kN·m) to a beam at the top of a barrier excluding M_w;

M_c—Cantilever barrier's bending bearing moment (kN·m/m) to the longitudinal axle of the bridge.

Where using the formula above, M_c and M_w shall not vary widely within its height range. For other situations, a strict yield line analysis shall be adopted.

Background:

Figure D.3.1-1 and Figure D.3.1-2 include only the ultimate flexural carrying capacity of the concrete components. Hoops shall be provided to resist shear and/or diagonal tension. It should be noticed that the bridge deck also resists the tension caused by the component of the crash load F_t,; Therefore, the ultimate flexural carrying moment of the bridge deck M_s shall also be determined.

In this analysis, it is assumed that the failure mode of the bridge deck occurs within the range of the barrier and does not extend out of the bridge deck. This means that the bridge deck must have sufficient load carrying capacity to ensure that failure modes of the yield line occur within the range of the barrier. If the failure mode extends out of the bridge deck, then the load carrying capacity formula will lose efficacy.

This analysis is also based on the assumption that the barriers are long enough for the failure mode mentioned in the figure to occur. For shorter barriers, a yield line may occur long the joints the barrier and the bridge deck. This failure mode is permissible and the load carrying capacity of the barrier shall be calculated using appropriate analysis.

This analysis is also based on the assumption that the positive and negative resistant bending moment of the barrier wall and the positive and negative resistant moment of beams are equal.

R_w is the system carrying capacity of the concrete barrier. By comparing it with the load born by the barrier, the applicability of the structure can be determined. It may be seen from the yield line analysis in Equation(D.3.1-1) and Equation(D.3.1-2) that the flexural strength M_b, M_w and M_c are all related to the system carrying capacity R_w, which is the 'nominal carrying capacity' corresponding to the 'nominal load' of the barrier.

Where the width of the concrete barrier varies with its height, the M_c in above formula shall be the average height of the barrier.

D.3.2 Under failure conditions, non-elastic analysis method shall be adopted for the beam barrier design, and possible failure modes of beam barriers are shown in Figure D.3.2.

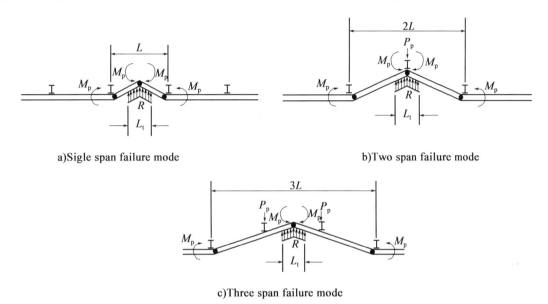

Figure D.3.2 Possible failure modes of beam barriers

1 If end posts are excluded from the failure mode the critical nominal resistance R shall be the minimum value of Equation (D.3.2-1) and Equation (D.3.2-2) for barriers with various spans.

1) The number of spans in failure mode is the odd N:

$$R = \frac{16M_p + (N-1)(N+1)P_pL}{2NL - L_t} \quad (D.3.2\text{-}1)$$

2) The number of spans in failure mode is the even N:

$$R = \frac{16M_p + N^2P_pL}{2NL - L_t} \quad (D.3.2\text{-}2)$$

Where:

L—Post, the length of one span (m);

M_p—Bending bearing moment of inelastic yield line (kN·m) for all beams constituting plastic hinge;

M_{post}—Plastic bending bearing moment of a single post (kN·m);

P_p—The shear born by the single post corresponding to the M_{post} located at the Y above the bridge deck (kN);

R—The total limit resistance strength of the fence, i.e. the nominal resistance (kN);

L_t, L_L—Distribution length of vehicle crash load F_t, F_L (m).

2 For the impact at the end of the crossbeam that causes damage to the end posts, for any number of beam spans, the critical nominal resistance R of the barrier shall be calculated in accordance with Equation (D.3.2-3).

$$R = \frac{2M_p + 2P_p L(\sum_{i=1}^{N} i)}{2NL - L_t} \qquad (D.3.2\text{-}3)$$

Background:

This design method can be adopted for concrete and metal beam barrier. The post at each end of the plastic structure must be able to withstand the shear of the beam.

For multi-beam systems, each beam has an effect on the yield mechanism shown in Figure D.3.2, it's the size of which depends on the rotation of the beam corresponding to its longitudinal position. For example, the beam at bottom does not suffer from yield damage in general, and therefore it is negligible where calculating the total ultimate resistance of the barrier.

After determining the specifications of main beams and posts, the following tasks shall also be completed:

Complete the joint design of the top beam and the vertical post which can withstand the bending moment caused by the vertical load and the eccentric load;

Check the connection of beams and posts under longitudinal crash loads;

Complete the design of plastic bending moment of the post, including the connection between the post and the flange and between the flange and the anchor bolt.

D.3.3 The resistance strength of each component of the combined-type barrier shall be determined in accordance with the provisions of D.3.1 and D.3.2. Beam resistance strength shall be determined by one-span R_R and R'_R of two or more spans. The resistance strength of the post at top of the concrete wall and the anchor bolt shall also be determined.

The resistance strength of the combined barrier shall be the smaller value determined by the two failure modes shown in Figure D.3.3-1 and Figure D.3.3-2.

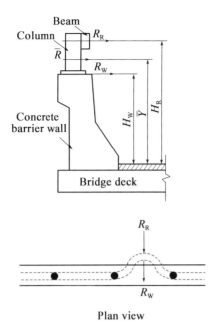

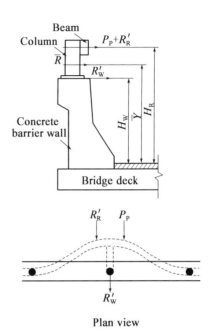

Figure D.3.3-1 Failure mode I of combined barriers-crash occurred in the middle of the span

Figure D.3.3-2 Failure mode II of combined barriers-crash occurred at the post

1 Where the vehicle crash occurs at the middle of the span of the metal crossbeam as shown in Figure D.3.3-1, the resistance strength R_R of the crossbeam and the maximum strength R_w of the concrete wall shall be added to determine the synthetic strength $\overline{R}$ and the effective height $\overline{Y}$, as shown in Equation (D.3.3-1) and Equation (D.3.3-2).

$$\overline{R} = R_R + R_w \qquad (D.3.3\text{-}1)$$

$$\overline{Y} = \frac{R_R H_R + R_w H_w}{\overline{R}} \qquad (D.3.3\text{-}2)$$

Where:

R_R—The ultimate resistance strength of crossbeam with one span (kN);

R_w—The ultimate resistance strength (kN) of the concrete wall specified in Article D.3.1;

H_w—Concrete wall height (m);

H_R—Beam height (m).

2 Where the crash load of the vehicle occurs at the post as is shown in Figure D.3.3-2, the maximum composite strength $\overline{R}$ shall be the sum of the post load capacity P_P, the beam carrying capacity R'_R, and the reduced concrete wall carrying capacity R'_w, and the height is $\overline{Y}$, as is in Equations (D.3.3-3) and Equations (D.3.3-4).

$$\overline{R} = P_P + R'_r + R'_w \qquad (D.3.3\text{-}3)$$

$$\overline{Y} = \frac{P_P H_R + R'_R H_R + R'_w H_w}{\overline{R}} \qquad (D.3.3\text{-}4)$$

Among them:

$$\overline{Y} = \frac{P_P H_R + R'_R H_R + R'_w H_w}{\overline{R}} \qquad (D.3.3\text{-}4)$$

Where:

P_P—The ultimate lateral resistant strength of the post (kN);

R'_R—The ultimate lateral resistance strength of crossbeams with two spans (kN);

R'_w—The decreased resistance strength of the concrete wall to resist post load (kN);

R_w—The ultimate lateral resistance strength of the concrete wall specified in Article D.3.1 (kN).

Background:
It shall be recognized that the maximum effective height $\overline{Y}$ equal to the centroid height H_R of the beam can be obtained, but the simplified composite strength $\overline{R}$ can only equate to the the bearing capacity P_p of the post and the bearing resistance strength R'_R of the beam.

The analysis here does not consider the crash at the open interface of the concrete wall. Metal beams will help to distribute the load at this interface. If expansion joints are adopted at the minimum degree, the resistance strength of the beam can be improved.

For the crash at the end of the beam, the nominal resistance strength may be calculated by adopting the sum of the resistance strength of the concrete wall calculated by the Equation (D.3.1-3) and the resistance strength of the one-span metal beam calculated by the Equation (D.3.2-3).

D.4 The design of the bridge deck cantilever

D.4.1 The design of the bridge deck cantilever shall take the following limit state into consideration:

State I: The horizontal and longitudinal crash loads specified in Article D.2 serving as the limit state of carrying capacity for crashal loads;

State II: The vertical crash load specified in Article D.2 adopted as the limit state of bearing capacity for crashal loads;

State III: The load acting on the cantilever beam used as the limit state of the load carrying capacity of the variable load, according to the current *General Specifications for Design of Highway Bridges and Culverts* (JTG D60) for state I and state II, the load factor for dead load shall be 1.0.

D.4.2 The following limit states shall be taken into consideration for the bridge deck supporting the concrete barriers:

State I: The flexural resistance capacity M_s (kN · m/m) provided by the bridge deck cantilever and the pulling force T (kN/m) specified in Eq act at the same time and shall exceed M_c at the root of the barrier of the fence. Axial tension T can be expressed as:

$$T = \frac{R_W}{L_c + 2H} \tag{D.4.2}$$

Where:
  R_W—Barrier resistance strength (kN) specified in Article D.3.1;
  L_c—Critical length (m) of the yield line failure mode;
  H—Concrete barrier height (m);
  T—Pulling force per unit length of the bridge deck (kN/m).

State II: Bridge deck cantilever bearing vertical load shall be designed on the basis of the cantilever section of bridge deck.

Background:
If the bearing capacity of the bridge deck cantilever is less than the specified value, the yield line failure mechanism of the barrier is different from that shown in Figure D.3.1-1, and therefore Equation (D.3.1-1) and Equation (D.3.1-2) are incorrect. The purpose of the crash test is to preserve it without having to identify whether the limit strength of the barrier system has been achieved. This may result in over-designing the barrier system and a larger possibility that the deck may be over-design as well.

D.4.3 The following limit states shall be taken into consideration for the bridge deck of the beam barrier:

  1 Cantilever plate stress calculation

State I: the bending moment per unit length M_d and the tension per unit length of the bridge deck T, can be expressed as:

$$M_d = \frac{M_{pass}}{W_b + d_b} \tag{D.4.3-1}$$

$$T = \frac{P_p}{W_b + d_b} \tag{D.4.3-2}$$

State II: Impact shear force P_v and cantilever bending moment M_d can be expressed as:

$$P_v = \frac{F_v L}{L_v} \qquad (D.4.3\text{-}3)$$

$$M_d = \frac{P_v X}{b} \qquad (D.4.3\text{-}4)$$

Among them:

$$b = 2X + W_b \leqslant L \qquad (D.4.3\text{-}5)$$

Where:

M_{post}—Plastic bending carrying capacity of a single post (kN·m);

P_p—The shear force born by a single post corresponding to M post located at $\overline{Y}$ above the bridge deck (kN);

X—The distance from the outer edge of the post bottom to the studied section (m) as is shown in Figure D.4.3-1;

W_b—Base plate width (m);

T—Bridge deck tension (kN/m);

d_b—The distance (m) from the outer edge of the baseplate to the innermost row of bolts, as is shown in Figure D.4.3-1;

L—Post spacing (m);

L_v—Vertical distribution length of longitudinal load at the top of the barrier (m);

F_v—Vehicle vertical load (kN) born by the top of the barrier after the end of the crash load F_t and F_L.

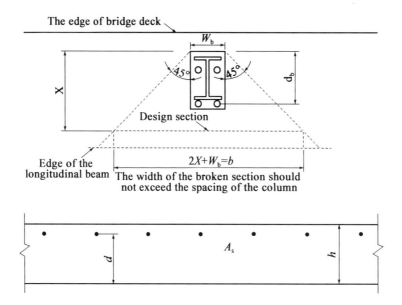

Figure D.4.3-1　Effective length of cantilever bearing concentrated post load (horizontal or vertical)

2 Resistant strength to impact shear

State I: Impact shear can be taken as:

$$V_u = A_f F_y \quad (D.4.3\text{-}6)$$

Resistance strength of bridge cantilever to impact shear can be taken as:

$$V_r = \Phi V_n \quad (D.4.3\text{-}7)$$

$$V_n = v_c \left[W_b + h + 2\left(E + \frac{B}{2} + \frac{h}{2}\right) \right] h \quad (D.4.3\text{-}8)$$

$$V_c = \left(0.166 + \frac{0.332}{\beta_c}\right)\sqrt{f'_c} \leqslant 0.332\sqrt{f'_c} \quad (D.4.3\text{-}9)$$

$$\frac{B}{2} + \frac{h}{2} \leqslant B \quad (D.4.3\text{-}10)$$

Among them:

$$\beta_c = W_b / d_b \quad (D.4.3\text{-}11)$$

Where:

V_u—Shear force (N) with partial coefficient at the section;

A_f—The area of the compression flange plate (m²);

F_y—Yield strength of the compression flange plate (MPa)

V_r—Resistance strength (N);

V_n—The nominal shear-bearing capacity of the section under consideration (N);

v_c—Nominal shear-bearing capacity of concrete provided by tension (MPa);

W_b—Baseplate width (m);

b—The length of the bridge deck length resisting post shear load $b = h + W_b$;

h—Bridge deck thickness (m);

E—The distance from the edge of the deck to the post's compressive stress resultant force action point (m);

B—The distance between the action point of the pulling force and the action point of the compressive force (m);

β_c—The ratio of the long and short sides of the concentrated load area or reaction area;

f'_c—Standard value of the concrete axial compressive strength (MPa);

Φ—Resistance coefficient = 1.0;

d_b—Distance from the outer edge of the base plate to the innermost row of bolts (m).

The assumed load distribution of impact shear is shown in Figure D.4.3-2.

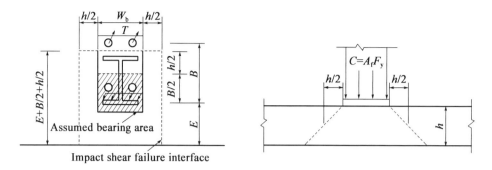

Figure D.4.3-2 Impact shear failure mode

Background:

1 Cantilever Board Design

The crash of the vehicle with the beam barrier system, such as the metal beam barrier system with wide flanges or tubular posts, creates a great concentrated loads and bending moments at the place where the posts are attached to the bridge deck. The previous version of American Bridge Design Code adopted a simplified analysis method to distribute the load on the barrier or the post to the bridge deck. For example, 'The effective length of the bridge deck facing the post load shall be: the Effective length of bridge deck without a low wall $E = 0.8x + 3.75$ feet; the effective length of deck with low wall $E = 0.8x + 5.0$ feet, where x is the distance from the post center to the survey point, measured in feet.'

2 Resistant Strength to Impact shear

Concrete bridge deck often cause damage due to impact shear forces caused by load C in the post flange. Proper thickness h, margin E, or base plate specifications (W_b or B or thickness) shall be provided to prevent such damage. The test results and experience show that in the event of bridge deck failure, the failure mode has been punching failure and losing the structural integrity between the concrete and the reinforcing bars. The adoption of various types of shear reinforcement bars can increase the limit strength of the connection between the post and the bridge deck, but cannot effectively reduce the shear, diagonal pulling force, or bridge deck cracks. The shear-bearing capacity can be improved by increasing the thickness of the bridge deck, the width, thickness or the margin of the base plate.

Wording Explanation for the *Guidelines*

1. The strictness in execution of the *Guidelines* is expressed by using the wording as follows:

    1) MUST—A very restrict requirement in any circumstances.

    2) SHALL—A mandatory requirement in normal circumstances.

    3) SHOULD—An advisory requirement.

    4) MAY—A permissive condition. No requirement is intended.

2. Expressions used for reference to standards are explained as follows:

    The standards for which a year is added to the standard number shall be the specific versions to be used. Otherwise they shall be the latest available versions.

References

1. AASHTO LRFD BRIDGE DESIGN SPECIFICATIONS(2012)

2. AASHTO ROADSIDE DESIGN GUIDE(2011)

3. AASHTO A POLICY ON GEOMETRIC DESIGN OF HIGHWAYS AND STREETS(2001)

4. 日本道路協会《防護柵の設置基準・同解説》(平成 20 年 1 月)

5. 日本道路協会《車両用防護柵標準仕様・同解説》(平成 16 年 3 月)

6. Il Ministro delle Infrastrutture e dei Trasporti ISTRUZIONI TECNICHE PER LA PROGETTAZIONE, L'OMOLOGAZIONE E L'IMPIEGO DEI DISPOSITIVI DI RITENUTA NELLE COSTRUZIONI STRADALI(2004 年 6 月)

Technical Terms in Chinese and English

序号	中文词汇	英文词汇
A		
1	安全风险	safety risk
2	安全评价	road safety audit
3	安全设计	safety design
4	安全性能评价	safety performance evaluation
B		
5	半刚性护栏	semi-rigid barrier
6	半挂车	semi-trailer
7	避险车道	escape ramp
8	边坡坡度	degree of foreslope
9	边缘线	edge line
10	标线	markings
11	标志板	sign panel
12	标志边框	sign border
13	标志基座	sign foundation
14	标志立柱	sign support
15	波形梁护栏	corrugated beam barrier
C		
16	侧风	crosswind

序号	中文词汇	英文词汇
17	车道	lane
18	车道数	number of lanes
19	车行道	traveled way
20	车行道边缘线	traveled way edge line
21	车行道分界线	lane line
22	车辆侧倾	vehicle roll
23	车辆碰撞荷载	vehicle impact load
24	车辆驶出路外事故	run-off-road crashes
25	车辆尾部	rear of the vehicle
26	车辆性能	vehicle performance
27	出口编号	exit number
28	出口匝道	exit ramp
D		
29	大半径曲线	large radius curve
30	大型车辆	large vehicle
31	大型货车	large truck
32	单车道	single-lane
33	单坡型护栏	single slope barrier
34	虚线	broken line
35	导航	navigation
36	导流岛	channelization island
37	导向箭头	direction arrow
38	道路名称及编号	route names and route numbers
39	道路事故	accidents, crashes
40	道路线形	roadway alignment
41	道路中心线	roadway centerline
42	地脚螺栓	anchor bolt
43	电子不停车收费	electronic toll collection

续上表(continued)

序号	中文词汇	英文词汇
44	陡坡	steep grade
45	渡槽	aqueduct
46	对向车道分界线	centerline
47	多车道	multilane
48	地形	terrain
E		
49	二次事故	secondary accident
50	二级公路	Class-2 highway
F		
51	反光标线	retroreflective markings
52	反光交通标志	retroreflective signs
53	反光涂料	retroreflective painting materials
54	反射体	reflector
55	反应距离	perception-reaction distance
56	反应时间	perception-reaction time
57	防雪栅	snow fence
58	防护等级	protection level
G		
59	刚性护栏	rigid barrier
60	钢背木护栏	steel-backed timber guardrail
61	钢结构桥梁	steel bridge
62	钢筋混凝土 F 型护栏	F-shaped reinforced concrete barrier
63	挡土墙	retaining wall
64	高风险路段	high-risk section
65	路堤	embankment
66	高速公路	motorway
67	隔离设施	traffic separation devices
68	隔离栅	fencing

续上表(continued)

序号	中文词汇	英文词汇
69	公路	highway
70	公路改扩建项目	highway reconstruction and upgrading project
71	公路功能	highway function
72	公路几何设计	geometric design
73	公路交通安全设施	highway safety devices
74	公路交通特性	highway traffic characteristics
75	公路路侧	roadside
76	公路平面交叉	at-grade junction
77	公路土建工程	highway civil engineering
78	公路线形	highway alignment
79	公路养护	maintenance
80	固定性障碍物	fixed objects
81	观察角	viewing angle
82	滚动阻力系数	coefficient of rolling resistance
83	过渡标线	transition markings
84	过渡段	transition section
85	干线公路	arterial highway
H		
86	合流	merge
87	横断面	transverse profile, cross section
88	横向标线	transverse markings
89	横向荷载	transverse load
90	护栏	barriers
91	护栏标准段	standard sections of highway barrier
92	护栏端头	barrier terminals
93	护栏构件	barrier components
94	护栏过渡段	transition sections of highway barriers
95	护栏立柱	guardrail posts

续上表(continued)

序号	中文词汇	英文词汇
96	滑移倾覆	sliding and overturning
97	缓冲设施	impact attenuator
98	回填土	backfill
99	汇流鼻	nose of merging areas
100	混凝土保护层	concrete cover
101	混凝土护栏	concrete barrier
102	混凝土基础	concrete footing
103	混凝土墙式护栏	vertical concrete barrier
104	货车	trucks
	J	
105	积雪标杆	snow pole
106	急弯	sharp curves
107	集散公路	collector-distributor highway
108	计算净区宽度	suggested clear zone distance
109	既有设施	existing facilities
110	加减速车道	acceleration and deceleration lanes
111	驾乘人员	passengers and drivers
112	驾驶任务	driving task
113	减速标线	speed reduction markings
114	减速度	deceleration
115	减速丘	speed hump
116	减速丘标志	speed hump sign
117	减速让行线	yield line
118	减速让行标志	yield sign
119	建设标准	construction standards
120	建议速度	advisory speed
121	交通安全	traffic safety
122	交通安全设施	traffic safety facility

续上表(continued)

序号	中文词汇	英文词汇
123	交通标志	traffic sign
124	交通标志支撑结构	structural supports for highway signs
125	交通冲突点	conflict point
126	交通工程	traffic engineering
127	交通行为	traffic behavior
128	交通控制设施	traffic control device
129	交通量	traffic volume
130	交通流	traffic flow
131	交通流冲突	traffic flow conflicts
132	交通流向	the direction of traffic flow
133	交通流组织	organization of traffic flow
134	交通事故	crash, accident
135	交通条件	traffic conditions
136	交通运行状况	traffic operating conditions
137	交通组成	traffic composition
138	胶粘剂	glue
139	结构设计	structural design
140	金属镀层	metal coatings
141	金属构件	metal hardware
142	金属网状栏杆	metal mesh fences
143	金属梁柱式护栏	metal beam guardrail
144	禁令标志	regulatory signs
145	警告标志	warning signs
146	净空高度	height clearance
147	净区	clear recovery zone
148	净区宽度	clear recovery zone width
149	静态标志	static signs
150	救援电话	emergency call

续上表(continued)

序号	中文词汇	英文词汇
151	禁驶区线	no-passing zone markings
152	分流	diverge
153	分离式断面	separate roadways
154	风荷载	wind load
155	风力	wind force
156	服务区	rest area
157	集散公路	collector-distributor highway
K		
158	抗腐蚀能力	corrosion resistance capability
159	抗滑性能	skid resistance
160	抗剪强度	shear strength
161	抗拉强度	tensile strength
162	可变信息标志	changeable message signs, variable message signs; dynamic message signs
163	可见度	visibility
164	小客车	passenger car
165	控制出入	access control
166	跨线桥	overpass
L		
167	栏杆	railings (pedestrian, bicyclists)
168	缆索护栏	cable barrier
169	里程	mileage
170	立面标记	object marker
171	立柱	column
172	连接件	connecting devices
173	连续下坡路段	long downhill grades
174	梁柱式护栏	beam barriers
175	路侧	roadside
176	路侧边坡	foreslope

续上表(continued)

序号	中文词汇	英文词汇
177	路侧护栏	roadside barrier
178	路侧条件	roadside conditions
179	路侧障碍物	roadside obstacles
180	路堤边坡坡度	embankment slope
181	路堤高度	embankment height
182	路段	section
183	路基	subgrade/earthwork
184	路面加铺	pavement overlay
185	路面状况	pavement conditions
186	路权、用地范围	right-of-way; road reserve
187	路网	road network
188	路线	route
189	路线几何特征	geometric features
190	路线线形	road alignment
191	路缘石	curb
192	轮廓标	delineators
193	旅游景区	scenic area, tourist attractions
M		
194	锚固	anchorage
195	锚筋	anchor rod
196	门架式	gantry
197	涵洞	culvert
198	摩擦梁	rub rail
N		
199	耐久性	durability
200	挠度值	deflection
201	能见度	visibility
202	逆反射材料	retroreflective material

续上表(continued)

序号	中文词汇	英文词汇
203	年平均日交通量	annual average daily traffic
204	农村公路	rural highway
P		
205	排水	drainage
206	排水沟	gutter
207	排水孔	drainage hole/drainage inlet
208	排水系统	drainage system
209	碰撞	collision
210	碰撞角度	impact angle
211	碰撞能量	impact energy
212	碰撞速度	impact speed
213	碰撞条件	impact condition
214	道路中心标线	centerline marking
215	平面布设图	layout plan
216	平曲线	horizontal curve
217	坡度	slope(横坡)/grade(纵坡)
218	坡脚	toe of the slope
219	坡长	slope length
Q		
220	气候气象	climate
221	气象条件	climate condition
222	汽车轮载	wheel load
223	汽车碰撞荷载	vehicle impact loads
224	砌石边沟	masonry ditch
225	浅碟形边沟	shallow v-shaped ditch
226	桥墩	bridge pier
227	桥梁	bridge
228	桥面板	bridge deck

续上表(continued)

序号	中文词汇	英文词汇
229	桥台	abutment
230	切线方向	tangential direction
231	渠化标线	channelization markings
232	渠化岛	channelization island
233	渠化设计	channelization design
234	曲线段	curved section
235	全寿命周期成本	life cycle cost
R		
236	人行道	sidewalk
237	人行地道	pedestrian underpass
238	人行横道线	pedestrian crossings
239	人行天桥	pedestrian overpass
240	人口稠密区	densely populated area
241	认读距离	recognition distance
242	日照	sunlight
243	柔性材质	flexible material
244	柔性护栏	flexible barrier
S		
245	四级公路	Class-4 highway
246	三级公路	Class-3 highway
247	色度性能	photometric characteristic
248	上跨桥梁	overpass bridge
249	设计交通量	design traffic volume
250	设计碰撞能量	design impact energy
251	设计速度	design speed
252	设计通行能力	design capacity
253	设计位移量	design displacement
254	设计要素	design element

续上表(continued)

序号	中文词汇	英文词汇
255	设计载荷	design load
256	设计最大弯矩	maximum design bending moment
257	伸缩缝	expansion joint
258	声屏障	sound barrier
259	省道	provincial highway
260	视距	sight distance
261	实车碰撞试验	vehicle crash testing
262	实车足尺碰撞	full-scale crash testing
263	实体安全岛	physical refuge island
264	使用寿命	service life
265	事故多发点	high crash frequency spots
266	事故概率	the probability of crashes
267	事故率	the frequency of crashes
268	事故类型	the type of crashes
269	视觉环境	visual environment
270	视线不良	limited sight distance
271	视线	sight line
272	视线诱导设施	visual guiding device
273	收费广场	toll plaza
274	受力验算	stress calculation
275	横向位移	lateral displacement
276	竖向位移	vertical displacement
277	竖向加速度	vertical acceleration
278	竖向净空	vertical clearance
279	双车道公路	two-lane highway
280	水平推力	horizontal thrust
281	瞬时风速	instantaneous wind speed
282	死亡的事故	fatal crash

续上表(continued)

序号	中文词汇	英文词汇
283	速度控制	speed control
284	隧道	tunnel
285	隧道洞口	portal
286	竖曲线	vertical curve
T		
287	逃生通道	escape route
288	特大型客车	extra large bus (overall weight over 25tons)
289	特大悬索桥	super large suspension bridge
290	特殊构造物	special construction
291	填方	fill
292	挖方	cut
293	填方高度	fill height
294	停车标志	parking sign
295	停车视距	stopping sight distance
296	停车位标线	parking space marking
297	通道	passageway
298	通行优先权	priority
299	通视三角区	sight triangle
300	同向行驶	same direction of travel
301	突起路标	raised pavement marker
302	土基	subgrade
303	土基压实度	degree of compaction
304	土路肩	soft shoulder
W		
305	挖方深度	cut depth
306	外边缘	outer edge
307	外侧车行道	outer lane
308	弯道	curve

续上表(continued)

序号	中文词汇	英文词汇
309	无信号灯控制	unsignalized
310	县道	county highway
311	现浇法施工	cast-in-place construction
312	限速值	speed limit
313	限制速度标志	speed limit sign
314	线形	alignment
315	线形指标	alignment features
316	线形组合	combination of horizontal alignment and profile
X		
317	乡道	township highway
318	厢式货车	van
319	消能设施	energy dissipation devices, breakaway devices
320	小半径曲线	small radius curves
321	小客车	passenger car
322	斜拉桥	cable-stayed bridge
323	信号灯	traffic signal
324	醒目度	visibility
325	悬臂式交通标志	cantilevered sign
326	悬空类交通标志	overhead sign
327	眩光	glare
328	积雪量	snow volume
Y		
329	养护管理	maintenance management
330	养护修复	maintenance
331	夜间视认效果	be visible at night, night visibility
332	一级公路	Class-1 highway
333	Ⅰ级铁路	Class-1 railroad
334	硬路肩	paved shoulder

续上表(continued)

序号	中文词汇	英文词汇
335	油罐车	tanker trailer
336	有效宽度	effective width
337	预告标志	advance sign
338	预拱度	camber
339	预加力	prestressing force
340	预制件	precast element
341	圆曲线半径	radius of a circular curve
342	端头	terminal
343	运行轨迹	trajectory
344	运行速度	operating speed
345	运行状态	operating condition
346	运营	operating
347	行车方向	direction of travel
348	行车视距	sight distance
349	行人	pedestrian
350	行驶速度	speed
Z		
351	匝道	ramp
352	窄桥	narrow bridge
353	照度	illumination
354	照明灯杆	lighting pole
355	振动标线	raised pavement markers
356	正常使用年限	useful service life
357	支撑结构	support structure
358	支路	branch
359	直线	tangent
360	指路标志	guide sign
361	人行横道指示标志	pedestrian crossing guide sign

续上表(continued)

序号	中文词汇	英文词汇
362	制动床	arrester bed
363	制动距离	stop distance
364	制动失效	brake failure
365	致残	leading to disability
366	致死	leading to fatality
367	中间带	median
368	中心圈	central circle
369	中央分隔带	central dividing strip, median
370	中央分隔带端头	median barrier terminal
371	中央分隔带护栏	median barrier
372	中央分隔带开口处	median barrier opening
373	中央分隔带开口护栏	median opening barrier
374	重型车	heavy truck
375	昼夜条件	day or night
376	主线	mainline
377	主要干线公路	all primary arterial highway
378	主要集散公路	main collector-distributor highway
379	专用车道	exclusive lane
380	桩号	station
381	自行车道	bikeway/bike path/bike route/bike lane
382	字符	word, legend
383	纵向标线	longitudinal markings
384	加速度	acceleration
385	最大纵坡值	maximum longitudinal grade
386	左向出口	left exit
387	左右转弯专用车道	left or right turning lane
388	作用点	point of action